PRIMARY MATHS PROBLEM SOLVING

AGES 6 TO 11

KEITH WINDSOR

CONTENTS

AUTHOR
Keith Windsor

PROJECT EDITOR
Christine Harvey

EDITORS
Mark Haslam, June Hall

ASSISTANT EDITOR
Jane Gartside

DESIGNER
Anna Oliwa

COVER AND ILLUSTRATIONS
Mathew Pilbeam

© 2003 Scholastic Ltd
Text © Keith Windsor 2003

Published by Scholastic Ltd,
Villiers House,
Clarendon Avenue,
Leamington Spa,
Warwickshire CV32 5PR

Printed by Bell & Bain Ltd, Glasgow

1 2 3 4 5 6 7 8 9 0   3 4 5 6 7 8 9 0 1 2

British Library Cataloguing-in-Publication Data
A catalogue record for this book is available from the British Library.

ISBN 0-439-98474-2

The right of Keith Windsor to be identified as the Author of this work has been asserted by him in accordance with the Copyright, Designs and Patents Act 1988.

AUTHOR'S ACKNOWLEDGEMENTS
Many people encouraged me to write this book, especially my family. The activities were developed with children, students and teachers in Essex: Howbridge Infant and Junior Schools, Ghyllgrove Junior School, Ryedene Community Primary School and St Margaret's Primary School, Bowers Gifford. Phil was a great inspiration to me, and Tricia worked on lots of the mathematical content.

INTRODUCTION

Alfred and Bill can together dig a hole in 24 days. If Alfred can only dig two-thirds as much as Bill, how long would it take each of them on their own to dig a hole the same size as the original one?

PROBLEM SOLVING FOR FUN

Recreational mathematics, which began to appear over 100 years ago, is clearly not the beginning of problem solving. It is however significant because it was an attempt to popularise mathematics and also categorise problems under headings such as arithmetic problems, geometry problems, practical puzzles. The problem above was created by Henry Ernest Dudeney, whose puzzles appeared regularly in monthly publications at the end of the 19th century. These puzzles were collected, updated and published in book form in the 1960s. Martin Gardner developed mathematical problem solving through regular writing in the *Scientific American* magazine and subsequent books such as *Mathematical Puzzles and Diversions*.

Recreational mathematics consisted mainly of clever puzzles; lots of which demanded prior mathematical knowledge, great skill and sometimes an element of 'trickery' to solve them. The sophisticated mathematical thinking required to solve these puzzles can turn recreational mathematics into an activity with a negative effect on the learner.

(Alfred would take 60 days and Bill would take 40 days, by the way. The solution is complex and needs application of fraction, ratio and proportion skills.)

PROBLEM SOLVING IN THE CURRICULUM

Investigational mathematics in schools has links with the 'puzzle process' and developed through the 1970s and 1980s with the 'New Mathematics' movement and the influence of the *Cockcroft Report* (1982).

Investigations allowed children to make their own discoveries about an open, mathematical situation with different paths, solutions and possibly an element of generality. For many teachers these activities were too open-ended and control over children's learning was felt to be lost. GCSE coursework is a development of this approach in a much more managed format.

What areas can be enclosed with 12 panels of fencing, each panel 2m wide?

The National Curriculum for England and Wales introduced a Using and Applying Mathematics strand along with Number, Algebra, Shape and Space, Measures and Data Handling (and, in the original 1988 National Curriculum, Logical Approaches). Using and applying mathematics categorised the investigative approach with three distinct areas: language, methods and reasoning (introduced at first as separate strands).

The focus on 'numeracy' or the facility to do mathematics has, with the development of the National Numeracy Strategy and the 2000 National Curriculum revision, resulted in using and applying mathematics being integrated into the National Curriculum programme of study. It now appears with problem solving and making decisions, and is linked with measures, shape/space and data handling.

PROBLEM SOLVING IN THIS BOOK

In developing their mathematical thinking, children need to estimate quantities of measure, play with shapes, handle information and explore numbers and patterns. In doing so they will discover some of the underlying structures that link areas of mathematics together.

The problems in this book are mainly focused on patterns in number and shape/space together with systematic thinking. They are about mathematics itself and the value of being able to think creatively about a situation that is new, but can be linked to previous knowledge and experience. There are no 'real life' situations here, but making decisions in this context will help the children to do so in real life. These are not word problems to be put into a mathematical format, although elements of this process will occur within the challenges.

Create a number sentence using 2, 3, 6, 8 and 9 to make 100.

The emphasis is on getting children to engage with the problem, make their own decisions where possible, persist, enjoy and begin to see the magic of mathematics through these challenges. This whole process is guided by a knowledgeable and enthusiastic teacher.

Some solutions are included in the description of each problem and relevant applications and links are suggested. Where appropriate, more comprehensive solutions are provided.

PROBLEM SOLVING IN THE CLASSROOM
WHAT IS PROBLEM SOLVING?

There are four stages:

1. 'Getting into' a task which has been explained by you, the teacher. The children need to know what to do to get started, and ideally then continue to work independently or with a partner.

2. Finding some answers, as problems will produce many possible outcomes.

3. Developing a structure for finding more, or all of the solutions.

4. Working on extensions to the task or beginning to set individual problems.

THE VALUE OF PROBLEM SOLVING

Problem solving can enthuse and excite children, provide creative opportunities, allow for achievement across the ability spectrum and develop confidence and independence. It may involve collaborative learning, recognising and applying previous knowledge and skills, and shifting the focus from learning to using what is learned. If children are able to make their own connections this may give meaning and value to many aspects of their mathematics.

PROBLEM SOLVING AS DECISION MAKING, REASONING, COMMUNICATION

Children will need to make decisions in school and out of school, decisions that may or may not depend on previous knowledge, skills and experience. Problem solving in mathematics can help to model the decision-making process through challenges with interesting starting points at an appropriate level for the whole class. These challenges are concerned with processes rather than skills or knowledge, and they encourage children to think, work cooperatively, make choices, and develop their own methods of recording. As confidence grows, children find ways of moving on from difficulties, learn from mistakes, search for methods and answers, and review and check their efforts. This confidence will enable them to tackle a variety of mathematical tasks independently.

How many ways can ten plastic elephants be put into three pots?

PROBLEM SOLVING AND TEACHING

Problem solving cannot be taught directly, but develops when children use existing skills and knowledge to start a problem, gain ownership of it, find solutions and eventually set and answer questions themselves.

Children are asked to solve problems in the classroom constantly, but usually in very short time spells on a narrow topic that has just been taught or revised. The problems in this book are not direct teaching activities in themselves, but they will challenge the children to think and provide you, the teacher, with evidence of their thinking. Many children who find mathematics difficult can solve problems with surprising creativity if given the confidence to do so. This approach can have a positive influence on their work and the atmosphere of the classroom.

TEACHING WITH PROBLEM SOLVING - SOME HINTS
SOURCES OF PROBLEMS

The National Numeracy Strategy *Framework for Teaching Mathematics* and the Scottish National Guidelines on Mathematics 5–14 are rich resources for problems, with ideas and good advice for teachers on managing problem solving. Some of the problems in this book have been adapted from examples in this guidance. Many published materials have suggestions for investigative work, which can be presented in different ways, supported with apparatus and extended to provide further problems. Websites offer a wealth of material for on-screen use and classroom application. Try putting a relevant number, problem name or resource name into a search engine, for example NGFL VTC resources exchange. Many games and puzzles involve challenging mathematical material and appear in some of the problems in this book.

FINDING A STARTING POINT

Mathematical development is not linear, nor does it follow one defined path. As a teacher you will know when an activity is appropriate for your children, so choose an activity that you find interesting, and make sure you are confident about the outcomes. Think carefully how you will introduce it and encourage the children to explore for themselves so that they 'get into' the problem. As children get involved in the task they will probably want to change the conditions and the questions. As the teacher and facilitator you must decide whether this will work. In general, get everyone to work from the same starting point and allow for planned deviation and extension later.

▼▲▼▲▼▲▼▲▼▲ ▼▲▼▲▼▲▼ ▲▼▲▼▲▼ ▲▼▲▼▲▼▲▼ ▲▼▲▼▲▼ ▲▼▲▼▲▼

Choose five digits at random, repeats allowed. Find the sum and double it, this is your target number. Try to make this total using some or all of the five digits.

▼▲▼▲▼▲▼▲▼▲▼▲▼▲▼ ▲▼▲▼▲▼▲▼▲▼▲▼ ▲▼▲▼▲▼▲▼▲▼ ▲▼▲▼▲▼

WHY YOU NEED TO TRY OUT PROBLEMS

You will need to 'have a go' at the problems in this book – or any others you wish to set – in order to present the task confidently. The process will also help you to decide whether you need to simplify the introduction and support the learning process, or how you will extend the problem when the children are ready. It is not necessary for you to find all the answers, but it is important to identify the questions that the children may ask and have the answers ready. This will help you to discover what helps the children to think, and consider issues like working alone or with a friend, and having time to complete the problem satisfactorily.

There may be an opportunity for you to tackle some problems that you have not tried before. In this case you can work alongside the children in order to demonstrate your personal commitment and own way of working. In doing so you will support their work and share their enjoyment in problem solving.

YOUR ROLE IN THE CLASSROOM

▲ Do make sure that you give the children confidence to start working on a problem through careful explanation and illustration.

▲ Do ask, and encourage children to ask, appropriate questions.

▲ Do intervene to clear up misconceptions and explain errors.

▲ Do step back and allow space for independent work.

▲ Do encourage the children to 'get into' the problem and make it their own.

▲ Do not interrupt so much that you stop the children working.

▲ Do not exercise control to such an extent that ownership of the problem moves back to you, the teacher.

▲ Do review the work in any session, praising where possible, but also encouraging steps towards more successful problem solving.

ALLOWING TIME FOR GETTING ANSWERS

Children need time to develop their mathematical thinking and should be encouraged to explore a situation without needing constant reassurance. Make it clear that you will give solutions, but only after everyone has had a chance to work on the problem. You can offer hints and encouragement without giving answers directly. In feedback and discussion, include children's suggestions and explain difficulties, as well as giving solutions.

The problems are presented in a way that suggests continuous challenge, the possibility of return and updating later and the opportunity for interactive display in the classroom.

HOW THIS BOOK CAN HELP

THE PROBLEMS IN THIS BOOK

There are two main sections of problem-solving resources in this book: suggestions for using physical resources to start off the problem-solving processes of reasoning, decision-making and communicating ideas (pages 9–23), and then a section of 25 problems using a number of the different resources (pages 25–75).

Solutions are offered for most of the long problems (see pages 76–100). Some of the solutions are 'complete', and provide every combination or pattern; for others I hope and expect you and the children may discover more possibilities. These pages are all photocopiable so they can be freely distributed to the children to help them check or develop their work. The other photocopiable resources provided on pages 101–110 link with activity outcomes and include grids, puzzle pages and ICT suggestions.

INTRODUCING THE PROBLEMS

Most of the problems in this book can be introduced without written instructions. A demonstration by the teacher with large hands-on materials can involve all the children effectively and give you the opportunity to highlight key points and deal with possible misunderstandings. All the children should begin with the same task, with support if necessary, use apparatus to help thinking where appropriate and be given the opportunity to interpret the problem in their own way. Once the children start on the problem, ten minutes without your help is a good strategy for developing confidence. This approach will encourage children to cooperate, explain details to each other, and discuss difficulties. These are key elements in the problem-solving process. Children can create their own data for many of the tasks and the input they have, together with the questions that you ask, determine the way that the problem develops.

USING RESOURCES AND APPARATUS

Key apparatus to facilitate problem-solving include objects, pictures, diagrams, tables and lists. Strategies for solution will involve guessing and checking, pattern spotting, reviewing, simplifying and reasoning. The first main section in this book contains lots of ideas for using resources to start off the problem-solving process. Using physical resources that the children can manipulate will encourage them to use apparatus at any age to help their thinking. The value of large demonstration materials for starters, display, prompts and solutions are emphasised throughout and ways to use resources to develop strategies for solving problems are made explicit in the explanations of the problems.

Nine sticks make the number 34 in 'calculator digits'. Make bigger numbers using all nine sticks.

CHANGING THE LEVEL

Most problems can be set for more than one ability level by changing the nature of the question asked through altering the number range or the resources allowed, for example. The majority of the problems have an 'easy' element as part of the task, allowing wide inclusion and the introduction of problem solving to any age group. While the mathematics in many problems may be very simple – adding three or four single digits, perhaps – the need to work systematically, make decisions about a method and record outcomes creatively can greatly increase the sophistication of a problem. Level can be difficult to determine, so to see if a problem is right for your class, try it yourself.

Problems can be differentiated in various ways: by changing values or the number of values, by varying the introduction and the examples shown, by offering individual support, by using appropriate mathematical vocabulary, or by the provision of practical resources. Most of the longer problems include ideas for simplifying the problem and for making it more challenging.

RESOURCES FOR STARTING PROBLEMS

In this section some mathematical classroom resources are described and discussed in the context of starting off problems, although all of them may also be used to support children's thinking. The resources are flexible, movable and multi-purpose which makes them ideal for children to work with, encouraging them to create their own problem-solving situations.

Some of the materials are large items that can be placed on the floor, stepped on, moved around and left as temporary display or prompts for classroom work. Desktop materials should mirror this apparatus on a smaller scale so that the children move from explanation to application without interruption. The whiteboard, magnetic board or overhead projector can be part of this process of making the problem clear and displaying the details, but the opportunities for children's involvement are more limited.

Your objective should be to include as many children as possible in the initial mathematical discussion so that they:

1. have a clear picture of the task
2. have begun to work on the problem, as a group and individually
3. are able to continue work on the task without further instruction.

Materials on the floor allow for this interactive explanation, give an opportunity to leave the problem details displayed and can be the focus for a group to continue the activity.

Each item of apparatus is discussed with suggestions for starting off problems across the range. In some cases these problems have been graded as easy, intermediate or expert to give an indication of the entry level. However, the problems can be used flexibly and adjusted to the needs of individuals with appropriate support. When children get into problem-solving they will frequently surprise you with their ingenuity, creativity and ability to perform at much higher levels than expected.

The resources are grouped under seven headings:

▲ digit cards 0–9
▲ number tiles 0–24
▲ circles
▲ paper strips/lolly sticks
▲ target boards
▲ dominoes
▲ write-on/wipe-off boards.

DIGIT CARDS 0-9

Digits are the building blocks for our number system. They represent the components of a number, or its place value. Large digit cards are flexible materials that allow you to create any number, positive or negative, fraction or decimal.

Take five digit cards at random.

We can:
- ▲ associate object or names with the digits
- ▲ place them in order
- ▲ sort them into odds and evens
- ▲ add, subtract or multiply pairs (sum, difference and product)
- ▲ turn over one number and try to make it from the other four, using some or all of the operations
- ▲ create two-digit numbers, order them, mark them on a 0–100 line, find prime numbers
- ▲ make the largest and smallest three-digit numbers
- ▲ find two digit numbers which are in the 7 times table.

Digit cards may be in calculator format:

We can use digit cards to clarify the place value of any number (lots of zeros needed):

$$268 \rightarrow 200 + 60 + 8$$

Make number sentences if we include operations cards:

Create missing digit problems by turning cards over:

| 2 | x | 4 | = | 2 |

ACTIVITIES WITH DIGIT CARDS

Easy

Shuffle one set of 0–9 cards. Turn over two and find the sum/difference, record your answers and repeat the process. After five examples reshuffle, continue until you have 100 answers for the sum and difference.

Intermediate

▲ Shuffle one complete set with two extra cards chosen at random. Turn over three and make a two-digit number and a one-digit number, find the sum and difference, record your answers and repeat the process. After four examples reshuffle, continue until you have 10 different answers for the sum and difference.

▲ Shuffle two sets of cards (20 altogether) and deal them out in pairs to make 10 two-digit numbers. Place these in order and then mark their positions on a 0–100 line (with or without numbers marked in). Reverse all the digits in your two-digit numbers and repeat the process.

Expert

Select three cards at random from a double set of digit cards, make a two-digit number and a one-digit number and find their product. What is the largest product you can make from your three chosen digits? Extend this to four cards and find the largest product for two 2-digit numbers.

NUMBER TILES 0-24

Number tiles represent the positional value of numbers. They can be used for number activities on the floor, as components of a number track or line, or to construct regular grids of different sizes, or random arrays for investigation, hiding and revealing numbers. Each arrangement has its own features.

Number track – like stepping stones in numerical order, the spacing may or may not be regular.

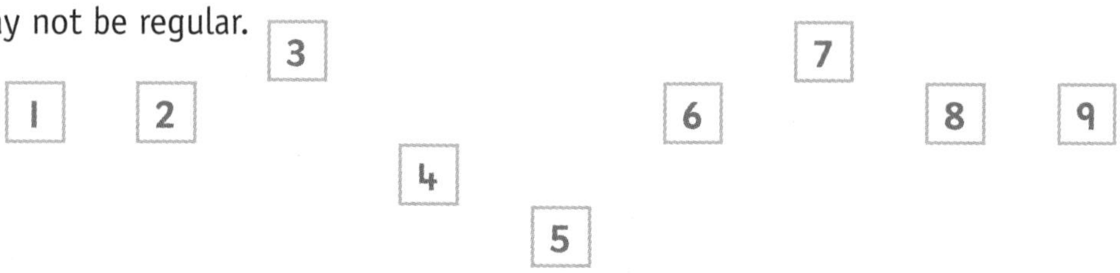

| 3 |
| 1 | 2 |
| 4 |
| 5 |

| 7 |
| 6 | 8 | 9 |

Number line – regular spacing is essential, the numbers are aligned next to markers and zero is included. Number lines are used for measuring.

| 0 | 2 | 4 | 6 | 8 | 10 | 12 | 14 | 16 | 18 | 20 | 22 | 24 |

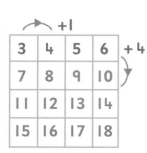

+1

3	4	5	6	+4
7	8	9	10
11	12	13	14
15	16	17	18

Figure 1

5	3	8
11	6	1
4	2	9

Figure 2

17	3	13
7	11	15
9	19	5

Figure 3

Pattern number grid (*Figure 1*) – numbers in a regular arrangement and used for sequencing, calculating, and highlighting the times tables and other patterns (see Grid patterns activity in the longer problems, page 44).

Random number grid (*Figure 2*) – here used as a target board, has no pattern to the numbers.

Magic square (*Figure 3*) – the rows, columns and diagonals all have the same sum (in this case 33).

Odds and evens – tiles show even numbers one way, odd numbers the other.

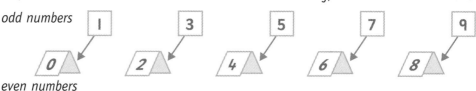

odd numbers

| 1 | 3 | 5 | 7 | 9 |
| 0 | 2 | 4 | 6 | 8 |

even numbers

Step patterns and sequences – this example shows counting in 3s from 2.

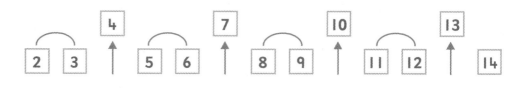

| 2 | 3 | 4 | 5 | 6 | 7 | 8 | 9 | 10 | 11 | 12 | 13 | 14 |

Addition arithmagon – the aim is to find the missing ▶ numbers to make the totals given in the squares.

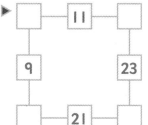

Easy
Hide a tile from the set and get children to ask questions to identify the number. You can only answer 'yes' or 'no', so the questions must be considered carefully – practice will be necessary! You can use the other tiles to help in the elimination process, for example if you are asked '*Is the number an odd number?*', answer 'yes', so you can lay out or turn over all the even numbers to show that the missing number is not there. This procedure for checking with tiles helps to develop the thinking process and gives the children a structure for refining guesses. You may give the children a grid with numbers 0–24 to mark off the numbers that have been eliminated, or let them make jottings to support the mental process.

3	12	8
15	4	19
1	21	7

◀ **Intermediate**
Choose nine tiles randomly from the set and arrange them in a 3 × 3 grid.
Cover one tile and try to make that number using any of the other tile numbers with any appropriate operations, (add and subtract first, then include multiplication and division). You may find that some numbers are not possible, or, more likely, that some numbers can be made in different ways. Here is a set of answers for this random grid:

$3 = 15 - 12$ $12 = (21 + 15) \div 3$ $8 = (19 + 1) \div 4 + 3$

$15 = 21 - 7 + 1$ $4 = (15 + 12 + 1) \div 7$ $19 = 12 + 8 - 1$

$1 = 19 \div (12 + 7)$ $21 = 3 \times 7$ $7 = (21 + 19 + 15 + 1) \div 8$

Expert
Lay out four tiles that make an equal step sequence:

3 8 13 18

▲ What is the 10th number in this pattern?
▲ Can you find the 20th number?
▲ What would the 100th number be? Can you check this? (A calculator is helpful for this activity!)

CIRCLES

Children can use large counters, plastic bottle tops (for example red and green tops from milk cartons), picture discs, counters from a game (for example draughts).

Develop estimation and counting. How many circles are there in this group? Count them and rearrange to check.

◀ Draw polygons by joining points marked around a circle.

Use counter stacks to score in a game. ▶

The partitions of 4 are   1, 1, 1, 1;   1, 1, 2;   2, 2;   1, 3;   4.

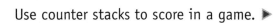

2	3	4
5	9	1
6	7	8

◀ Cover five numbers in this grid to leave a total of 20.

Explore number properties: rectangles, squares and triangles.

Place circles around a circle, then continue the pattern (these are hexagonal ▶ numbers).

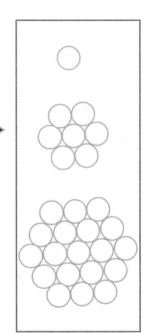

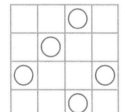 ◀ Patterns on a grid, for example the three times table. This can be shown with circles on a grid.

ACTIVITIES WITH CIRCLES

Easy

Use three different-sized circles (for example, those from a Logiblocks set). Draw around them for practice, create a picture, make an overlapping design or put circles inside circles (concentric circles).

 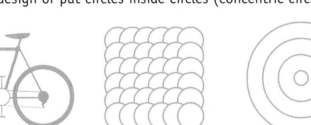 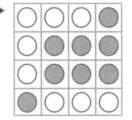

Intermediate

Play three in a line and continue until all the counters ▶ are used. Count up the lines of three for each player.

◀ **Expert**

Mark points on a circle, and join all the points to every other point. Count the diagonals and regions for each number of points. The example shows 5 points on the circle, with 10 diagonals and 16 regions. Tabulate results, then predict and test for patterns.

PAPER STRIPS/LOLLY STICKS

Collect sticks or rods that are of an equal length. Lolly sticks for construction purposes are good for the children to use. You can cut paper or card strips with a trimmer from A4 sheets, make sure that they are constant width as well as length. Geostrips or Meccano pieces work well if they are all the same length. A large supply is very useful for demonstration, display and children's use in the classroom. In these suggestions and activities, all the materials are referred to as 'sticks'.

Sticks are good for exploration and make creative mathematical pictures:

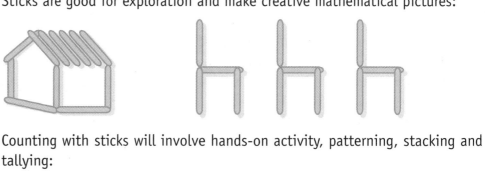

Counting with sticks will involve hands-on activity, patterning, stacking and tallying:

You can make grids and rectangles with sticks:

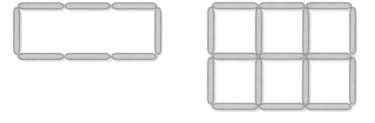

Polygons are fun when made with practical materials: ▶

You can use sticks for digit numbers:

This leads to number sentences for recording practical activity:

Sticks can help us with growing patterns:

ACTIVITIES WITH STICKS

Easy

You have 16 sticks. How many different computer digit numbers can you make? What are the biggest numbers in your set?

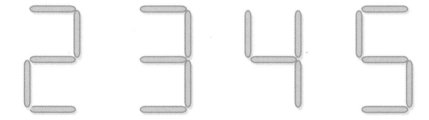

Intermediate

With 20 sticks what number sentences can you construct? You don't have to use all the sticks, but you can't have more than 20.

Expert

Can you make filled-in rectangles with sticks? Record your findings, including the number of sticks used in each one.

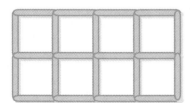

TARGET BOARDS

Any array of numbers in a grid can be used as a target board for mental mathematics, activities with number sentences and games with dice. The numbers can be positive, negative, fractions, decimals or measures.

3	11	18
21	4	6
19	8	13

◄ Make a target board by selecting nine numbers from a 1 to 24 set of tiles and arranging them in a 3 × 3 square on the floor.

Ask the children *'What do you notice about the numbers in this grid?'* Give the children the opportunity to talk about the numbers they see and how their positions in the grid affects their thinking about them. They may spot some patterns even if the numbers are chosen randomly. Some children will see the numbers as labels: house numbers, ages, birthdays and dates, and this makes valuable discussion material.

Your questions could be:
▲ What special numbers are there? (odd, even, square, prime, factors, multiples)
▲ What pairs make 10 or a multiple of 10? (key mental strategy)
▲ Can you find three numbers making 17, 23, 28, 31, 40, 47? (include other totals)
▲ If I cover one number can you make it using some of the others? (This target is included in the grid.)
▲ Is it possible to make 100 with these numbers? (This could be the activity for the whole class to try.)

You could:
▲ Use markers, stepping, pointing, or turn tiles over to stress the mathematics that is taking place.
▲ Encourage all children to contribute questions and answers, including asking some children to set challenges for others.
▲ Roll two or three dice and use the numbers to generate values on the board.
▲ Make a large version of the board for display with children's solutions.
▲ Get children to copy the board, and work on set problems or further challenges. One group can work on the floor with the tiles.
▲ Repeat the activity with target boards as bingo cards, this makes a good mental and oral starter.

There are many variations to the target boards ► activity.

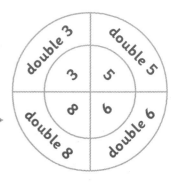

QUESTIONS

▲ How could I score 24 with 3 darts?

▲ What is the largest score with two darts?

▲ Can you list all the possible scores with 3 darts, from the lowest to the highest?

In other versions of the dartboard, numbers can be repeated, doubled or trebled. More values can be included in different sections or as inner and outer bull numbers. A 'real' dartboard presents lots of challenging mathematical possibilities.

$3\frac{1}{2}$	4.0	$\frac{3}{4}$
6.25	$3\frac{1}{4}$	2.75
$1\frac{1}{4}$	3.0	4.5

◄ Children need practice with the notation and calculation aspects of decimals and fractions. A target board can include a whole range of decimals, fractions and percentages for work on equivalence and simple calculation.

A challenging problem is to make 10 using any of the decimals or fractions in this target board. Consider the use of a calculator (with fraction input) to assist children in this task.

20min	1h 20min	2h
1h 40min	2h 40min	40min
2h 20min	1h	3h

1m	18cm	1.3m
0.72m	1m 37cm	2.03m
1m 67cm	38cm	115cm

Use the measures target boards (above) for familiarisation with units, work on place value, equivalence, estimation, and addition and subtraction.

DOMINOES

▼A▼A▼A▼A▼A▼A▼A▼A▼A▼A▼A▼A▼A▼A▼A▼A▼A▼A▼A▼A▼A▼A▼

Dominoes are a versatile resource that can be used for counting, sorting, matching, playing games, solving puzzles and setting problems at various levels.

▼A▼A▼A▼A▼A▼A▼A▼A▼A▼A▼A▼A▼A▼A▼A▼A▼A▼A▼A▼A▼A▼A▼

SUGGESTIONS FOR WORKING WITH DOMINOES

Fill space and create patterns.

Make stacks to compare and count. ▶

◀ Build bridges for counting growing patterns.

Play games with matching dots. ▶

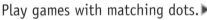

◀ Form groups as a problem-solving activity.

Use them to represent numbers in number sentences.

 + **=**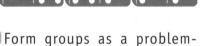

A set of double six dominoes has 28 different tiles:
7 tiles with one or more sixes (double six down to six/zero)
6 tiles with one or more fives (double five down to five/zero)
5 tiles with one or more fours (double four down to four/zero)
4 tiles with one or more threes (double three down to three/zero)
3 tiles with one or more twos (double two, two/one, two/zero)
2 tiles with one spot (double one and one/zero)
1 tile with no spots (double zero).

    Arrange them in that order to check the set is complete. There are 168 spots on a complete set of double six: *How many on a set of double nine dominoes?*

ACTIVITIES WITH DOMINOES

Easy

▲ Sort the dominoes into two sets:
   1. those with an even number of spots
   2. those with an odd number of spots.
▲ Sort the dominoes into three sets:
   1. those with more than seven spots
   2. those with exactly seven spots
   3. those with less than seven spots.
▲ Set out number cards 0–12, place dominoes with the matching number of spots on each card. What do you notice?
▲ Make a track of dominoes where the joining edges make a total of 6. Repeat this for totals of 7 or 8.

Intermediate

▲ Put the dominoes into sets that total 15. Will all the dominoes be used?
▲ Use a set of dominoes face up and find all the pairs which total 13. Try other totals.
▲ Play a game by taking six dominoes each from a set placed face down. The person with the highest double starts. Take turns to match dominoes on any edge of the double. If you can't go, pick up another domino. The winner is the first one to use all their dominoes. If no one can finish, the winner is the person with the least score on their remaining dominoes.

   As an alternative you can count scores of dominoes left and keep a record of this. The person with the lowest score at the end of the several games is the winner.

   You can also score by adding ends of dominoes during play and looking for multiples. A version of this is called 'fives and threes'.
▲ Use dominoes as two-digit numbers (for example 2 and 4 would be 24). Choose one each, the person with the highest score keeps both dominoes. Repeat this seven times to complete a game (this is called 'Comparison snap').

Expert

▲ Try making domino squares of any size, where each side totals 15. How many different squares can you make?
▲ Choose ten dominoes and, using them as two-digit numbers, put them all in order on a number line. Reverse all the dominoes (for example 24 becomes 42) and reorder them on the number line. Set a time limit to make this a real challenge.

WRITE-ON/WIPE-OFF BOARDS

These boards allow children to respond individually to your prompts and then display the results for you to check. Number use predominates but other possibilities are estimation, drawing lines, shapes, angles, jottings, collecting data, marking routes and plans. You can use them as a teacher to set further work, hide numbers, pass around information and list key vocabulary. Many are commercially produced, although laminated card provides an adequate write-on/wipe-off surface.

SUGGESTIONS FOR USING THE BOARDS

Numbers

▲ Write three numbers between _ and _. (Give values, point to a counting stick or hundred square and so on.)

▲ What do you think this number is? (For example, it's bigger than 13, odd and a multiple of 3.)

▲ How many numbers can you fit on your board? (For example, start with 1 in the top left corner.)

▲ Can you write the numbers from 20 to 50 on your board? (Arrange them in rows with the board this way round.)

▲ Answer these three questions then add the numbers together (half of 32, 30 – 13, double 11).

▲ Make guesses on your board: how many legs in the room today? (including chairs and tables)

▲ Write your date of birth. (How many days until your next birthday?)

> My birthday 13/01
>
> Today is 23/09
>
> Days to my birthday
>
> 7 + 31 + 30 + 31 + 13

Pictures

▲ Draw a mathematical picture and describe it for your partner to try to copy without seeing yours.

▲ Use your board for partner symmetry-drawing. (I draw half the shape, you reflect it in the mirror line.)

▲ Draw the shape that I will get after I unfold this cut-out. (Fold paper in four, cut out a triangle from the centre.)

▲ Trace this route on your board, starting in the bottom-right corner: forward 2, left turn 90°, forward 3, ...

▲ Draw these shapes on your board: large triangle, small circle, ... (Put the small circle inside the large triangle touching one of the edges.)

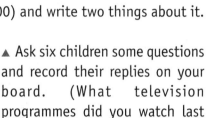

Words

▲ What does this word mean? (For example, polygon) Write an explanation or draw some examples.

▲ Write a sentence which contains these three key mathematical words: quadrilateral, angles, total.

▲ Choose a big number (between 200 and 300) and write two things about it. You can use a calculator to help you.

less, fewer
factors, multiples
capacity, volume

▲ Ask six children some questions and record their replies on your board. (What television programmes did you watch last night?)

▲ Find mathematical words and phrases that go together (this could be played as a pairs card game).

Shapes

▲ Fit four squares together in four different ways and record on your board. Turn your board around to check that they are different.

▲ Make a plan to show where you sit in the classroom. The top of your board should face this window.

▲ Show me three-quarters by shading a rectangle. Write some equivalent fractions and draw diagrams for them.

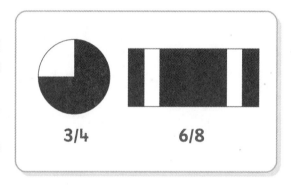

3/4   6/8

OTHER SUGGESTIONS

▲ Use as TRUE/FALSE indicators. Mark one side T and the other F and ask the children to respond to questions you pose.

▲ *Guess the number on my board?* The children ask ten questions with 'yes' or 'no' answers and use their boards for jottings.

▲ Place toys on your board in a Carroll diagram with these four sections: red, not red, rolls, does not roll.

▲ Write an extension activity to pass around (try to make 20 using 1, 2, 3, 4, 5).

▲ Use the boards as clock faces, eg: *This is a digital time, you draw the analogue time*, or for compass points.

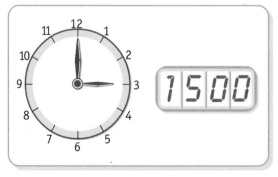

LIST OF LONG PROBLEMS

LONG PROBLEMS

The 25 'long' problems in this section each include advice on:
- ▲ the level of the problem and changing the level
- ▲ how to get started and what resources to use
- ▲ how to keep the problem going
- ▲ suggestions for recording and display
- ▲ differentiation
- ▲ a summary of the problem's outcomes and the mathematics underlying it.

The section begins with a sample problem with more explanation of each part of the process, but a few particular points are worth highlighting.

LEVELS

Each problem has an indication of the level of working: easy, intermediate, expert. Easy problems should be accessible to children in the first years of primary school, intermediate problems demand greater mathematical knowledge and expert problems are meant to challenge children with more advanced skills and understanding.

RESOURCES/GETTING STARTED

Resources that the children can use to support and challenge their thinking are suggested for all the problems, except those that can be solved mentally or with pencil/paper – a valuable resource in itself. The apparatus may be for introducing the activity, or essential for individuals to use, or as an option within the working process.

SIMPLIFYING AND CHALLENGING

The suggestions given for simplification may also provide an alternative way of introducing the problem or a version of the task to present before starting on the main, set problem.

Challenges for each problem contain further related work to extend children's thinking.

MATHEMATICS/SUMMARY

For each task key mathematical outcomes are summarised, including general statements that arise directly from the problem situation. More details are given in the solutions, which are provided for most of the problems.

THREES AND FOURS

▼▲▼

PROBLEM: *What numbers, up to a maximum of 30, can you make by adding 3s and 4s together? You can use 3s or 4s, or a mixture of both, but addition is the only operation.*

Example: 16 is 4 + 4 + 4 + 4 and 13 is 3 + 3 + 3 + 4.

▼▲▼

The problem can be set as a simple practical task that helps to develop number sentence recording, a pencil and paper (or calculator) exploration, or as challenging exercise in developing a general statement. The activity offers the opportunity for calculation practice leading to repeated addition, groupings and use of brackets representing multiplication.

LEVEL
Easy
Solve the problem with structured apparatus and limited totals.
Intermediate
Find specified totals using pencil/paper/calculator and record solutions.
Expert
Find any total and make a general statement about the solution.

RESOURCES
You will need Multilink in two colours, with Multilink track or Unifix track (lengths of ten join together) or 2cm squared paper cut into strips. The tracks can be used for marking off totals found and recording ways of making these totals. Giant Cuisenaire also fits 2cm square paper. If 'standard' Cuisenaire is used the paper strips need to have 1cm squares or you could use a metre ruler or ideally a metre rule with track (Metlink).

GETTING STARTED
For practical demonstration ◄ use some Cuisenaire 3-rods and 4-rods or make Multilink towers in two colours. You will also need a number track to

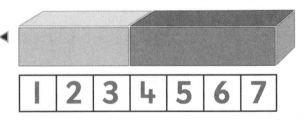

fit the rods, with numbers in the squares up to 30.

Ask the children what totals they can make using two or more rods where the rods can be the same colour, or different colours. Demonstrate suggestions first by making a tower and counting, for example 3 add 4 makes 7 so that is one total using 3s and 4s. Then demonstrate this on a number track by matching the rods to the squares to show that 3 + 4 = 7 (or 4 + 3 = 7).

▼▲▼▲▼▲▼▲▼▲▼▲▼▲▼▲▼▲▼▲▼▲▼▲▼▲▼▲▼▲▼▲▼▲▼▲▼▲▼

This visual prompt will generate other suggestions from the children. You must decide how many examples to explain and whether you want to suggest a method of recording.

Making 10 produces 3 + 3 + 4 or 3 + 4 + 3 or 4 + 3 + 3, each of these providing a satisfactory solution. For larger totals it is possible to combine different amounts of 3s and 4s, producing answers where the numbers are different, not just in a different order, for example 19 = 4 + 3 + 3 + 3 + 3 + 3 or 19 = 4 + 4 + 4 + 4 + 3.

Your final instruction for children might be: 'Place blocks on your number track to make different totals and record your answers.' In other words: 'How many rods of each colour did you use to make your total?'

Limit the number of rods used initially to ten, as some children will just collect them without getting started on the problem. If you are using cubes, sort them in two colours to make a clear distinction between the 3s and 4s.

KEEPING THE PROBLEM GOING

Children will need encouragement in the search for patterns, to find totals that have been missed and look for more than one solution for the higher numbers.

RECORDING/DISPLAY

Children may record in lots of ways using colours, drawings, coding and numbers. As soon as children are familiar with simple number sentences you can encourage this method of representing the rods in the order that they are placed to make the total:

3 + 3 + 3 + 3 + 4 = 16 or later using brackets (3 × 4) + (4 × 1) = 16
3 + 3 + 3 + 3 + 3 + 3 + 4 = 22 or (3 × 6) + (4 × 1) = 22.

You may want the children to develop their own system of checking which totals have been made but if they have a number track they can mark off the totals completed and also indicate how the totals are produced. This provides a useful visual assessment check for you, where each total marked on the track can be backed up by evidence in the children's recording.

Look for patterns or systems developing in the way the children tackle the problem. Their work will provide good evidence of informal jottings supporting mental mathematical activity. You may choose to display solutions to encourage the children and indicate the totals that have not been found or have more than one possible solution. This gives an opportunity to use the examples for explanation before continuing with the problem.

CHALLENGE

Try making 43, 53, 79, 91 in different ways. This is much harder as the intermediate steps are missing.

▼▲▼▲▼▲▼▲▼▲▼▲
SOLUTIONS
Page 76

LINKED PROBLEMS
▲ Two numbers, page 48
▲ Make twenty, page 54
▲ Three rings, page 56
▲ Seven digits, page 72

FOUR SQUARE PUZZLE

PROBLEM: *Use any of these shapes and fit them together to make a rectangle with no gaps. The shapes can be placed in any position inside the rectangle.*

LEVEL

Easy

Complete a 2-D shape jigsaw by filling in given rectangles with cut-out shapes.

Intermediate

Create the shapes initially by combining four squares, and then use them to make rectangles of different sizes.

RESOURCES/GETTING STARTED

Use large squares on the floor to create the five different possible shapes. Start by placing four squares on the floor and invite children to fit them together, each child producing a different shape until all have been found. There will be discussion about shapes that look different, but are the same when turned around or flipped over. The large squares are good for constructing the pieces, but for explanation of transformations you will find it easier with cut-out versions of the pieces, which you can make from A4 paper or card with 6cm squares as the basis.

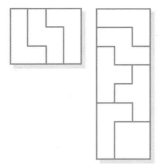

◀ The puzzle allows for the use of two of each of the shapes apart from the 4 × 1 rectangle, so that clear guidelines are set for the problem whilst providing challenge with the limited number available.

When the pieces have been created, discussed and displayed, use some of them, with children's input, to create a rectangle. This can be done initially by playing with the shapes, fitting them together and filling gaps. This is a process that children need to see clearly, take part in and follow. Encourage them to include the more complex shapes, looking for appropriate spaces as they build. You might create two rectangles for display and leave them on the floor.

You can give the children a set of pieces to cut out for each puzzle, and outlines of the rectangles to fit the shapes into. A photocopiable version is provided on page 101.

KEEPING THE PROBLEM GOING

Review progress by bringing the class together and looking at solutions found, getting the children to explain how they overcame difficulties and worked within the constraints of the task. The activity will not be completed in one session, so make time for revisiting the problem while the children are motivated and involved. Puzzle pieces can be made available in the classroom for further informal work.

RECORDING/DISPLAY

For recording purposes, squared or dotty paper gives the required framework for a scale drawing of the rectangle and the component pieces. Using different colours for each of the pieces creates a ready-made display of children's work. This can be added to as the children find more solutions over the period of time spent on this problem.

SIMPLIFICATION

Allow children to copy the rectangles you created as a first step towards solving their own problems. It is helpful if the children can walk around to get different views of the shapes and their positions. Lots of rectangles can be made with the 2 × 2 squares, 4 × 1 rectangles and the L-shapes only. The children can cut the required shapes from large squared paper.

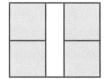 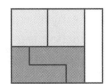 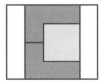

CHALLENGE

Fill a 6 × 6 square with all nine shapes. Although the problem may seem difficult at first, there are several different ways to complete the square. If children complete the square with a different combination of shapes then a new puzzle is created!

MATHEMATICS/SUMMARY

Persistence is required to successfully fit the shapes into rectangular grids and record the solutions. The activity requires the ability to recognise 2-D shapes in the context of the space occupied. The children will be sliding, flipping and turning shapes in completing their rectangular jigsaw puzzle. The solutions on page 78 include examples of rectangles (or squares) containing three up to nine shapes.

RESOURCES
Page 101

SOLUTIONS
Page 78

LINKED PROBLEMS
▲ L-shapes, *page 32*
▲ Symmetrical shapes, *page 46*
▲ Pentominoes, *page 50*
▲ Hexomino cubes, *page 68*

CATERPILLARS

PROBLEM: *Using two colours of Multilink cubes or prisms, how many different caterpillars can be made by joining them together?*

LEVEL

Easy

As a class, or in a group, choose three cubes or prisms (of two colours) at random and make a caterpillar. Repeat this several times and discuss possible variations.

Intermediate

Given lots of cubes or prisms in two colours, choose colours appropriately to make all the possible caterpillar combinations.

RESOURCES/GETTING STARTED

Place equal numbers of two colours of cubes or prisms in a feely bag. Start with one child who chooses one cube or prism from the bag. Three selections are made, and joined in order of selection, to produce a three-segment caterpillar. The front and back of the caterpillar need to be identified easily, so that all possible outcomes can be counted. Isos prisms are ideal for this problem.

back ... *front*   *back* ... *front*

You may get the child to predict the outcome by making a three-segment caterpillar before choosing from the bag (the prediction is unlikely to be correct). This activity can be repeated with the whole class making a predicted model before one child chooses (it is highly likely that at least one child in the class will be correct). Join in this activity by making a choice yourself, this shows that you cannot possibly know the answer beforehand. By repeating the activity, or using the class predictions to find the missing caterpillars, a set is produced that can be sorted and displayed on the floor for everyone to see. For the three-segment caterpillar there are eight possibilities which can be grouped in sets of 1, 3, 3 and 1 caterpillars:

front

back

Note, for example, that a green–green–yellow caterpillar (starting from the front) is different from a yellow–green–green caterpillar.

KEEPING THE PROBLEM GOING

Encourage systematic thinking by suggesting starting points, next steps and key things to look for. The feely bag provides a rich source of predicting and testing activities, as you can repeat the task with variations on future occasions. This is one activity where mathematical ability does not guarantee correct predictions! Making sets of outcomes is important as it allows for comparisons by placing caterpillars next to each other.

RECORDING/DISPLAY

Recording can take the form of freehand drawing and this works well as the focus is on the order of colours and number of segments, not scale or accuracy. Squared paper can be used, and you could get the children to cut out the three or four segments to allow for moving around in the sorting and checking process. The models made can actually form a complete display in themselves provided the Multilink cubes or prisms are not otherwise immediately required.

SIMPLIFICATION

Make sure that all children understand the predicting and testing process, and ask as many individuals as possible to make choices and discuss them. The explanations will help others and build confidence for future activities with more demanding mathematical content.

You may want to start with two segments and use the four possibilities as an illustration of the problem and a structure for solving it.

CHALLENGE

There are endless variations but many produce large numbers of outcomes. Try five segments with two colours as the next step. This produces 32 outcomes which can be organised in to groups of 1, 5, 10, 10, 5 and 1 as the colours are changed.

MATHEMATICS/SUMMARY

For two colours the pattern is: 1 segment, 2 caterpillars; 2 segments, 4 caterpillars; 3 segments, 8 caterpillars; 4 segments, 16 caterpillars. This pattern relates to the structure of the Flags problem, and the grouping of the colours gives the rows in Pascal's triangle, linking with the Pyramid problem. For a more detailed explanation and other variations see the Flags problem and the Caterpillars solution on page 79.

▼▲▼▲▼▲▼▲▼▲▼▲
SOLUTIONS
Page 79

LINKED PROBLEMS
▲ Flags, *page 34*
▲ Pyramids, *page 66*

L-SHAPES

▲▼▲▼▲▼▲▼▲▼▲▼▲▼▲▼▲▼▲▼▲▼▲▼▲▼▲▼▲▼▲▼▲▼▲

PROBLEM: *How many L-shapes, made from three squares, can you fit onto a 3 × 3, 4 × 4 or 5 × 5 square grid?*

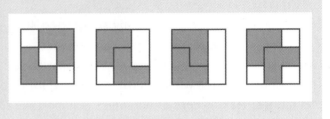

▲▼▲▼▲▼▲▼▲▼▲▼▲▼▲▼▲▼▲▼▲▼▲▼▲▼▲▼▲▼▲▼▲

LEVEL

Easy

Play as a game for two players on a 4 × 4 grid, placing L-shapes on the grid in turn until it is impossible to fit any more in.

Intermediate

Set the task to find the minimum and maximum number of L-shapes for various square grids as a challenge, starting with a 3 × 3 square. The minimum number of L-shapes will leave spaces (or vacant squares), but must have no spaces into which another L-shape could fit. The maximum number would normally have only one or two squares not covered by part of an L-shape.

RESOURCES/GETTING STARTED

This suggested starter is suitable for all children as a fun way of introducing the activity and setting subsequent problems. You need a 4 × 4 grid on the floor with large L-shapes constructed from three squares the same size as the grid squares.

▲ Explore the different ways in which L-shapes can be placed on the grid.

▲ Choose two children to play the 'L-shape game', where the object is to place the last L-shape on the grid.

▲ Discuss strategies and play again.

▲ Suggest possible maximum and minimum numbers of L-shapes that would fit on the grid.

▲ Get the children to play in pairs with desktop materials cut from a large card grid.

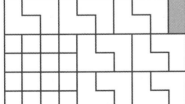

▲ Continue to explore the maximum and minimum values for smaller and larger grids, looking for strategies and patterns.

You can cut out a 4 × 4 grid and 14 L-shapes from a rectangular grid drawn with horizontal and vertical lines. Use the width of a ruler as a constant measure in both directions to produce the squares.

KEEPING THE PROBLEM GOING

Key questions include:

▲ How do you know that you have found the maximum and minimum numbers?

▲ How do you place shapes in the corners?

▲ What is the link with multiples of 3 and the squares on the grid?

▲ Can you fit in all the numbers of L-shapes between the maximum and minimum?

In order to help with the transformation aspects of the task, it may be helpful to colour code the L-shapes according to the four positions that an L-shape can occupy, for example:

RECORDING/DISPLAY

Coloured shapes make good display material for the children to add their comments. Two colours in the game means that you can identify 'who went where?' but not the order of play. The moves could be tracked by numbering the L-shapes as they are placed on the board.

SIMPLIFICATION

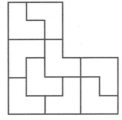

Some children will benefit from an exploration activity with the L-shapes before getting into the game or problem. Making a picture, fitting two or more together, symmetry and tessellation could all be part of this constructive session.

When L-shapes fit together other outlines are created; encourage the children to develop these and use as puzzles for others to try.

CHALLENGE

Rectangular grids, other than the squares, offer opportunities for further exploration and another possibility is a large L-shape into which smaller L-shapes fit. The problem could be changed around: *'Given ten L-shapes what is the maximum/minimum grid size on which they will fit?'*

MATHEMATICS/SUMMARY

This activity helps children to visualise aspects of 2-D space by focusing on one particular shape and thinking about fitting that shape into grids of different sizes. There are no clear answers or conclusions, but enthusiastic children will raise a lot more questions through participation in the task. The equivalent 3-D shape can be constructed from three cubes, hence the name 'tricube'. Nine tricubes will make a 3 × 3 × 3 cube in many different ways.

SOLUTIONS
Page 80

LINKED PROBLEMS
▲ Four square puzzle, *page 28*
▲ Symmetrical shapes, *page 46*
▲ Pentominoes, *page 50*
▲ Hexomino cubes, *page 68*

FLAGS

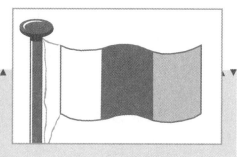

▼▲▼▲▼▲▼▲▼▲▼▲▼▲▼▲▼▲▼▲▼▲▼▲

PROBLEM: *How many flags can be constructed from a given template and a number of possible colours?*

▼▲▼▲▼▲▼▲▼▲▼▲▼▲▼▲▼▲▼▲▼▲▼▲▼▲▼▲▼▲▼▲▼

LEVEL

Easy

Find the number of different flags that can be made from three sections using two colours, with repeated colours allowed.

Intermediate

Find different flags with three sections using three colours, with repeated colours allowed.

Expert

Find all the possible flags with three sections using four colours, where each section is a different colour.

The three sections need to be horizontal or vertical stripes for consistent outcomes. 'Repeated colours allowed' means that more than one section can be the same colour on any flag, (so the whole flag could be one colour). 'Each section is a different colour' means that no two sections will be the same colour on any flag.

RESOURCES/GETTING STARTED

A4 sheets of coloured paper make an excellent introduction to this problem. As well as providing ready-made colours, the flag can be constructed with A4 sheets of coloured paper placed next to each other horizontally or vertically. Use a metre ruler or similar as a flagpole to determine which way round the flag is positioned. This avoids confusion over whether a red–white–blue flag is different from a blue–white–red flag. The pole should be included in all the children's recorded work.

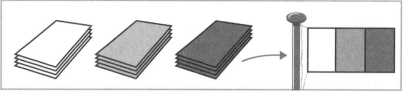

Arrange stacks of chosen coloured paper on the floor and build up flags by selecting sheets and placing them together. This provides a good visual picture for comparison of possible outcomes and allows children to make decisions based on the examples that they can see. They can physically and mentally move the sheets to change flags that are displayed or create new ones. The flags produced by this method can be left as an opening for children's own efforts or removed if you want them to find their own starting points.

▲▼▲▼▲▼▲▼▲   ▼▲▼▲▼▲▼▲▼▲▼▲▼▲▼▲▼▲▼▲▼▲▼▲▼▲▼▲▼▲▼▲▼▲▼

You may want to mirror the demonstration by getting the children to use small rectangles of coloured paper when they work on the problem individually, and this makes neat display material if glued down. This is an alternative to using colouring pens on pre-drawn grids. You do not need to produce worksheets with lines of ready counted flag templates, which can be limiting and may suggest the number of possible outcomes. Let the children draw their own flags and experiment, before moving to a fixed-size flag and layout. Making each of their new flag designs on a separate small piece of paper has great organisational value and allows for constructive errors without rubbing out or starting a whole new sheet.

KEEPING THE PROBLEM GOING

You must encourage the children to develop systems. One way is to organise and display the individual flags that have been made. You can then ask questions like:

▲ 'Have you got the one with two red and one yellow stripes?'
▲ 'Could you check your answers with someone else?'
▲ 'Can you find four more solutions?'
▲ 'Is there another one starting with blue?'

SIMPLIFICATION

Use fewer sections and build up the number of colours to emphasise the pattern. For example, with two sections the pattern will be: 1 colour, 1 flag; 2 colours, 4 flags; 3 colours, 9 flags.

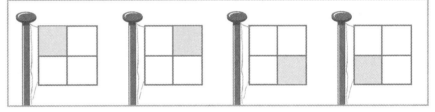

CHALLENGE

With a 2 × 2 square flag how many different outcomes are there for two colours?

MATHEMATICS/SUMMARY

Key skills for this activity are organising, checking and knowing when you have found them all (proof).

There are two rules for simple situations involving permutations as these problems do:

▲ If colours are repeated with 's' (for sections) and 'c' (for colours) then the number of possibilities is c^s, meaning $c \times c \times c \times \ldots \times c$ (s times). So, for the easy problem with three sections and two colours that can be repeated, there are 2^3 or 8 solutions.

▲ For the intermediate problem with three sections and three colours that can be repeated, there are 3^3 or 27 solutions.

▲ If colours are not repeated and there are s sections and c colours, then the number of possibilities is $c(c - 1)(c - 2) \ldots s$ times. So, for the expert problem, with three sections and four colours with no repeats, the number of possibilities is $4 \times (4 - 1) \times (4 - 2) = 4 \times 3 \times 2 = 24$.

▼▲▼▲▼▲▼▲▼▲

SOLUTIONS
Page 81-82

LINKED PROBLEMS
▲ Caterpillars, page 30
▲ Pyramids, page 66

NUMBER MAZE

▼▲▼▲▼▲▼▲▼▲▼▲▼▲▼▲▼▲▼▲▼▲▼▲▼▲▼▲▼▲▼▲▼▲▼▲▼▲▼

PROBLEM: *Find routes through the maze and the associated number totals.*

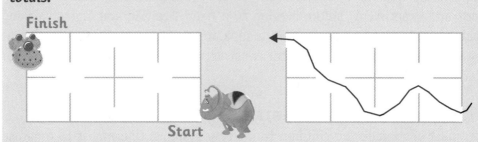

In one version of the problem, an elephant travels from room to room picking up buns to make a given total. How many routes are there?

▼▲▼▲▼▲▼▲▼▲▼▲▼▲▼▲▼▲▼▲▼▲▼▲▼▲▼▲▼▲▼▲▼▲▼▲▼▲▼

LEVEL

2	5	6
3	4	2
5	16	3

◀ **Easy**

Begin with addition only on a 3 × 3 grid, adding numbers up to six. Starting with zero, find different routes and the sum of the numbers along each one.

Intermediate

Include addition and subtraction to reduce the start number to the lowest possible value on a 4 × 4 grid.

▶

(30)	–8	+1	–19
–5	+2	–15	+3
+1	–7	+3	–6
–20	+2	–8	?

?	+3	×2	–4
+7	×3	–9	+6
×4	+1	–3	×2
–5	×2	+6	?

◀ **Expert**

Use addition, subtraction and multiplication with varied starting and finishing numbers on a 4 × 4 grid.

RESOURCES/GETTING STARTED

The easy and intermediate level activities can be started as a game for two children with the class watching. On the floor, use an appropriately sized grid containing a start number (in one corner) and a target number (in the opposite corner). Prepare a set of cards with the numbers and operations (+3, –2 and so on) which will be placed on the grid. This can be done according to a preset plan, or as a random activity (a good task for a child). A dice is rolled to determine the direction of travel (if odd move left or right, if even move up or down). The path is followed by the children taking turns until the square with the target number is reached. Both children complete the maze and the nearest to the target number wins. This sets the challenge for the children to work on, tracing possible routes to find the best path (giving a total nearest to the target number).

Using the 4 × 4 grid at the expert level is too complex to demonstrate on the floor. A starting number less than seven could involve negative numbers in

△▽△▽△▽△▽△▽   ▼▲▼▲▼▲▼▲▼▲▼▲▼▲▼▲▼▲▼▲▼▲▼▲▼▲▼▲▼▲▼▲▼▲▼

the solution, making an interesting challenge. Children could use a calculator to check answers.

KEEPING THE PROBLEM GOING

Variations on this activity will make the task a regular feature of your problem solving sessions. There is a complex array of possibilities even in a simple maze. Support children by indicating a good starting point and a system for ensuring that all routes are considered.

RECORDING/DISPLAY

Routes through the maze can be recorded on a blank grid as paths, perhaps in different colours with respective totals for comparison. Mazes displayed on the wall make interesting interactive material that children can explore as a giant game board. The activity makes a good basis for children developing their own number maze to try out with younger children.

SIMPLIFICATION

Use addition only and explain the activity in terms of gathering objects to try to reach a target total. Place plastic counting toys, for example elephants, on the squares to represent the amounts to be added, the starter number forming the basis of their counting. The children can collect the elephants in a basket as they move through the maze, counting on as they go. This encourages the children to add on to the number they already have in their basket, comparing their total with the target number when the last square is reached. Using just +1 and +2 as the operational numbers (or groups of objects) will give a range of different outcomes.

CHALLENGE

Include division in the maze, at first 'halve' or 'divide by 2', as this produces fractions such as halves, quarters and eighths. If other division numbers are used, two possible strategies which have the same result in general are:
▲ Perform the division and round to the nearest whole number, this value is carried into the next square, for example $13 \div 4$ gives 3.25, so 3 is carried into the next square.
▲ Change the number carried from the previous square to the nearest whole number that divides exactly by the amount on the grid square, for example $17 \div 3$ is changed to $18 \div 3$, so 6 is carried into the next square.

Both of these suggestions involve good practice for estimation and rounding, and provide a useful context for possible calculator use.

MATHEMATICS/SUMMARY

Each of the three levels of the activity involve finding a route through the maze and using associated operations. By changing the numbers in the maze, a new set of calculations is produced with different outcomes. This generates lots of mental (and calculator) mathematical practice.

SOLUTIONS
Page 83

LINKED PROBLEMS
▲ Find four numbers, page 40
▲ Four by four grids, page 52
▲ Times-table sums, page 74

SQUARES AND TRIANGLES

▲▼▲▼▲▼▲▼▲▼▲▼▲▼▲▼▲▼▲▼▲▼▲▼▲▼▲▼▲▼▲▼▲▼▲▼▲

PROBLEM: *Two squares and two equilateral triangles with the same edge lengths make many 2-D shapes when joined edge to edge. With six squares and eight triangles a range of 3-D closed shapes is possible.*

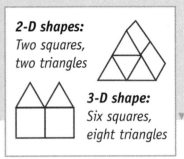

2-D shapes:
Two squares, two triangles

3-D shape:
Six squares, eight triangles

▼▲▼▲▼▲▼▲▼▲▼▲▼▲▼▲▼▲▼▲▼▲▼▲▼▲▼▲▼▲▼▲▼▲▼▲▼

LEVEL

Easy

What solid shapes can you build using these six squares and eight triangles? Can you build a house for a teddy using these (14) pieces?

Intermediate

With two squares and two triangles can you find 12 different 2-D shapes and record them? Shapes can be made from two or more pieces.

Expert

Find 12 different solid shapes, which use exactly six squares and eight triangles and draw the net for each one you discover.

RESOURCES/GETTING STARTED

Demonstrate with large squares and equilateral triangles with matching edges. Set out 2-D shapes on the floor, and include some simple nets of 3-D shapes. You can use sticky tape as hinges to turn the nets into solids and hence demonstrate the move from 2-D to 3-D. The advantage of having separate squares and triangles is that the children can experiment with the placing of faces that will build solid shapes, hence get a better visual picture of the move from 2-D to 3-D. This works well if you take a solid shape and break it down to its 2-D form or net. Polydron or Clixi facilitates the joining of pieces, but separate desktop-sized squares and triangles of card (joined with tape if necessary) are still useful for exploration and developing thinking.

Strategy: Join two squares. Fix one triangle, move the other. This gives five different 2-D shapes.
▼

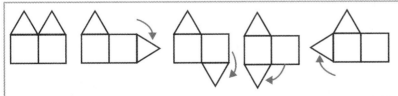

KEEPING THE PROBLEM GOING

For some children it will help if you suggest a system for organising the arrangement of squares and triangles, and the way that shapes are put together. Once a starting point has been found then the children can use this as a basis for the next solution.

Make sure that you get involved in the 3-D construction activities to show the children that you too have to work on new problems and manipulate practical materials. It is often difficult to fix the last piece in a solid closed shape without collapsing the whole structure. Patience and dexterity are required along with the ability to remember how the solid was constructed in the event of a total disaster!

RECORDING/DISPLAY

Children can record 2-D shapes freehand on plain paper, as grid paper will not help to combine triangles and squares. As long as the shapes are distinct and the connections are clear then this is sufficient recording. Deter children from drawing around shapes, it will help their thinking to connect the parts of the shape together using the sketchbook approach. Some children will be able to visualise the shapes and continue the problem on paper with minimal use of apparatus. Make sure that the children see all the possibilities for the 2-D shape problems. They should display models of the 3-D shapes with their nets to reinforce the connections and demonstrate the range of outcomes.

SIMPLIFICATION

Two squares and one triangle, or two triangles and one square produce enough 2-D outcomes to make an interesting simplification of the problem. Ready-cut shapes can be placed together and glued down as a record of children's work.

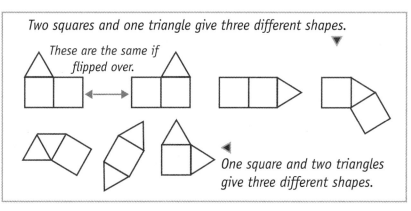

Two squares and one triangle give three different shapes.

These are the same if flipped over.

One square and two triangles give three different shapes.

CHALLENGE

Try two squares and three triangles to discover how many 2-D shapes can be constructed.

For the 3-D models constructed, the nets can be recorded freehand, as this will give a reasonable picture of the component pieces and how they are positioned. A challenge is to rebuild original shapes from the nets that have been recorded. This is a complex process with some of the irregular solids. Using cut-out card squares and triangles, accurate solid shapes can be built and joined with tape to make pleasing models.

Five squares make an open cube.

Eight triangles fit around the top and one square completes the solid.

MATHEMATICS/SUMMARY

The great variation in possible solids made from six squares and eight triangles is surprising and most of these will not be named or well known, so there is a real sense of children and teachers making new discoveries.

SOLUTIONS
Page 84

FIND FOUR NUMBERS

PROBLEM: *Can you find four numbers in the grid provided (see Level below) whose total is exactly the required number?*

LEVEL

1	5	3	6
7	6	1	4
5	3	5	7
4	7	6	2

◀ **Easy**

Provide a 4 × 4 grid containing single-digit numbers. Ask the children to find sets of four numbers, which total 20 exactly. In this grid a total of 20 can be made using 1, 6, 6 and 7.

Intermediate

Find various totals in a 4 × 4 grid where the four numbers are contained in an L-shape made from four squares. Examples of L-shape totals in this grid are 42, 44, 45 or 52. ▶

8	12	9	10
11	15	13	11
14	9	15	8
12	13	10	14

2	10	9	4
12	50	15	21
5	25	3	20
17	13	16	8

◀ **Expert**

Make a total of 100 using any operations with four numbers from the grid. Two ways of making 100 are 50 + 25 + 20 + 5 or (3 × 15 × 2) + 10.

RESOURCES/GETTING STARTED

For each problem, the grid should be set out on the floor with large number tiles so that all children can see it clearly. Ask: *'What happens if I add these four numbers together?'* pointing to four different squares or stepping on the numbers in turn. You can also specify numbers by their position, for example: *'Add the first number in the first column to the second number in the second column.'* Give the children time to think before getting responses and encourage participation: *'Who would like to set the next problem?'*

In the intermediate activity, you need to indicate some of the possible L-shapes on the grid to help children in their search for particular totals:

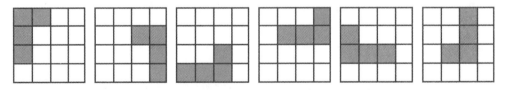

KEEPING THE PROBLEM GOING

When everyone has found at least one answer, bring the children back to the carpet to share their solutions and ways of working. Try changing the values in the grid, either during the session or as an opportunity to revisit the activity or set homework. Children can make their own grids and set problems for the rest of the class to try.

RECORDING/DISPLAY

No recording is necessary at the easy level; the focus is on mental mathematics with the numbers identified in the square. For the other problems a clear indication of the numbers chosen is needed to check that solutions are correct, both in the total and the numbers used. Shaded L-shapes will indicate totals for a given grid of numbers, and at the expert level the children will be writing number sentences using the values in the grid. All three activities could make an ongoing classroom challenge in a large display format.

SIMPLIFICATION

Using the large tiles on the floor, place counting objects on the squares with digit cards for the numbers alongside. Children can pick up objects, and count to get the total. Use repeated 1s, 2s, 3s and 4s and find four squares next to each other with a total of 10. Use a container for the collection, this helps to focus on the amount required and also gives the facility for adjustment. (*You need one more. Put those two back and pick up three instead.*)

1	2	1	3
3	2	4	1
2	3	2	3
4	1	2	1

CHALLENGE

There are lots of possibilities to extend the problem with different numbers in the grid, variation of shapes that contain the numbers and changing targets. The children can be involved in setting their own problems and altering the conditions. Targets can be selected with the aim of getting as near as possible to that value. At the intermediate level, challenge the children to find *all* the totals included in the L-shapes on the grid.

A further challenge is to find four numbers that total 34 in a magic square. A photocopiable sheet of magic squares is provided on page 102.

MATHEMATICS/SUMMARY

A lot of calculation work in mathematics lessons involves working with two numbers. It is good to extend the thinking to sets of four. These activities demand that the children use mental strategies and hold totals in their heads. The grids provide a framework that can be scanned to find values fulfilling the conditions of the problem.

RESOURCES
Page 102

SOLUTIONS
Page 85

LINKED PROBLEMS
▲ Number maze, *page 36*
▲ Four by four grids, *page 52*
▲ Times-table sums, *page 74*

TWO BLOCKS

PROBLEM: *Using 2 × 1 blocks, can you construct rectangles and look for patterns?*

LEVEL

Easy

Can you make rectangles using up to twelve 2 × 1 blocks?

Intermediate

Construct different sized rectangles with no fault lines.

Expert

Find a rule for a growing pattern using rectangular arrangements of 2 × 1 blocks. The blocks are arranged in increasing numbers to create rectangles, which are all two squares wide and any length depending on the number of blocks used.

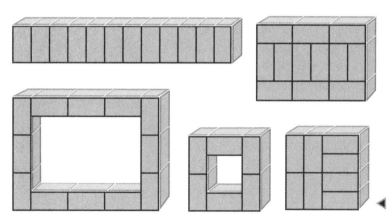

RESOURCES/GETTING STARTED

The red blocks from a giant Cuisenaire set are perfect for demonstrating these three problems. This means that standard size Cuisenaire sets can then be used by the children to continue the problem with continuity of materials. For the easy level problem, you have to decide rules for the construction of rectangles and whether all the blocks must be used in each case (the last example above uses just eight).

A fault line is a straight line from one side of a rectangle to the other. The blocks need to be turned to eliminate fault lines and you will need to demonstrate this by starting to construct a rectangle. Once the rules are clear, let the children explore and play to develop their own systems. You may need a lot of materials, but rectangular card strips 2 × 1 are a reasonable substitute. Some children will be able to work with freehand jottings directly on squared or dotty paper once the activity is clear.

Outline the problem without giving too many answers, choosing four blocks for example and taking

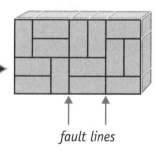

fault lines

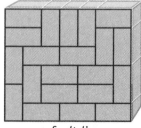

no fault lines

suggestions for possible arrangements but not displaying them all. You can do this by using only one set of four blocks so that the children see some of the solutions, but still need to adopt their own strategies to find others systematically.

Five arrangements for four 2 × 1 blocks.

KEEPING THE PROBLEM GOING

In the easy problem, you should encourage thinking about groups and types of rectangles as a sorting and categorising activity.

The intermediate problem has less structure, but it may be helpful to offer a grid size (for example 8 × 8) in which it is possible to create a rectangle without fault lines.

In the expert problem, determine whether values are correct for the numbers attempted and then establish one arrangement for one block, two for two blocks and so on, as a way of building up the pattern in a manageable way. This systematic approach will be valuable for many other problem situations and children do need to be persuaded to look at smaller values as the next step in discovering patterns, rather than moving to larger numbers.

RECORDING/DISPLAY

Clearly for each problem in this set the children need to present drawings of rectangle constructions on squared/dotty paper, although some informal jottings on plain paper may be useful for children happy with the sketchbook approach. For all the problems, arrange to display solutions at some stage to act as a review of the outcomes and also encourage discussion, additions and extension.

CHALLENGE

Use three-block rectangles (3 × 1 blocks or light green rods in the Cuisenaire set) to make larger rectangles using 12 blocks, to create rectangles with no fault lines and to explore the growing pattern, in this case with rectangles of width 3.

MATHEMATICS/SUMMARY

The features of a rectangle are reinforced by the easy and intermediate level activities. Squares are special rectangles where both pairs of opposite sides are the same length.

The Fibonacci sequence (1, 1, 2, 3, 5, 8, 13, ...) generated in the expert level problem occurs in many mathematical activities where patterns are generated.

▾▲▾▲▾▲▾▲▾▲▾▲
SOLUTIONS
Page 86

GRID PATTERNS

▼▲▼▲▼▲▼▲▼▲▼▲▼▲▼▲▼▲▼▲▼▲▼▲▼▲▼▲▼▲▼▲▼▲▼▲

PROBLEM: *What pattern do you get on a consecutive number grid if you shade in numbers in equal-step sequences?*

▼▲▼▲▼▲▼▲▼▲▼▲▼▲▼▲▼▲▼▲▼▲▼▲▼▲▼▲▼▲▼▲▼▲▼

LEVEL

Easy

Shade odds and evens on different width grids.

Intermediate

Try patterns of 2s, 3s and 4s on different width grids.

Expert

Find a way of predicting the pattern for any equal-step sequence from two to six on different width grids.

RESOURCES/GETTING STARTED

For the purposes of this activity, a grid is defined as a number rectangle for counting numbers starting at 1. The numbers are filled in each row in order, starting at the beginning of the next row when each previous row is completed. The hundred square is one example of a consecutive number grid on which equal-step sequence patterns can be identified. However, the patterns (such as fives in vertical columns) are particular to the 10-column arrangement of the hundred square.

This activity looks at number grids with various widths and the patterns that occur on them when we shade equal step sequences. In general, the grid width (the number of columns) needs to be at least one more than the step for the sequence being investigated.

1	2	3	4	5	6
7	8	9	10	11	12

1	2	3
4	5	6
7	8	9
10	11	12
13	14	15

1	2	3	4
5	6	7	8
9	10	11	12
13	14	15	16
17	18	19	20
21	22	23	24

◀ The sequence patterns do not have to be the multiplication table patterns and this is a good way of exploring equal-step sequences starting at any number. This means for a pattern of 3s you could shade the numbers 3, 6, 9, 12, 15, 18, ... or 1, 4, 7, 10, 13, 16, 19, ... or 2, 5, 8, 11, 14, 17, ... You may need to clarify and practise these patterns before starting the activity. Use a large number line and indicate the step of 3, or miss out two numbers between each number in the sequence. A good method for reinforcing this is to practise counting loudly each sequence number and quietly each missing number. Stressing the pattern numbers verbally: **1**, 2, 3, **4**, 5, 6, **7**, 8, 9, **10**, ... will help to emphasise the numbers that need to be shaded in the grid.

Number floor tiles are ideal for starting this problem at the easy/intermediate level as they can be laid on the floor to

▲▼▲▼▲▼▲▼▲▼▲   ▼▲▼▲▼▲▼▲▼▲▼▲▼▲▼▲▼▲▼▲▼▲▼▲▼▲▼▲▼

demonstrate the grid, and individual tiles can be turned over to illustrate the shading process. The children should generate their own grids wherever possible. This is a valuable activity in itself as the patterns at the ends of the rows are a key check for accuracy. The grids need to continue far enough for the pattern to be absolutely clear, so that numbers that should be shaded in the next row can then be predicted with confidence.

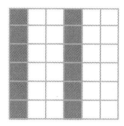

Shading 1, 4, 7, 10, … on a 6-column grid.

KEEPING THE PROBLEM GOING

Each level of this problem includes opportunities for making general statements from observation of the pattern. Encourage the children to be systematic by collecting examples of grids and looking for similar patterns, this is a good activity for sharing out the investigation. ('You try the grid with four columns, I will try the grid with five.')

RECORDING/DISPLAY

Recording is implicit in this activity and shaded grids provide ready-made outcomes. Squared paper (2cm) is convenient to work with and easy to see on a display. The grids can be sorted and arranged in a format that encourages thinking about the general solutions.

CHALLENGE

Use different starting numbers for the grids to vary the way that the pattern is created, for example starting with 0 in the first square. Suggest how the grid patterns are created for sequence patterns larger than 6.

MATHEMATICS/SUMMARY

The number line provides the basis for the equal-step sequences and emphasises the infinite nature of each repeating pattern. The activity stresses that the number of different patterns is the same as the sequence step in each case, for example in the sequence of 4s there are four different grid patterns.

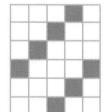 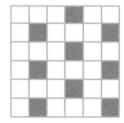 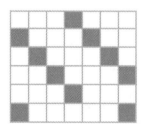 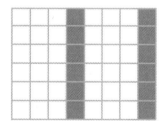

SYMMETRICAL SHAPES

PROBLEM: *Given these 2-D shapes (square, rectangle and L-shape), what shapes can you create by joining two or three together edge to edge? Which of the shapes have line symmetry? Which of the shapes have rotational symmetry?*

LEVEL
Easy
Create shapes that are built from the given pieces and record them.

Intermediate
Find ten different shapes that have at least one line of symmetry and record them on squared paper.

Expert
Find as many shapes as you can with line symmetry and/or rotational symmetry.

RESOURCES/GETTING STARTED
The 2-D shapes need to be cut accurately for the problem to work best. The rectangle is made from two of the squares and the L-shape from four squares or two of the rectangles. A good way to produce the shapes (or get children to produce them) is using a grid constructed on card. Rule the grid with horizontal and vertical parallel lines on card by using the width of the ruler both ways, this ensures that a square grid is produced without formal measuring. Cut out sets of shapes to use for the problem. This creates an interesting question itself about the maximum number of sets that can be made. If you produce the grid then the children can do the cutting to share the task and give some practice, but show them the method of constructing the grid, as this will be useful for other practical tasks.

Place a set of pieces on an OHT and invite suggestions for making shapes. You can also use large shapes on the floor, blank number tiles work well even

 though the squares are not joined.

▲ Get the children to describe a possible shape for you.
▲ Work from their suggestions.
▲ Explain line and rotational symmetry if this is part of the problem set.
▲ Leave some shapes on the OHT or floor as examples.
▲ Demonstrate how to record appropriately to illustrate accuracy and scale.

KEEPING THE PROBLEM GOING

Make sure that there are lots of materials so that solutions can be kept and new ideas developed from existing ones. Intervene when necessary to confirm rules of operation, illustrate a good technique or demonstrate particularly pleasing solutions. Emphasise that different views of shapes may suggest that the shapes are different and decide how much explanation is needed about rotation and reflection.

RECORDING/DISPLAY

This is an opportunity to introduce scale drawing or using square grids to record. Many children find it hard to translate from the object to a representation (diagram) and rely on drawing around objects. This is unreliable and does not give a true picture of the constructed shape. For some this will be the first mathematical diagram that they draw. A key reason for recording is so that the child can explain their thinking and resume work when interrupted. The test is *'Can you make your shape from the picture you have drawn?'* Developing this skill may be a key feature of the activity. When the problem is completed you need to collect all the different shapes together and use them for discussion about variation, symmetry and transformations.

SIMPLIFICATION

Make symmetrical shapes by using squares and 2 × 1 rectangles. There are lots of possibilities!

CHALLENGE

Try using four L-shapes to create symmetrical shapes, some of which may have 'holes' or spaces. This activity helps to make the link between line symmetry and rotational symmetry.

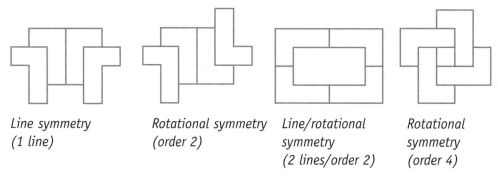

Line symmetry (1 line) *Rotational symmetry (order 2)* *Line/rotational symmetry (2 lines/order 2)* *Rotational symmetry (order 4)*

MATHEMATICS/SUMMARY

Transformations feature highly in this work on constructing symmetrical shapes. The moving of shapes reinforces the idea of balance in symmetry and changing from lines to rotations by adjusting parts. Slide and turn (or translation and rotation) are the building blocks of tessellation and packing, and reflection and symmetry are clearly linked.

SOLUTIONS
Page 88

LINKED PROBLEMS
▲ Four square puzzle, page 28
▲ L-shapes, page 32
▲ Pentominoes, page 50
▲ Hexomino cubes, page 68

TWO NUMBERS

PROBLEM: *I'm thinking of two numbers. Can you work out what they are from the information that I give you, and then make up some problems of your own?*

LEVEL

Easy
Find two whole numbers that add up to 20.

Intermediate
The sum of two numbers is 25, the product is 156. What are they?

Expert
Two prime numbers have a difference of 6. Their sum is divisible by 11. Can you find three (or more) examples?

$$\blacksquare + \blacktriangle = 25 \qquad \blacksquare \times \blacktriangle = 156$$
$$10 + 15 \longrightarrow \qquad 10 \times 15 = 150$$
$$11 + 14 \longrightarrow \qquad 11 \times 14 = 154$$
$$12 + 13 \longrightarrow \qquad 12 \times 13 = 156$$

RESOURCES/GETTING STARTED

Encourage a systematic approach from the start. For the easy level, you may choose the two numbers at random and then wait for the children to come up with the correct answer, this is the first stage of the problem-solving process. Place two cards with your chosen values in an envelope so that the children know when they have found the answer. This makes a good activity for children to try themselves. You may start to give clues: *'The first number is much bigger than the second'*, *'Both numbers are even'*, leading eventually to *'The difference between the numbers is 12'.* Show that 16 and 4 are the only values possible with these clues. Identifying sum and difference gives scope for lots of activities with number.

At the intermediate level, the introduction of 'product' involves a range of numbers that will go beyond mental mathematics, hence the use of a calculator is required. Finding two particular numbers requires understanding of the mathematical language used and an ability to 'scan through' one set of outcomes to identify the numbers that satisfy the other condition. It helps if the children can visualise all the pairs of numbers with a sum of 25 and choose two to test their product, this gives a starting point for the next stage of the problem solving.

$$10 \times 1 = 10$$
$$9 \times 2 = 18$$
$$8 \times 3 = 24$$
$$7 \times 4 = 28$$
$$6 \times 5 = 30$$

Product increases as numbers get closer together

(and $5.5 \times 5.5 = 30.25$)

For example, 5 and 20 have a sum of 25, but the product is 100 which is clearly too small. With experience the children will find that if the numbers are closer together then the product is larger.

A better guess is 10 and 15 with product 150 and now we are very close to the solution. Using a range of numbers and number properties can vary these questions and link in with teaching of a particular new skill or element of mathematical knowledge.

For the expert level, the children need to know about primes and have access to a list of them (in order), and then be able to scan the list to find pairs with a difference of 6. Some of these pairs will have a sum that is divisible by 11, for example 41 and 47. The properties of numbers from 1 to 100 are listed as a photocopiable resource on page 110.

KEEPING THE PROBLEM GOING

Children often find it difficult to make the initial guesses, which 'gets them into' the problem. Emphasise that any two numbers that satisfy one condition will make a starter for the process of refinement.

Questions need to be generated to keep these problems going. A set of numbered cards each with a different problem can be passed around the class and shared from one pair of children to another. The aim is to encourage the children to make their own problems and add them to the set of cards. This creates more challenges for the children to try, and demonstrates which of them really understand the mathematics within the task.

RECORDING/DISPLAY

Jottings to aid mental process will be a key feature of this activity. A display entitled 'We found all these pairs of numbers that ...' is good for summarising the work and can be added to, changed and developed as other problems are set.

CHALLENGE

▲ Extend to three numbers with extra conditions that identify possibilities and link them together.
▲ Use the whole range of number properties to describe the missing values, using the opportunity to teach/revise a new category.
▲ Get the children to invent their own problems for other children to try. This activity could include you, the teacher, but make sure that they have worked out the correct answers!

MATHEMATICS/SUMMARY

These problems represent a progression through the increasing knowledge and skills that are required to solve multi-step problems.

The product of two numbers can represent the area of a rectangle, for example, if the length and width must total 25, the area could be 10 x 15 or 8 x 17 and so on. The maximum area is a square, and this is equivalent to finding the largest product.

RESOURCES
Page 103 and 110

LINKED PROBLEMS
▲ Threes and fours, page 26
▲ Make twenty, page 54
▲ Three rings, page 56
▲ Seven digits, page 72

PENTOMINOES

PROBLEM: *Pentominoes are 2-D shapes created from five squares joined together edge to edge. These can be used as jigsaw pieces to create puzzles containing from two up to twelve pentomino shapes. The pentomino shapes are sometimes labelled with letters for identification purposes and as a shorthand mechanism for setting and solving puzzles.*

V T W X U Z F P I N Y L

LEVEL

Easy

Fit two pentominoes together to make different shapes.

Intermediate

Fill a square 5 × 5 with five pentominoes to make a challenging puzzle.

Expert

Find solutions to the 5 × 5 puzzle where all the pieces are different.

RESOURCES/GETTING STARTED

Finding all the pentominoes (12) is quite challenging in itself, but this does not have to be the starting point for the activity. Fitting all the 12 pentominoes together in a rectangle is a very difficult puzzle. Many children will be disheartened by lack of success and give up. By starting with more straightforward problems and involving the children in decisions about their own puzzles we can encourage the problem-solving approach without the frustration. These suggestions give access levels that allow many children to work with pentominoes and appreciate what a challenging puzzle is. The activities work well with ICT and examples given can easily be created using the Draw facility in Word on a PC (see page 104).

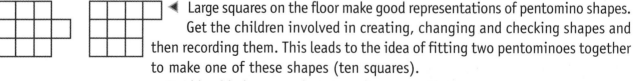

◀ Large squares on the floor make good representations of pentomino shapes. Get the children involved in creating, changing and checking shapes and then recording them. This leads to the idea of fitting two pentominoes together to make one of these shapes (ten squares).

Double-sided squares (squares where one side ▶ is a different colour from the other) allow you to turn over five and adjust the puzzle outcome. This helps to reinforce the idea that the five squares in a pentomino must be all joined edge to edge.

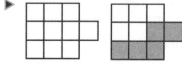

Once the children are confident with the range of shapes and the ways they fit together, creating a 5 × 5 square with five pentominoes is not difficult. The challenge is to make a puzzle, record a solution and then set it for others to solve. This means that the creator of the puzzle must think about the shapes that are included in terms of complexity, repeats and so on. Exclude the I-shape and encourage children to think about the more complex shapes as puzzle pieces, W, X, F, U, T for example.

RECORDING/DISPLAY
Initial recording can be freehand on plain paper as long as it helps the children to identify solutions and check for repeats. Cut-out squares fitted together give a good picture of the shapes and colour can be used. For more accuracy use squared or dotty paper, which means that scale drawing is required. Any display of solutions, especially in colour, will provide a striking record of the children's creativity with the possibility of almost infinite additions. All the pentomino shapes (except I) are used in these four solutions:

U N N L L

V Z Z Y Y

U X L F P

W Y P L T

KEEPING THE PROBLEM GOING
The activity lends itself to children's input. You could ask them to create shapes from two or more pentominoes, draw the outline that contains the pieces and then set this as a puzzle for others in the class to solve. Stress that these puzzles may never have been set or solved before; this is a real opportunity to discover some mathematics for themselves. Solutions may be unique or more than one solution may be found making the puzzle more interesting.

If you want to set an on-going challenge then continue with rectangles increasing in size and the number of pentominoes needed to fill them: 3 × 5 for three shapes, 4 × 5 for four shapes and so on. Questions like *'Can you find a solution where all the pieces are different?'*, *'Is there a solution without a P-shape?'* and *'Will it work with a W included?'* all help to keep the problem going. The solutions on page 89 include all possibilities for the easy level and some examples of pentominoes filling 5 × 5 rectangles – the children will find many more.

MATHEMATICS/SUMMARY
The 12 pentominoes will fit together to make four different sized rectangles containing 60 squares (3 × 20, 4 × 15, 5 × 12, 6 × 10).

A challenging puzzle uses all the pentominoes together with a 2 × 2 square (one example of a tetromino) to fill an 8 × 8 square. An example of each of these appears on solutions page 89.

There is a wealth of material available for this topic, which is a good example of 'new mathematics'. In the 1950s, Solomon Golomb suggested the term 'polyominoes' to include all the 2-D shapes that could be made by joining squares together, edge to edge. For further information make a web search on 'pentominoes' or 'polyominoes'.

▼▲▼▲▼▲▼▲▼▲

RESOURCES
Page 104

SOLUTIONS
Page 89

LINKED PROBLEMS
▲ Four square puzzle, *page 28*
▲ L-shapes, *page 32*
▲ Symmetrical shapes, *page 46*
▲ Hexomino cubes, *page 68*

FOUR BY FOUR GRIDS

▼▲▼▲▼▲▼▲▼▲▼▲▼▲▼▲▼▲▼▲▼▲▼▲▼▲▼▲▼▲▼▲▼▲▼▲▼

PROBLEM: *On a 4 × 4 grid, how many different routes can you find and follow?*

▼▲▼▲▼▲▼▲▼▲▼▲▼▲▼▲▼▲▼▲▼▲▼▲▼▲▼▲▼▲▼▲▼▲▼▲▼

LEVEL

Easy

Beginning at any square, can you visit all the other squares just once, and return to your starting point? Record your path on squared paper.

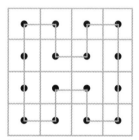

Visit every square

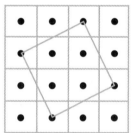

Four counter square

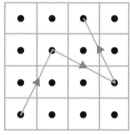

Knight's move

Intermediate

Place four counters on the grid at the corners of a square. How many different positions can you find?

Expert

Using the knight's move in chess, how many squares can you visit on a 4 × 4 grid? You can start at any square you choose, but you cannot move to a square that has been visited already.

RESOURCES/GETTING STARTED

Large squares or blank floor tiles make an ideal starting point for all these problems. Place the squares a short distance apart to allow room for moving. Identify a starting square and mark it so that all the children can see. Invite suggestions for solving the problem *'Who can see a way of visiting every square and returning to the starting point?'* Ask a child to step on the grid and demonstrate by walking around. The other children will help you to check that the solution is correct, if not invite a different child to try. When a route has been found ask the group, *'Can you remember this?'*, *'How can we record it?'* Listen to suggestions and try them out before using paper strips to connect the squares in order, one child following the solver around the grid to mark the route. This gives a picture on the floor of a possible recording method, which can be modelled on squared or dotty paper by joining points with lines.

A similar introduction works for the square of counters and the knight's move versions of the problem, and suggests a way of working for the children.

Large counters placed in the centre of chosen locations on the grid can be tested for accuracy using rulers or strips to join the points. This indicates a good method for the children to record squares on their own grids.

For the knight's move, explain the L-shape path (two steps forward, one step left or right) and use longer strips to record on the floor-grid. These strips

should measure the actual distance ▶
from the first square to the last
square of the move. This helps to
give a picture and a measure of the
possible moves.

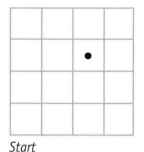

Start

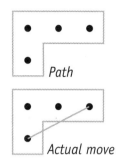

Path

Actual move

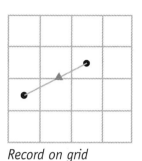

Record on grid

KEEPING THE PROBLEM GOING

Spend time on the floor-grid to ensure that children understand the problems. Show how a solution on the floor is transferred to squared paper in a scale diagram. The children's view of the grid may cause difficulty in the transfer to paper, emphasise the plan view, identifying direction and starting point. In the first problem, encourage children to look for the diagonal routes as these provide more possibilities and interesting outcomes for recording. In the intermediate problem, the corners of the square are much more difficult to find when the edges are not horizontal and vertical. Suggest that children join points on a grid to test their counter positions.

RECORDING/DISPLAY

The children's work on 2cm squared paper grids provides an ideal display of all three problems. Group similar solutions together as they may look different from other viewpoints. This leads to valuable discussion about the similar routes, counter positions and paths for the knight's moves.

SIMPLIFICATION

A 3 × 3 grid does not work well because of the limited number of routes. For support, allow children to work on the large grid (on the floor or desktop) and record by using the paper strips.

CHALLENGE

The knight's move problem can be extended to any larger grid up to an 8 × 8 chessboard where the visit to every square is a classic problem.

MATHEMATICS/SUMMARY

There are many routes possible for the easy problem, 16 examples are given on page 90.

Consider whether you can make a square with the first two counters in any position on the grid. You may want to challenge the children to find difficult (or impossible) starting points if you feel confident. It is good to demonstrate your own involvement in the task and show that you do not always know all the answers!

The maximum number of knight's moves possible on a 4 × 4 grid appears to be 14. Examples of this, and other numbers, are given on page 90. Can you prove that covering 16 squares is not possible?

SOLUTIONS
Page 90

LINKED PROBLEMS
▲ Number maze, *page 36*
▲ Find four numbers, *page 40*
▲ Times-table sums, *page 74*

MAKE TWENTY

PROBLEM: *Using four groups of objects, four rods or four number cards, can you make a total of 20?*

LEVEL

Easy

Choose four rods from a set of 1 to 8 to fill a number track to 20 exactly.

Intermediate

Put 20 objects into four groups, all different, and with a maximum group size of 8.

Expert

Using digit cards from 1 to 8, find all the sets of four that make a total of 20 when added together.

RESOURCES/GETTING STARTED

For the easy level, provide number tracks or strips of squared paper to fit Cuisenaire or giant Cuisenaire (structured rods in ten colours). Explain that the four rods must be all different. Demonstrate a possible solution, for example:

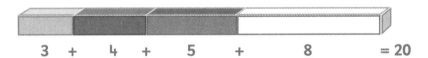

3 + 4 + 5 + 8 = 20

For the intermediate level, you need counting and sorting apparatus such as plastic cars, elephants or dinosaurs in various colours. Elephants are far more interesting than cubes and much more likely to engage the learner in this

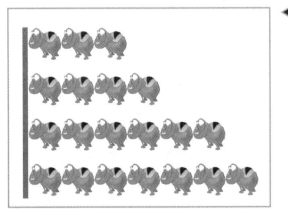

problem. Make sure that there is space for the objects to be placed into groups. Let the children decide how to do this, for example four piles, four mats or four rings. For explanation, encouragement or summary, the objects can be organised in rows with a base line to link with graphical format. This facilitates adjustment to find a new solution, for example move one off the '3' group and add it to the '4' group.

Encourage the children to use digit cards, which they can make themselves. The cards can be used as labels for the practical apparatus or to solve the problem mentally. The cards allow for movement and the opportunity to 'fiddle with numbers' – important aspects of this and many other problems. The cards are also valuable for sharing or demonstrating solutions.

You may start the task by demonstration without giving one of the answers exactly. If you do put rods, objects or cards together, make a total that is almost right as this will encourage children to think for themselves and give a clue to a correct solution. For example, 4 + 5 + 6 + 7 = 22 can be adjusted to 20 by changing the 4 to a 2, or by changing the 5 to a 3, giving two correct solutions.

KEEPING THE PROBLEM GOING

Decide if you are going to set a target number of solutions (in this case there are seven distinct possibilities). Once one answer has been found you can encourage children to build on that solution by adjusting the practical materials as suggested, or changing numbers by adding to one and taking from another. Look for other answers that arise as this may set a further challenge later.

RECORDING/DISPLAY

The three different levels of access provide varied display solutions. Children will develop their own way of recording, checking and presenting solutions. The use of colour works well and it is possible to represent some of the solutions as 2-D shapes with areas corresponding to numbers on the cards.

SIMPLIFICATION

Try any three numbers ▶ making 12 to make an easier starting problem. Have lots of cards available so that the children can make up sets of three, each with a total of 12. If zero is not counted there are 12 distinct sets, not counting arrangements of

Sets of numbers making 12 (12)	1 1 10	1 2 9	1 3 8	1 4 7	1 5 6	2 2 8	2 3 7	2 4 6	2 5 5	3 3 6	3 4 5	4 4 4
Arrangements for each set (55)	3	6	6	6	6	3	6	6	3	3	6	1

numbers within the sets. If change of order is counted differently there are 55 arrangements, for example (2, 2, 8) makes 12, but so does (2, 8, 2) and (8, 2, 2).

CHALLENGE

Other possibilities using digit cards 1–8:
▲ Make a total of 16 with three cards (five solutions)
▲ Use four cards to make a total of 18 (eight solutions).
▲ Make every number from 10 to 26 with four cards selected from 1–8 using addition only (see solution page 91).

MATHEMATICS/SUMMARY

Partitioning and recombining are the key mathematical elements in this task. In general, partitions do not follow a simple mathematical pattern.

The seven possible groups for making 20 from 1–8 are: (1, 4, 7, 8), (1, 5, 6, 8), (2, 3, 7, 8), (2, 4, 6, 8), (2, 5, 6, 7), (3, 4, 5, 8), (3, 4, 6, 7).

▽▲▽▲▽▲▽▲▽▲▽▲
SOLUTIONS
Page 91

LINKED PROBLEMS
▲ Threes and fours, page 26
▲ Two numbers, page 48
▲ Three rings, page 56
▲ Seven digits, page 72

THREE RINGS

▼▲▼▲▼▲▼▲▼▲▼▲▼▲▼▲▼▲▼▲▼▲▼▲▼▲▼▲▼▲▼▲▼▲▼▲▼

PROBLEM: *I have three rings in which to place all of the numbers from 1 to 9. How can I do it so that the total in each ring is 15?*

▼▲▼▲▼▲▼▲▼▲▼▲▼▲▼▲▼▲▼▲▼▲▼▲▼▲▼▲▼▲▼▲▼▲▼▲▼

LEVEL

Intermediate

Use digit cards, wooden numbers, cut-out digits or magnetic numbers on a board to find all the solutions by rearranging and changing the numbers.

◀ **RESOURCES/GETTING STARTED**

Place three hoops on the floor, use large digits 1–9 and place cards in the three rings. A random arrangement makes a good starting point, although you may want to make a first guess at organising the numbers. 'Let's put a large and a small number in this ring, some of the middle numbers in here and the rest in the third ring.'

This arrangement gives totals of 13, 11 and 21. Get the children to add the numbers in each ring and mark the totals. Small write-on/wipe-off boards are good for this as they make clear labels that can be placed alongside the ring and the total can be changed as the problem develops. Explain that the unequal totals indicate that adjustment is required. Encourage the children to make suggestions, then explain their thinking and finally demonstrate this practically. One strategy is to start with the largest group and distribute some of the numbers to the other groups, so moving 4 from group C to group B will give (1, 5, 7), (2, 4, 9) and (3, 6, 8) with totals of 13, 15 and 17. Exchanging the 1 and 3 from groups A and C balances the values and one solution to the problem has been found. ▶

In this case there are three numbers in each ring but this does not always happen. Try starting with 6 and 9 as the numbers in your first ring, leaving 1, 2, 3, 4, 5, 7 and 8 to be placed in the other two rings. The children can take the problem on from there.

KEEPING THE PROBLEM GOING

Encourage the children to make a guess and then adjust their totals by moving the numbers around – a practical demonstration of partition and regrouping. Try not to intervene unless children are completely lost, in which case it may help to use a simpler version of the problem. Practical apparatus that changes the number values into

A   13

B   11

C   21

objects does not really work here, as the conditions for the solving the problem are too complex, hence the focus on mental facility. Having digits to move around does help this process considerably. One key discovery is that if two groups total 15 then the third group does also, although checking is always recommended!

RECORDING/DISPLAY

Children can develop their own methods of recording; jottings to help with mental calculation and organisation will be evident. Set up an interactive display where the numbers can be changed regularly to show different solutions. This will also encourage children to develop their own problems with different starting values and variable number of rings. With some digit/ring combinations the totals for the possible regroupings may not always be equal. In these cases, the target for the problem should be to get them as close as possible.

SIMPLIFICATION

Using repeat digits you can set a similar challenge: 1, 1, 1, 2, 2, 2, 3, 3, 3 in three rings with a total of 6 in each ring. This could be solved with Cuisenaire rods with a 6-rod beside each ring, against which to match shorter rods to get equal totals. ▶

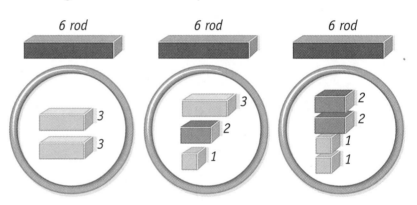

6 rod   6 rod   6 rod

CHALLENGE

The next set of consecutive numbers starting at one that will give equal groupings in three rings is 1 to 11 with totals of 22. Finding all the solutions is a real challenge! Some of them are listed on page 92.

MATHEMATICS/SUMMARY

This activity encourages 'fiddling with numbers', mental calculation and adjustment. The reward of finding a new solution is great. With careful choice of numbers there are lots of similar problems to set. Of course, there are more solutions possible if the totals have to be close, rather than equal.

There are nine different solutions to the three rings making 15:

159 267 348	12345 69 78	1257 348 69
159 2346 78	1239 456 78	1347 258 69
168 249 357	1248 357 69	1356 249 78

Any set of nine consecutive numbers will produce nine different solutions, for example 4 to 12 in three rings with a total of 24 in each ring. The solution will have exactly the same structure as above, with 4 replacing 1, 5 replacing 2 and so on.

▼▲▼▲▼▲▼▲▼▲

SOLUTIONS
Page 92

LINKED PROBLEMS
▲ Threes and fours, *page 26*
▲ Two numbers, *page 48*
▲ Make twenty, *page 54*
▲ Seven digits, *page 72*

CROSSOVER POLYGONS

PROBLEM: *What happens when we connect points marked around a circle with straight lines in different orders? What polygons and crossover polygons are produced?*

LEVEL

Intermediate

Join a set of points in the order of five numbers generated randomly using five digit cards to produce 5-sided polygons and crossover polygons.

Expert

Using fixed grids of six dots, explore all the different polygons and crossover polygons that can be produced. It is best to complete the intermediate level problem before moving on to the expert level.

RESOURCES/GETTING STARTED

Mark four points on the floor using large counters in an irregular quadrilateral arrangement (that is, not in a straight line). These points could be on the circumference of a large circle. Discuss ways of walking in a straight line from one point to all of the others and back to the starting point. Illustrate this by connecting the points with string or paper strips to clarify the path taken. In general, there are three possible outcomes for four points.

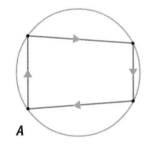

A

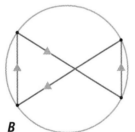

B

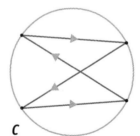

C

The three routes produce one irregular quadrilateral and two crossover quadrilaterals. In both of the crossover quadrilaterals, two triangles appear because of the intersecting lines travelling from point to point, not because there is a point fixed there. You may want to discuss this with the children, as similar situations will occur regularly in this activity. In a square or rhombus the two crossover polygons would be identical apart from the rotation through 90°.

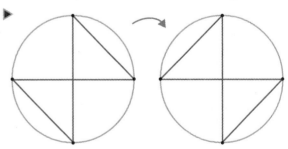

If we number the four points that we used to generate the quadrilaterals, then the path that produces A would be 12341, B would be 13241 and C would be 12431. So we have a code to describe the 2-D shape produced.

Using digit cards 1–5 and five marked points we ▶ can generate pentagonal crossover polygons. The method is mark and number the points, shuffle the cards, deal out in random order, use this code to generate the shape. Key questions would be *'How many shapes are there?'* and *'Do some different codes produce the same crossover polygons?'*

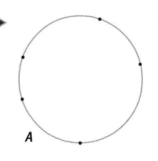

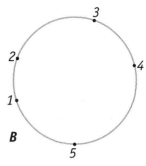

KEEPING THE PROBLEM GOING

Get the children to trial lots of code numbers first and then compare and discuss results. *'How did you get that shape?'* Some children will be able to manipulate the numbers without the digit cards to produce all the possibilities for five dots.

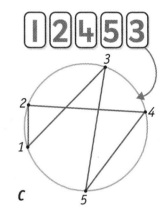

RECORDING/DISPLAY

For each problem, the sets of points need to be placed in the same positions for consistent comparison of outcomes, otherwise shapes will appear to be different just because of the arrangements of the dots. This can be done with a photocopiable sheet, tracing paper or using a dotty grid to position the starting dots – this is recommended. The points should also be spaced in an irregular arrangement to create the maximum number of possibilities.

A large version of the problem makes an effective display and emphasises the 'magic number' aspect of the work.

CHALLENGE

Rearranging the initial placement of the dots (but keeping the order of the numbers the same) can change the view of the outcome but not the structure of the joined up shape. By moving the relative positions of the dots around a circle you can distort the shape (similar to changing grid layouts with fixed coordinates).

  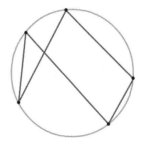

What happens to the number of outcomes if you space six points equally around the circle and join them with continuous paths?

MATHEMATICS/SUMMARY

The activity produces picture outcomes from numerical data, an example of graphical representation. Each polygon and crossover polygon has a code, or set of codes, that determines the way the shape is constructed.

▽△▽△▽△▽△▽△

SOLUTIONS
Page 93

LINKED PROBLEMS
Triangles, page 64

TWENTY-THREE

PROBLEM: *The answer is 23. What was the question?*

LEVEL

Intermediate

Produce number sentences that have an answer of 23 using appropriate values and operations. Include objects to suggest a story, for example 23 books, 23 legs, 23 elephants, 23 people or 23 cars.

Expert

Include a range of measures to encourage mathematical creativity in the construction of suitable questions, for example 23 minutes, 23 litres, 23 metres or 23cm^2.

RESOURCES/GETTING STARTED

There are no special resources required for this problem, but you may want to prepare for the activity by introducing the notion of '*Here is an answer, what was the question?*' with examples in words as well as numbers and units.
Two possible starting points are:

▲ Use a small number or key word and give some examples of questions that would produce that answer. '*List everything you know about the number 7, or triangles. How can we turn this into questions with the answer 7 or triangle?*'

▲ Revise or re-teach aspects of measures and use this question setting situation as a way of assessing understanding of the range covered. This makes a good activity for children in pairs, where ideas can be shared and discussed to arrive at a satisfactory question situation.

KEEPING THE PROBLEM GOING

Making up questions is very hard for children whose mathematical confidence is low. This problem situation will need strong teacher support and suggestions of possibilities, without giving too much specific information. For example, you may link this to use of vocabulary: '*Can you tell me something about 23 using the words "less than"?*' With discussion this will open possibilities for a whole set of questions.

Once the children are clear about the structure of the task and begin to think of questions with a specific answer, it gives you the opportunity to recognise misunderstandings and errors that are possible. Use the children's ideas to move on and create more possibilities by gathering the class or group together after short periods of working. Discussion is a vital part of developing, as well as starting, this activity.

RECORDING/DISPLAY

A web diagram with 23 as the central feature will display the great variation possible in this task.

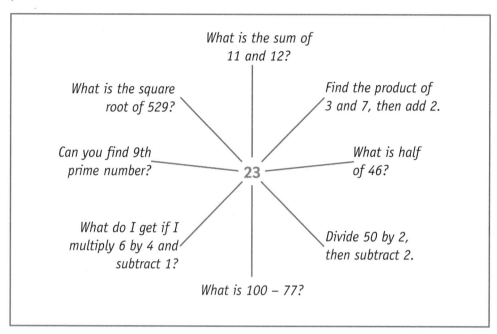

What is the sum of 11 and 12?

What is the square root of 529?

Find the product of 3 and 7, then add 2.

Can you find 9th prime number?

23

What is half of 46?

What do I get if I multiply 6 by 4 and subtract 1?

Divide 50 by 2, then subtract 2.

What is 100 – 77?

SIMPLIFICATION

As preparation for the activity, make separate question and answer cards for the children to match, but include several questions that have the same answer.

CHALLENGE

A bigger number, fraction or decimal provides a clear extension to this task and will emphasise the place value aspect of any measures used. Encourage the children to suggest other units to use and supply example questions. This gives the task a personal challenge factor and develops children's ownership of the problem.

MATHEMATICS/SUMMARY

This task links well with 'think of a number' problems and multi-step questions that encourage an algebraic approach.

The key question is 'What do we want children to know about this number?' and the work will demonstrate that every number has some special characteristics. At some stage repeat this activity for another number to emphasise the range of information that we want children to access, and the way it links with other aspects of the curriculum. Page 105 gives photocopiable information about 43 to illustrate the uniqueness of each number in our counting system, and page 110 lists number properties up to 100.

RESOURCES
Pages 105 and 110.

SQUARE BORDERS

PROBLEM: *Given 20 squares joined edge to edge in a continuous border, what areas can you enclose?*

LEVEL
Intermediate
Find and record different borders and the area enclosed by each one.

Expert
Produce examples of 20 square ▶ borders each with areas of between 7 to 16 squares.

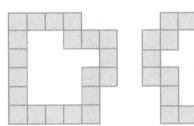

RESOURCES/GETTING STARTED
You will need 20 large squares (10cm edge is ideal) for demonstration on the floor and small squares for the children to use. You may choose to start with a border that encloses a rectangle, although a less structured approach can be helpful in defining the problem and beginning the process of solving it.

Take 20 squares and begin by joining them edge to edge to make a track that eventually turns back to the starting point. With help from the children, manipulate the squares so that the path of 20 squares joins on to the starting square. Explain that this is a border. Check the number of squares in the border and the area inside the border by counting.

The area enclosed will always be a whole number of squares because of the definition of the border, in which every square is attached to exactly two other squares. Square tiles can be used to check the area enclosed, but let the children explain how they see the area (that is, the rectangles that make up

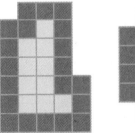 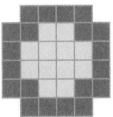

the area), as different strategies will be used, especially in the more complex examples.

◀ Different colour tiles are excellent for clarifying the exact area enclosed and linking the process of changing border shape with that of producing different areas.

Demonstrate how the squares can be moved, whilst maintaining the border of 20 squares to produce a new shape and possibly a different area. This will lead to a discussion of how the alteration of the border increases or decreases the area, but you may want to let the children start on the problem before suggesting further strategies.

KEEPING THE PROBLEM GOING

Key questions are:

▲ 'Has anyone found an area of ...?'

▲ 'Can you find two different borders with the same area enclosed?'

▲ 'Is this the smallest area possible?'

At some stage invite a child to reproduce their solution with tiles on the floor as part of a summary session. Take this opportunity to look at variations and transformations.

Try to get two different 20 square borders with the same area ▶ and discuss the links between the two.

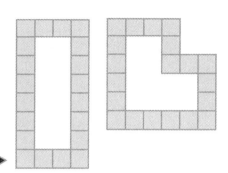

RECORDING/DISPLAY

Use squared or dotty paper for recording, with the tiles clearly defined and the enclosed area highlighted. Small squares stuck onto paper or card will produce a display that can summarise the solutions to the problem. Blank magnetic squares on a suitable surface are excellent as they can be moved easily to illustrate the development of the task.

SIMPLIFICATION

Several borders can be made with 12 squares suggesting a simplification of the problem or an introduction to the activity.

CHALLENGE

Find the largest and smallest possible areas for borders with different numbers of squares, for example 14, 16 or 18 squares.

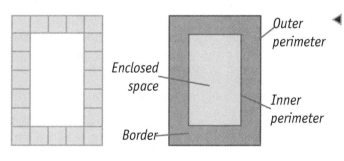

Outer perimeter

Enclosed space

Inner perimeter

Border

◀ MATHEMATICS/ SUMMARY

The number of squares in the border is not generally related to the area enclosed. It is possible, through this activity, to see how the area can be increased or decreased by changing the position of the border squares.

For each shape created there is a border, enclosed area, an inner perimeter and an outer perimeter.

With borders of 20 squares, the inner perimeter will be 16 units and the outer perimeter 24 units.

SOLUTIONS
Page 94

LINKED PROBLEMS
Twelve sticks, page 70

TRIANGLES

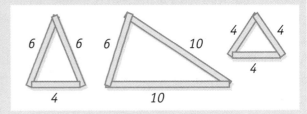

PROBLEM: *Given sticks that are 4cm, 6cm and 10cm long, what triangles can you make?*

LEVEL

Intermediate

Work with a limited number of sticks, make triangles practically and record solutions freehand.

Expert

Use pencil and paper only, sketch triangles and list characteristics.

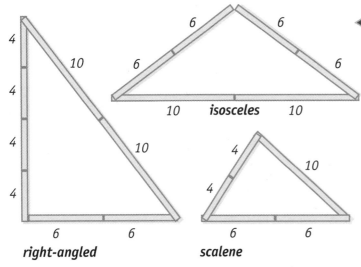

right-angled   *isosceles*   scalene

◀ **RESOURCES/GETTING STARTED**

Demonstrate with sticks, rods or card strips cut to lengths of 40cm, 60cm and 100cm. Invite suggestions for triangles that can be constructed with the rods. Ask them to visualise then explain or demonstrate their thinking, helping out if necessary but allowing time for adjustment and rethinking. This process will produce four or five triangles, which you can leave as prompts for individual work. Identify side lengths and decide how you want the children to indicate these on their own work.

This is an excellent activity for showing similarity, congruence and suggesting which lengths are possible to make triangles. Cuisenaire rods (purple, dark green and orange) make perfect desktop material for children to work on the problem. Expect periods of exploration before the children get into the problem, you may actually plan for this before you set a particular challenge.

For the intermediate level, three rods of each length is a manageable number, producing lots of different outcomes. The expert level problem could be set after a period of teaching or review of triangle characteristics, or as follow-on from the intermediate problem. This could occur six weeks later when your starting point would be: *'Remember those triangles we constructed? How many can you draw and identify as a paper, ruler and pencil activity?'*

Make sure that you remove any display material if you want to make this a key assessment activity!

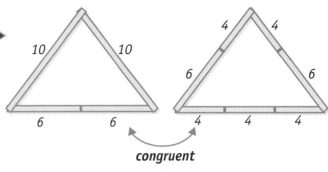

KEEPING THE PROBLEM GOING

Check for triangles that are exactly the same ▶ (congruent) and those that have the same angles but are different sizes (similar). Move the triangles around or change the child's view of them to check this. Increase the number of sticks available but suggest a limit for the length of side of the triangle so that there is a clear goal for solutions.

congruent

RECORDING/DISPLAY

Freehand drawing is the best way of recording as the lengths and angles can vary greatly. At a later stage or as a follow-on activity you may want the children to produce some scale drawings. Construction of triangles with ruler and compasses will produce

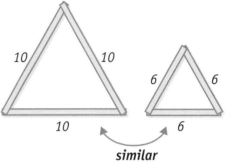

similar

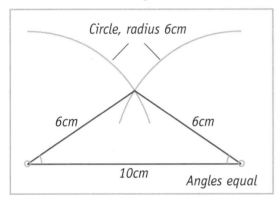

◀ accurate drawings where the angles can be measured.

Strips of paper, preferably a different colour for each length, mounted on a different colour paper background make a good visual display in which the components of each edge of the triangle are clear.

SIMPLIFICATION

Begin with making triangles from lots of rods that are all the same length – 10cm rods are ideal.

CHALLENGE

Find the perimeter of each triangle constructed, and list the triangles in perimeter order. This gives an indication of size, which may or may not correspond with the area, making a good discussion point. Try making triangles that use all three rods of each length, that is all with perimeter 60cm.

MATHEMATICS/SUMMARY

The realisation that we can only construct a triangle if the lengths of the two shorter sides total more than the length of the longest side is a key outcome from this activity. This is known as the 'triangle inequality' or $a + b > c$ where c is the longest side.

As the combinations of rods produce so many different side lengths to generate triangles, no further solutions are given for this activity. Scalene acute and scalene obtuse, isosceles acute and isosceles obtuse, right-angled and equilateral triangles are all possible with up to three of each of the 4cm, 6cm and 10cm rods.

▽▲▽▲▽▲▽▲▽▲▽▲
LINKED PROBLEMS
Crossover polygons, *page 58*

PYRAMIDS

PROBLEM: *In a pyramid shape with four boxes along the bottom, pairs of numbers are added to produce the number in the box above. This process is continued until the final total is placed in the top box of the pyramid (see example, right). What final totals are possible if the input numbers 1, 3, 6, and 7 are placed in any order?*

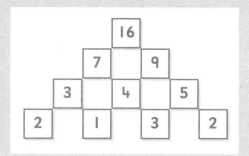

LEVEL

Intermediate

Find the possible solutions in the top box and begin to think about why different totals are produced.

Expert

Devise a rule for getting the top box number from the input numbers directly.

RESOURCES/GETTING STARTED

Large floor tiles make an excellent starting material as they can be used as numbers or blank tiles when turned face down, and you can step onto the blank tiles to show which answers are required. Set the input numbers using the tile values or placing numeral cards on blank tiles. Begin with the tiles in the second row, 'What number goes in this box if we add those two numbers?' You can record answers on the tiles as you move around or challenge the

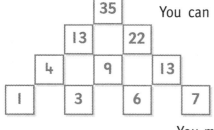

children to work mentally and give you any value in the pyramid when prompted. Move on to the next row and eventually the top box value. Rerun the process to ensure that all children understand the problem and choose others to give answers. For the numbers 1, 3, 6 and 7 in this order the final total will be 35.

You may choose to work with different numbers in your demonstration so that the children start the problem themselves. Now ask *'What happens if I change the order of the input numbers?'* and *'Will the final total remain the same?'* This is the basis of the investigation. The large tiles can be used in discussion to try out some solutions, demonstrate an example to the class or provide practical material for a group of children to work with.

KEEPING THE PROBLEM GOING

You need to know the possible answers so that help can be given if calculation is a problem. The initial problem asks what happens if you change the order of the input numbers, but not the values. Further questions can explore adding 1 to each starting number, doubling all starting values, getting to a set target number and so on.

RECORDING/DISPLAY

Some children may need help with the layout of their recording, but most will initially be able to create their own boxes on plain paper. This approach encourages jottings to help with calculations and boxes can be adjusted to fit the size of the numbers. Squared paper gives children a framework for filling in numbers. A spreadsheet is excellent for calculating and displaying possible arrangements – details appear on page 106.

SIMPLIFICATION

Use three numbers at the base of the pyramid, this may also be helpful for introducing the problem for the first time. This means that two calculations are required in the second row and the top box number is the sum of these two answers. As a check for you (and a challenge for the children) the top number in a 3-box pyramid is the sum of the first and last input numbers plus twice the middle number. With input numbers a, b and c the values in the second row are $(a + b)$ and $(b + c)$, giving a top box sum of $(a + b + b + c)$ or $(a + 2b + c)$.

This algebraic approach can be demonstrated with objects placed in the input boxes: coloured counters, cubes or Cuisenaire rods. The sum of two boxes then becomes the objects grouped together, demonstrating the general formula for the pyramid in a practical way.

$8 = 1 + 2 + 2 + 3$

$1 + 2 = 3$

$5 = 2 + 3$

1   2   3

CHALLENGE

▲ Include some larger input numbers, fractions or decimals as appropriate.
▲ Start with five boxes at the base of the pyramid and look for a general rule.
▲ Find the numbers in the bottom row given the top box number, there are lots of possible answers, especially if negative numbers are included.
▲ Try using just the tiles 1 to 24, with no number appearing more than once in the pyramid.

MATHEMATICS/GENERALITY

The structure of the pyramid links to Pascal's triangle (a triangular pattern of numbers in which each number is the sum of the two above it) and the numbers in each row give the general solution to the problem. Further details are given in Solutions, page 95.

▼▲ ▼▲ ▼▲ ▼▲ ▼▲
RESOURCES
Page 106

SOLUTIONS
Page 95

LINKED PROBLEMS
▲ Caterpillars, *page 30*
▲ Flags, *page 34*

HEXOMINO CUBES

▼A▼▼A▼A▼A▼A▼A▼A▼A▼A▼A▼A▼A▼A▼A▼A▼A▼A▼A▼A▼A▼

PROBLEM: *Can you construct six special hexominoes to fit into a grid of 36 squares?*

▼A▼A▼A▼A▼A▼A▼A▼A▼A▼A▼A▼A▼A▼A▼A▼A▼A▼A▼A▼

LEVEL

Intermediate

Find all the 'special hexominoes' (see the illustration below) and use some of them, with repeats, to fill a 6 × 6 grid, recording your findings. (All the possible hexomino shapes appear in Solutions, page 96.)

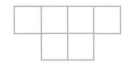

This is a hexomino

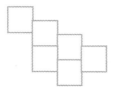

This is not a hexomino

Expert

Find outcomes with only two repeats or no repeats at all (that is, all six pieces different). Record your solution and set this as a puzzle for others to try.

▲ RESOURCES

Hexominoes are 2-D shapes made from six squares joined edge to edge.

If we use cubes to build the shapes we create solid versions of the hexominoes that have a depth of one cube. No cubes should be added above this initial layer. Special hexominoes all have a 2 × 2 block as part of their construction which can be made to hide all the 'studs' or connecting pieces which normally protrude from the shapes made with cubes. Two extra cubes are added to this 4-block and this means that no studs show when the special hexomino is completed. It is much easier to place these shapes together and move them around when solving the problem. It also means that it is easier to change one hexomino into another by altering the positions of the two extra cubes.

 **+**

2 × 2 block (no studs)   *2 extra cubes*   *Special hexomino*

GETTING STARTED

Place four large squares on the floor in a 2 × 2 grid, this is the basis for building the special hexominoes. Demonstrate how four Multilink cubes fit together to make this block without any studs showing. Two other squares need to be added to this 2 × 2 block. Ask the children where you can place them. As the children make suggestions, demonstrate by placing the squares on the floor and then using Multilink cubes. Talk about shapes that may be the same, even if they look different, by moving squares around. There are opportunities for discussion of rotation and reflection here. Leave one or two

completed hexominoes on the floor and set the problem: ▶
*'Using Multilink cubes, make all the different special
hexominoes that you can find, then try to solve the puzzle,
fitting six special hexominoes together on a 6 × 6 grid with
no spaces. Repeats are allowed'.*

KEEPING THE PROBLEM GOING

Use 2cm grid paper to cut out the 6 × 6 grids, this gives an exact template for
the Multilink cubes. Check that the children are constructing shapes without
studs showing. Encourage them to change pieces as they are solving the puzzle,
this adjustment is a good strategy and may help them to find any shapes not
previously discovered. The key is to create spaces that include a 2 × 2 square
so that one of the special hexominoes will fit in, the last piece being the most
difficult.

RECORDING/DISPLAY

Encourage children to record solutions as soon as they complete the practical
activity. You will then be able to suggest alterations, refinements or further
challenges. Each completed square is a potential puzzle challenge for other
children and this can lead to variations in the solutions for a given set of
pieces, all of which should be recorded. There are lots of opportunities for
stunning colour display material here, with scale drawings or computer versions.
The special hexominoes can be labelled with letters for easy identification.
This provides a mechanism for setting further problems, an example appears
on photocopiable page 107.

4 cubes

5 cubes

6 cubes

6 cubes

6 cubes

CHALLENGE ▲

Using the 2 × 2 block as a basis, '3-D' shapes can be constructed that can then
be combined to make a cube. For example, a 3 × 3 × 3 cube of 27 Multilink
cubes can be constructed from these five shapes: one 2 × 2 block, one 2 × 2
block with one extra cube, and three 2 × 2 blocks each with two extra cubes,
making 4 + 5 + 18 = 27 cubes altogether. Constructing such a puzzle is a high
level task, recording the solution is even more challenging!

MATHEMATICS/SUMMARY

The eight special hexominoes are particularly suitable for puzzle work because
of the nature of their construction. There are 27 other shapes that can be
constructed from six squares joined edge to edge.

▽▲▽▲▽▲▽▲

RESOURCES
Page 107

SOLUTIONS
Page 96

**LINKED
PROBLEMS**
▲ Four square
puzzle, *page 28*
▲ L-shapes, *page 32*
▲ Symmetrical
shapes, *page 46*
▲ Pentominoes,
page 50

TWELVE STICKS

PROBLEM: *Using 12 sticks, all the same length, what shapes can you create by placing them end to end in a continuous path?*

LEVEL

Intermediate
Make shapes that only contain right angles and record them on squared paper.

Expert
Make shapes with at least one right angle, or line or rotational symmetry.

RESOURCES/GETTING STARTED

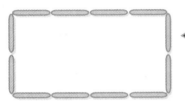

◄ Make a rectangle with rods on the floor, strips on a magnetic board or sticks fixed to any vertical surface. It really is helpful if you can move the sticks around easily as this allows you to change one shape to another.

Check with the children that all 12 sticks have been used and introduce/ recall the word perimeter as appropriate. You may want to consider the area of rectangular shapes and explain the links with perimeter. Demonstrate how you can change the area whilst keeping the perimeter fixed, for example move one corner in, and check the new area and perimeter. ▶

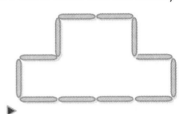

◄ Get the children to investigate their own shapes using practical materials, for example lolly sticks. The sticks must be all contained in the perimeter with no diagonals.

Lolly sticks and rods are suitable but paper or card strips are suitable for pairs to share. Provide plenty of materials so that solutions can be laid out in preparation for recording.

KEEPING THE PROBLEM GOING

The children will learn much from each other's work so it is important to share findings without giving too many answers. Often a suggestion of one shape will lead to variations, for example finding all the shapes with areas of five squares.

Some children will be tempted to create pictures, so you must decide whether this adds to, or detracts from the activity. You may consider using the sticks in artwork to tap the creative potential of the task.

RECORDING/DISPLAY

Indicate ways of recording on squared paper, dotty paper or plain paper; you must decide whether the shapes need to be accurately drawn with a ruler, or sketched with enough detail for future revision. Make sure that the children have enough space for this activity and consider letting them work on the floor, as this allows for shapes to be seen by others. With lots of sticks you can create an instant display that is excellent for discussion, comparison and giving children a feel for the measurements involved.

Centimetre squared or dotty paper is suitable for recording using a scale diagram, but this may need some explanation. You might want to encourage the plain paper sketchbook jottings approach if the children are confident and able to calculate the area from their drawings. When displaying shapes it is better if the scale is constant to allow for direct comparison and to emphasise the diversity of 12-stick perimeters that are possible

SIMPLIFICATION

There are lots of shapes possible with fewer sticks but fewer possibilities ▶ for rectangular shapes. Eight sticks produce three different rectangular shapes, so this is a good starting point. ◀ With ten sticks in the perimeter there are six different possibilities.

10 sticks

8 sticks

CHALLENGE

Try triangular shapes or shapes made with triangles and rectangles. Can you estimate or calculate any of these areas and hence place them in order of size?

MATHEMATICS/SUMMARY

The process of finding shapes from a given starting point involves adjustment, similar to that used for mental strategies used in number work. For most 2-D shapes the area and perimeter are not linked. For some regular shapes there is a simple relationship, for example for a square the area can be calculated from the perimeter by dividing by four and squaring the answer:

if perimeter of square = 36cm,
then side length = 36 ÷ 4 = 9cm,
so area of square = 9 × 9 = 81cm².

For most regular polygons, the calculation of area from perimeter is complex, involving Pythagoras' theorem and trigonometry, although scale drawing may help with estimates of area.

The largest area for 12 sticks is produced from a dodecagon (12-sided polygon). With more sticks the number of sides on the regular polygon increases and the shape appears approximately circular.

▼▲▼▲▼▲▼▲▼▲
SOLUTIONS
Page 97-98

LINKED PROBLEMS
▲ Square borders, *page 62*

SEVEN DIGITS

PROBLEM: *Use 1, 2, 4, 4, 5, 8 or 9 to make number sentences using any operations. You can only use a digit once in any number sentence (except 4), and the whole number sentence must be made from these digits. You do not need to use all the digits in each number sentence, for example 4 + 4 = 8 is OK. Digits can be combined to make other numbers, for example 44 or 12.*

LEVEL

Intermediate/expert

This depends on the number of digits used in solutions, as the challenge increases dramatically as more digits are included. Children need mental calculation skills with one-digit and two-digit numbers, knowledge of place value and understanding of order of operations for recording solutions.

RESOURCES/GETTING STARTED

Use large digits for introducing the problem and leave some solutions for children to see. Provide digit cards for individuals or pairs, as manipulating the cards really does help thinking and explanation. Decide whether calculators are appropriate for checking solutions or as an aid to finding more answers.

$$4 + 1 = 5$$
$$9 = 1 + 4 + 4$$
$$4 \times 4 + 2 = 1\,8$$
$$4\,9 \div (8 - 1) = 5 + 2$$

Show the children the digits and get them to construct a number sentence by moving digits and introducing appropriate signs for operations. The usual starting point uses three digits and you can indicate the variations that are possible: 8 + 1 = 9, 1 + 8 = 9, 9 – 1 = 8, 9 – 8 = 1. These may all be regarded as one 'number sentence family' solution. Get the children to suggest ways of building on from this starting point by adjusting or replacing digits. Examples like 4 + 4 + 1 = 9 or 2 × 4 + 1 = 9 are different solutions with the same mathematical content. You must judge when most of the children understand the task so that you don't display too many answers and take over the problem from individuals. Encourage careful use of jottings with errors or 'near misses' treated positively – mistakes may provide the key to further answers, for example: ▼

KEEPING THE PROBLEM GOING

The task is difficult at the outset, but gets easier as solutions are shared and variations

$$4 + 4 = 8 \checkmark$$
$$4 + 4 + 5 = \enclose{circle}{13} \times (\text{ no } 3)$$
$$\text{add } 8$$
$$4 + 4 + 5 + 8 = 2\,1 \checkmark$$

are discovered. The key difficulty is using only the digits given to complete a number sentence. Answers will be found that use other digits, or repeats of digits included already. A strategy of adjustment is useful here where an unlisted number is replaced by a calculation using the digits that are allowed, for example: ▶

Children need concentrated effort and plenty of time to succeed in finding more complex answers, but when sentences are found that no one else has discovered the sense of achievement is considerable.

$$4 \times 8 = \boxed{32} (\boxed{3} \text{ not available})$$

Strategy: use other digits to make 32

$$\boxed{32} = \boxed{9} \times \boxed{4} - \boxed{4} \text{ (but only two } \boxed{4}\text{s)}$$

$$\boxed{32} = \boxed{9} \times \boxed{4} - \boxed{5} + \boxed{1}$$

$$\text{So } \boxed{4} \times \boxed{8} = \boxed{9} \times \boxed{4} - \boxed{5} + \boxed{1}$$

RECORDING/DISPLAY

As the task progresses, encourage recording with some categorisation or system, for example using three digits, using four digits, using five digits and so on. Solutions can be written on strips and displayed on a board or get pairs of children to write solutions on each side of a strip of cards and hang the strips up to produce a mathematical mobile for the classroom. Instant display can be good for motivation, but you may want to wait until all children have had time to develop their own answers before showing others.

SIMPLIFICATION

You may want to count variations as different if this is appropriate to your class, for example $4 + 4 + 1 = 9$ can be written as $9 - 4 - 1 = 4$. Using more digits makes the problem easier especially if 0, 1, 2 and 3 are included. You could limit the operations, for example to addition and subtraction only, to establish the appropriate level of working.

EXTENSION

Ask the children to use as many digits as possible in their number sentences with seven digits as the ultimate challenge. You may want to score the sentences produced by counting the number of digits used as an incentive. This means that lots of smaller sentences are valued, as well as the ones using more digits, for example $4 \times 2 + 1 = 9$ scores four points, $14 \div 2 + 1 = 8$ scores five points. There are lots of possibilities, including some with the digits in numerical order, for example $12 + 4 - 4 + 5 - 8 = 9$. It is also possible to make any two-digit total using the other seven digits, for example $45 = (9 \times 4) + 8 + 2 - 1$. Some children could choose their own set of digits to create a problem to challenge others.

MATHEMATICS/SUMMARY

Manipulating numbers with confident use of mental strategy skills are crucial factors in this activity. Order of operations are a key element of the task as the number sentences become more complex. It is possible to make every one- and two-digit number by using all the other digits (see Solutions, page 99).

SOLUTIONS
Page 99

LINKED PROBLEMS
▲ Threes and fours, *page 26*
▲ Two numbers, *page 48*
▲ Make twenty, *page 54*
▲ Three rings, *page 56*

TIMES-TABLE SUMS

PROBLEM: *What is the largest and smallest total of the products of digits 1 to 9 arranged in a 3 × 3 square grid?*

LEVEL

Expert

Find the sum of the six horizontal products (in circles) and six vertical products (in diamonds) of digits 1 to 9 placed randomly in a square grid. Rearrange the digits to produce a larger or smaller total and continue until maximum and minimum arrangements have been found. This problem demands

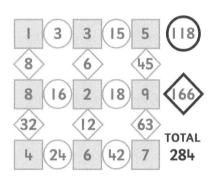

competence with all the multiplication facts up to   9 × 9 and an ability to add a string of two-digit numbers competently, using a calculator if necessary. In the above example, the sum of the horizontal products (the circled numbers) is 118, and the vertical products 166, giving a total product sum of 284.

RESOURCES/GETTING STARTED

Use the large number tiles or digit cards 1 to 9 and place them on the floor in a random 3 × 3 grid. As a starter activity stand on a tile and ask, for example, for 3 times that number, move about getting answers in the 3 times-tables randomly from individuals. You can target questions at individuals according to the difficulty of the calculation. Change to 7 times each number and repeat your random step by step movements on the digits.

Explain the times-tables sums problem by placing a blank tile between adjacent numbers horizontally and vertically, asking for the product in each case. Demonstrate clearly that there are six horizontal products and six vertical products; get a child to write these on the board. Ask *'What do you think the total of these 12 numbers might be?'* This will focus the thinking on a sensible range of values (for example, 300 is 12 × 25 and this is a good estimate). This makes a good activity for pairs where aspects of the work are shared, and for many children a set of digit cards will help with organisation and clarify thinking.

KEEPING THE PROBLEM GOING

Encourage checking to ensure correct totals and look for unusually high or low values to spot children's calculation errors. As you work with the problem you will get a feel for the validity of children's answers. After the children have explored some random grids, suggest ways that the arrangements of numbers can be changed to increase or decrease the total. Use the class recording strategy suggested opposite to collect answers and provide motivation for working.

RECORDING/DISPLAY

Discussion of possible layouts for working will influence recording. You may want to indicate a specific way of organising the two groups of six products to help with calculation and checking. If not, this is part of the challenge for children to develop their own method that is efficient and accurate.

For a whole class record produce a list with a range of ▶ spaces for entering totals, separated in 5s and fix it to the wall or board. The children enter the total that they have found in the appropriate range and write their initials. Include totals that are below the minimum value and above the maximum value. This chart gives an example layout with values outside the minimum– maximum range, and space for the children to write in their solutions. The list:

▲ allows you to check progress of individuals or pairs
▲ demonstrates the range of possible values
▲ may produce duplicate totals with different arrangements of digits
▲ motivates children to work on the next answer.

150	185	220	255	290	325	360
155	190	225	260	295	330	365
160	195	230	265	300	335	370
165	200	235	270	305	340	375
			239 KW			
170	205	240	275	310	345	380
175	210	245	280	315	350	385
			284 JS			
180	215	250	285	320	355	390

SIMPLIFICATION

What happens if all the digits are the same, say 2? You can limit the range of calculation by using digits 2, 3, 4 and 5 for example, with repeats, or target any individual range of numbers. A 2 × 2 grid is good for demonstrating the structure of the problem, but the number of outcomes limits the possible range of answers. ▶

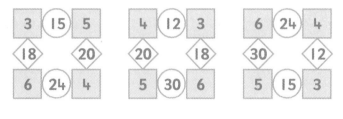

TOTAL 77   **TOTAL 80**   **TOTAL 81**

CHALLENGE

It is possible to target any number within a range of say 250–350. Any of these targets would make a challenging task, although many will be found in the process of looking for maximum and minimum.

Use a spreadsheet to generate formulae for calculating the sum of all the products. The digits can be rearranged easily by dragging and dropping. Each grid can be copied and pasted to produce a complete record of all attempts. Details of how this works are provided on page 109.

MATHEMATICS/SUMMARY

A key strategy here is to maximise or minimise the products by placing larger or smaller numbers next to each other. The centre number is clearly an important factor in this process. Demonstrate how this works in a plenary session with use of large digit cards that can easily be moved around. A range of possible answers is provided on page 108.

RESOURCES
Pages 108 and 109

SOLUTIONS
Page 100

LINKED PROBLEMS
▲ Number maze, *page 36*
▲ Find four numbers, *page 40*
▲ Four by four grids, *page 52*

THREES AND FOURS

Because 3 and 4 are small consecutive numbers the continuous pattern of totals starts at 6 (3 + 3).

It is possible to make all totals from 6 to 30 (and beyond) using 3s and 4s. The number of combinations increases as the totals get bigger.

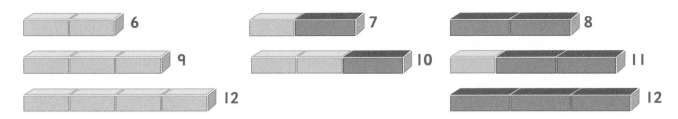

An addition table is another way of representing solutions.

+	3	6	9	12	15	18
4						
8			⑰			
12						
16		㉒				
20						
24				㊴		

⑰ ────► (3 × 3) + (4 × 2)

㉒ ────► (3 × 2) + (4 × 4)

㊴ ────► (3 × 5) + (4 × 6)

Given any number to express as the sum of 3s and 4s, one approach might be to ask:

▲ Is the number in the 3 times table? YES – then we can make it with all 3s.

▲ Does the number have a remainder of 1 when divided by 3? YES – then we can make it one 4 and all the rest 3s.

▲ Does the number have a remainder of 2 when divided by 3? YES – then we can make it with two 4s and all the rest 3s.

This exhausts all the possibilities, every number will fit in one of these categories.

Finding all solutions for one total produces a pattern in 3s and 4s:

43 = 4 + 3 + 3 + 3 + 3 + 3 + 3 + 3 + 3 + 3 + 3 + 3 + 3 + 3, ie (4 x 1) + (3 x 13)

43 = 4 + 4 + 4 + 4 + 3 + 3 + 3 + 3 + 3 + 3 + 3 + 3 + 3, ie (4 x 4) + (3 x 9)

43 = 4 + 4 + 4 + 4 + 4 + 4 + 4 + 3 + 3 + 3 + 3 + 3, ie (4 x 7) + (3 x 5)

43 = 4 + 4 + 4 + 4 + 4 + 4 + 4 + 4 + 4 + 4 + 3, ie (4 x 10) + (3 x 1).

The number of 4s goes up by three each time, while the number of 3s goes down by four. This is because the key value of 12 that can be exchanged using four 3s or three 4s to make different solutions. The rods make a very powerful demonstration of this process, allowing children to handle and manipulate numbers.

Here is one way of solving the problem *'Can we make every number from 6 to infinity?'*

We can make six	We can make seven	We can make eight
3 + 3	4 + 3	4 + 4
by adding 3s	by adding 3s	by adding 3s
9	10	11
12	13	14
15	16	17
18	19	20
21	22	23
24	25	26
27	28	29
30	31	32
33	34	35
36	37	38
39	40	41
42	43	44

and so on to infinity...

Finding a 'rule' for making any number bigger than 5 just using 3s and 4s with addition is a real challenge to children's thinking. There is no magic algebraic formula, but any written solution will either be based on building numbers in larger blocks or link to combining the 3 and 4 times tables with consideration of remainders in division by 3 and 4.

Any pair of starting numbers will produce lots of different totals. There will be a continuous pattern of answers eventually. With three numbers the possibilities are even greater.

Numbers with factors of 3 or 4 (or both) are rectangle, or composite, numbers. Prime numbers from 13 onwards can be expressed as the sum of two or more rectangle numbers, for example:

$43 = 27 + 16 = (3 \times 9) + (4 \times 4)$

$53 = 33 + 20 = (3 \times 11) + (4 \times 5)$

$79 = 39 + 40 = (3 \times 13) + (4 \times 10)$

FOUR SQUARE PUZZLE

There are many possible solutions. The shapes below are all viable solutions and show three ways of filling a grid where five grids are rectangles and two grids are squares (4 x 4 and 6 x 6).

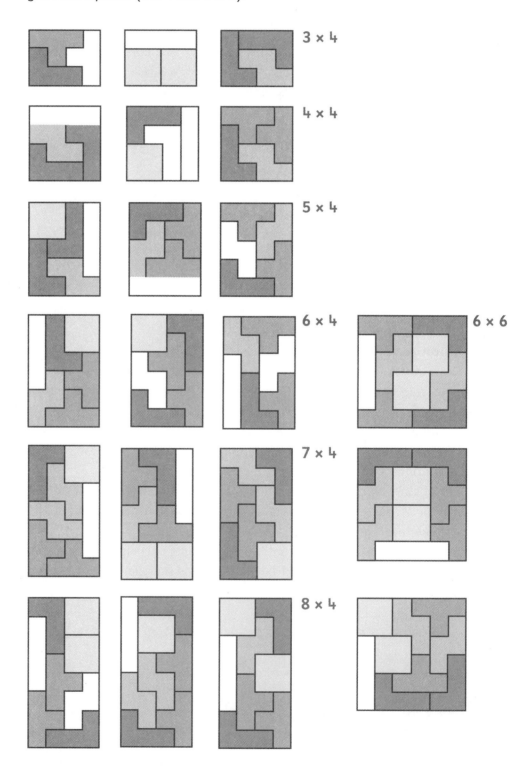

CATERPILLARS
(USING TWO COLOURS)

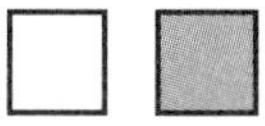

1 segment, 2 caterpillars

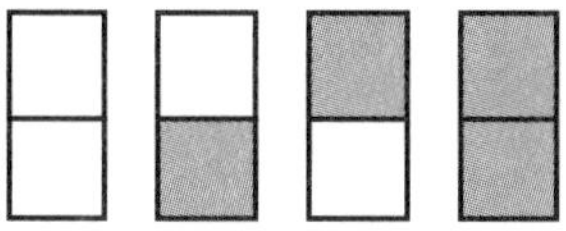

2 segments, 4 caterpillars

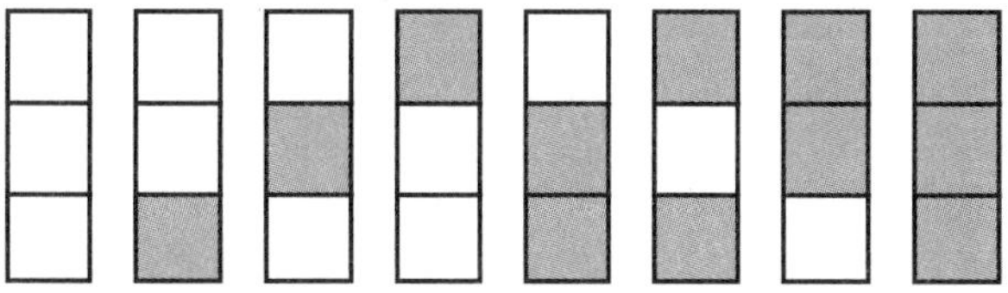

3 segments, 8 caterpillars

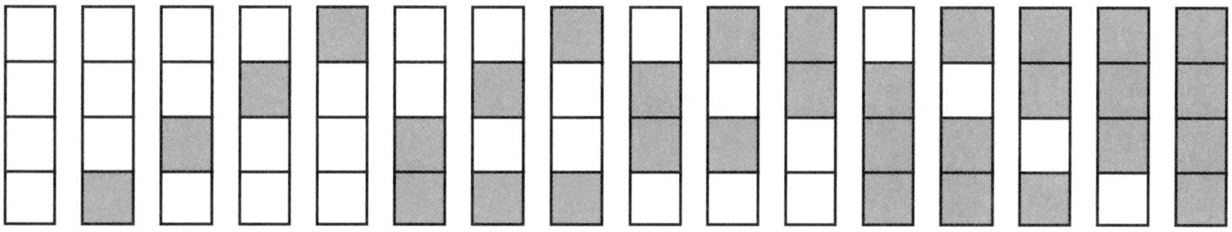

4 segments, 16 caterpillars

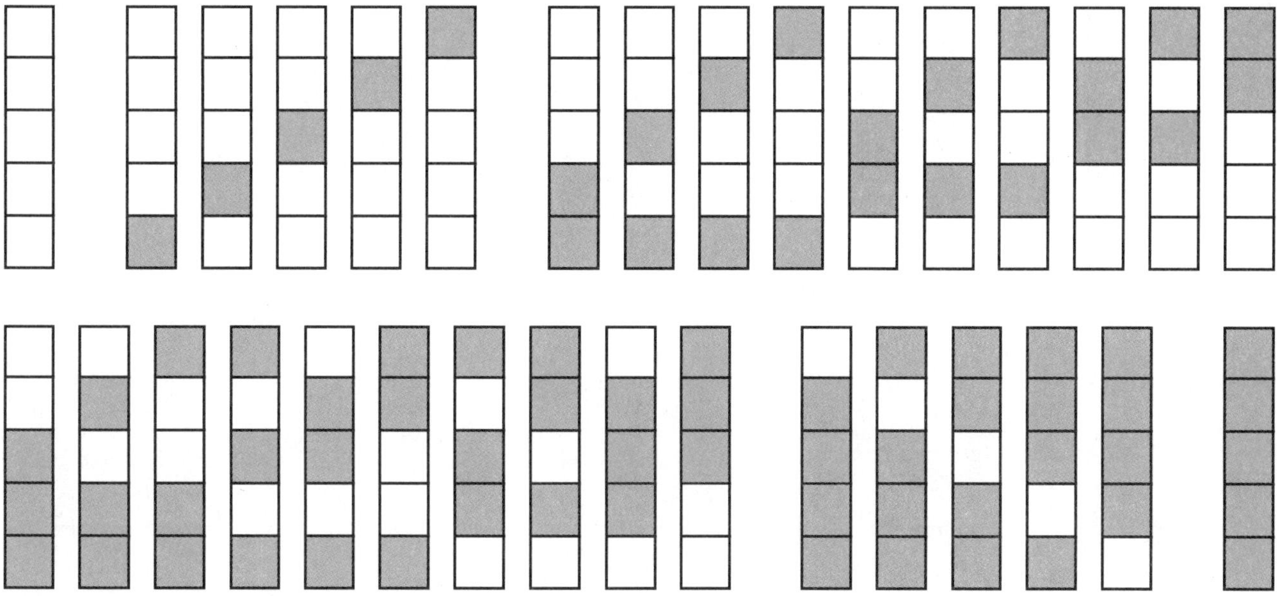

5 segments, 32 caterpillars

L-SHAPES

3 × 3 square

Min 2   2   2   2   2   2   Max 2

4 × 4 square

Min 3   3   4   4   4   Max 5

5 × 5 square

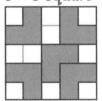 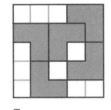 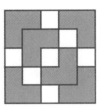 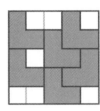 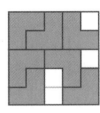 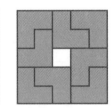

Min 5   5   6   6   7   Max 8

6 × 6 square

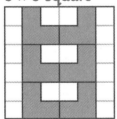 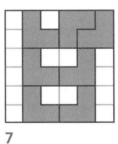 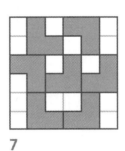 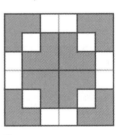

Min 6   7   7   8   8

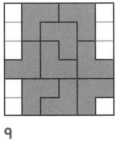 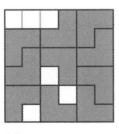 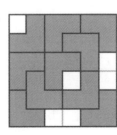 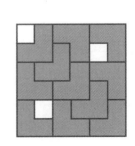 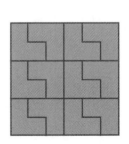

9   10   10   11   Max 12

FLAGS: 1

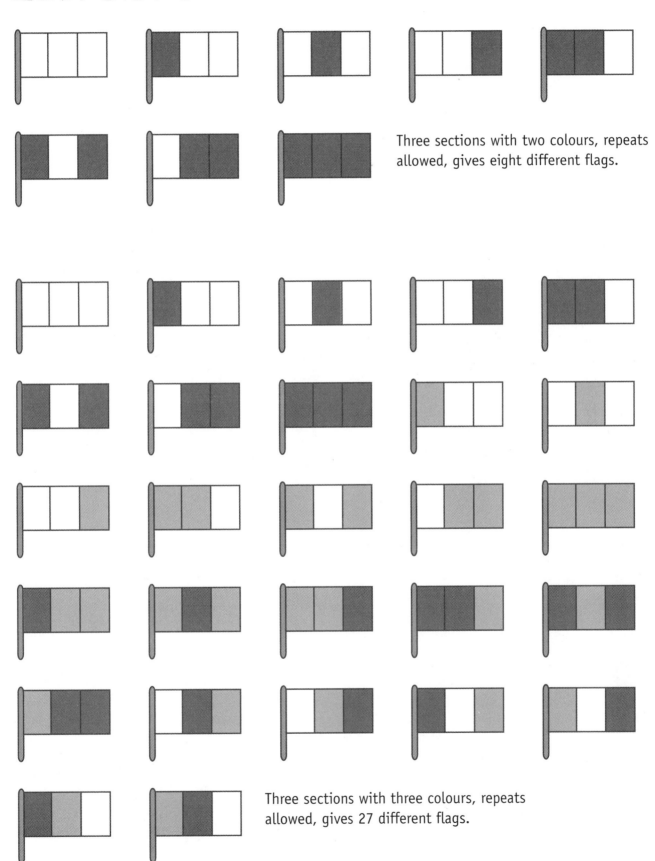

Three sections with two colours, repeats allowed, gives eight different flags.

Three sections with three colours, repeats allowed, gives 27 different flags.

FLAGS: 2

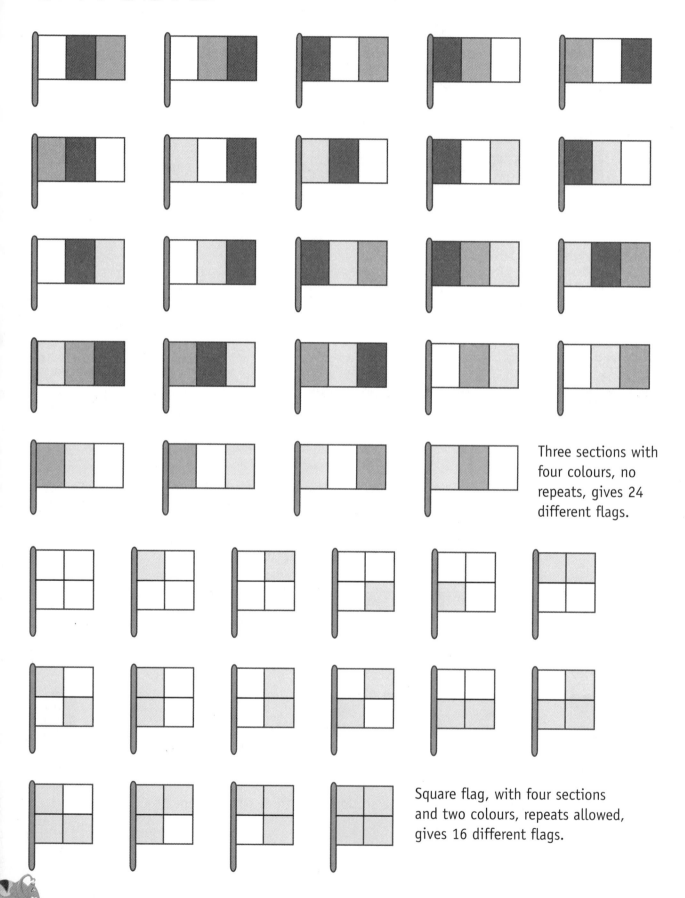

Three sections with four colours, no repeats, gives 24 different flags.

Square flag, with four sections and two colours, repeats allowed, gives 16 different flags.

NUMBER MAZE

Elephant routes

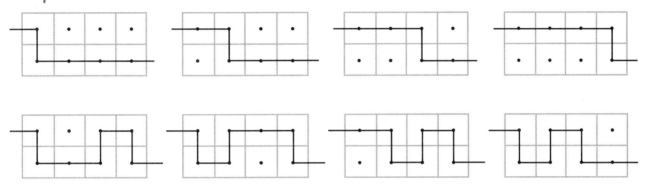

3 × 3 grid

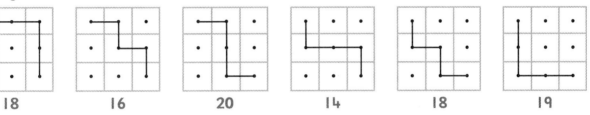

| 18 | 16 | 20 | 14 | 18 | 19 |

(30)	−8	+1	−19
−5	+2	−15	+3
+1	−7	+3	−6
−20	+2	−8	?

4 × 4 grid with addition and subtraction
There are 20 possible routes giving these final totals:
1, 5, 5, 3, 6, 6, 4, 14, 12, 11 (starting with −8)
9, 9, 7, 17, 15, 14, 16, 14, 13, 0 (starting with −5)

(1)	+3	×2	−4
+7	×3	−9	+6
×4	+1	−3	×2
−5	×2	+6	?

4 × 4 grid with addition, subtraction and multiplication
There are 20 possible routes giving these final totals:
20, 10, −8, 2, 18, 0, 6, 20, 16, 32 (starting with +3)
42, 24, 18, 44, 28, 56, 60, 36, 72, 60 (starting with +7)

SQUARES AND TRIANGLES

2-D shapes using two squares and two triangles:

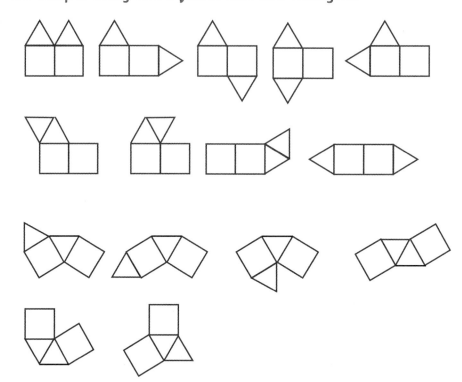

Net for a closed solid using six squares and eight triangles:

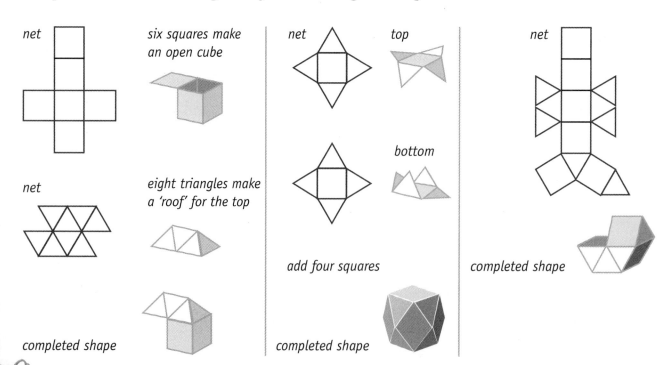

net

six squares make an open cube

net

top

net

net

eight triangles make a 'roof' for the top

bottom

completed shape

add four squares

completed shape

completed shape

FIND FOUR NUMBERS

Intermediate level

L-shapes have no lines of symmetry, so occur in eight different orientations on the grid:

For each orientation there are six positions, with different sets of numbers on the grid:

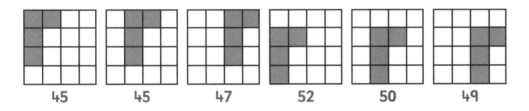

| 45 | 45 | 47 | 52 | 50 | 49 |

This gives a total of 8 × 6 = 48 possible positions. The totals for each orientation are listed:

44, 49, 38, 48, 53, 46

40, 46, 53, 48, 50, 45

50, 46, 44, 49, 51, 43

47, 51, 49, 47, 49, 46

42, 51, 45, 50, 47, 52

48, 49, 51, 43, 50, 45

42, 42, 54, 47, 48, 46

Expert level

Ten more ways of making 100

addition:
50 + 21 + 20 + 9
50 + 20 + 17 + 13
50 + 25 + 16 + 9

multiplication:
10 × 9 + 8 + 2
20 × 4 + 16 + 4
16 × 5 + 12 + 8

multiplication:
8 × 13 − 12 + 8
9 × 12 − 13 + 5
10 × 15 − (25 × 2)

division:
(50 × (9 − 5)) ÷ 2

TWO BLOCKS

Examples of different-sized rectangles with no fault lines

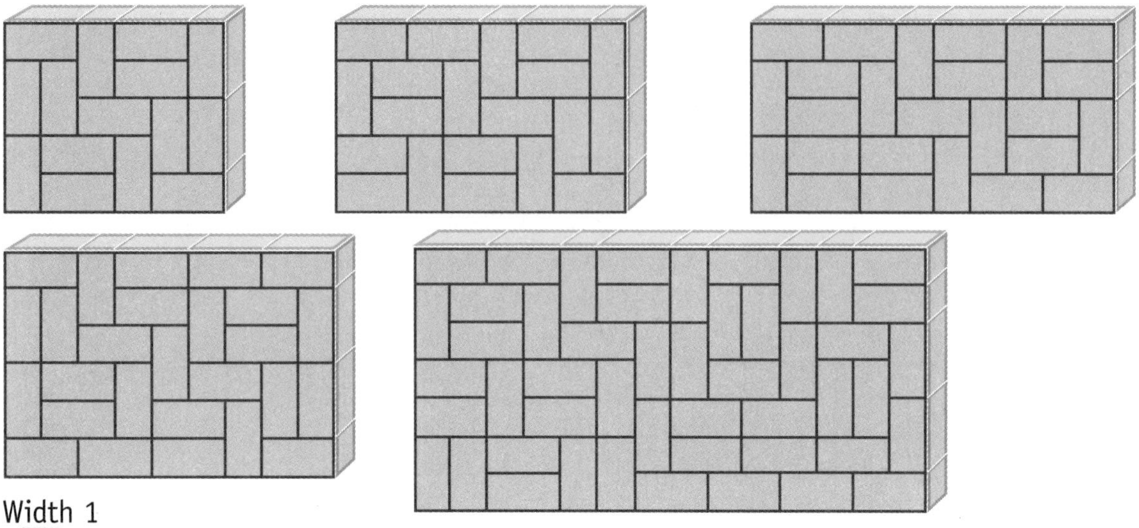

Width 1

1 arrangement

Width 2

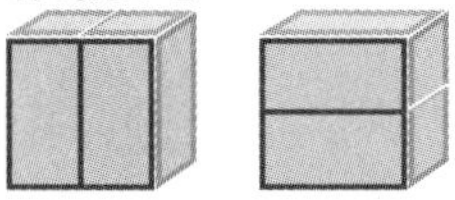

2 arrangements

Width 3

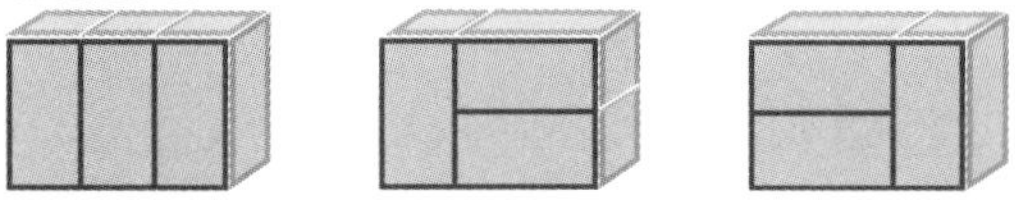

3 arrangements

Width	Arrangements
1	1
2	2
3	3
4	5
5	8
6	13

Width 4

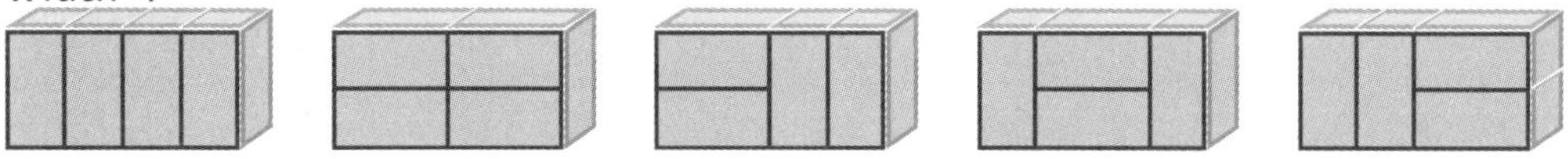

5 arrangements

Width 5

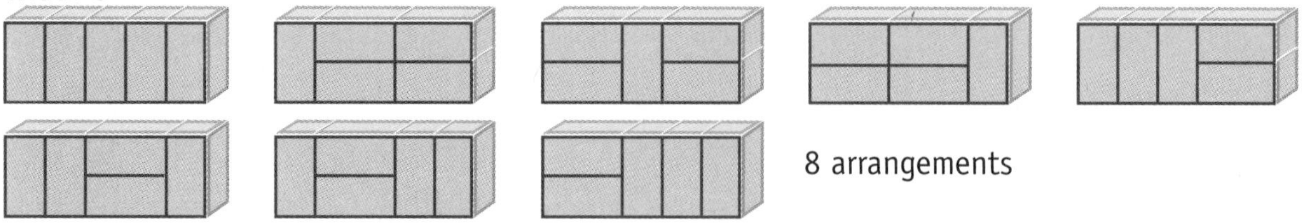

8 arrangements

Width 6

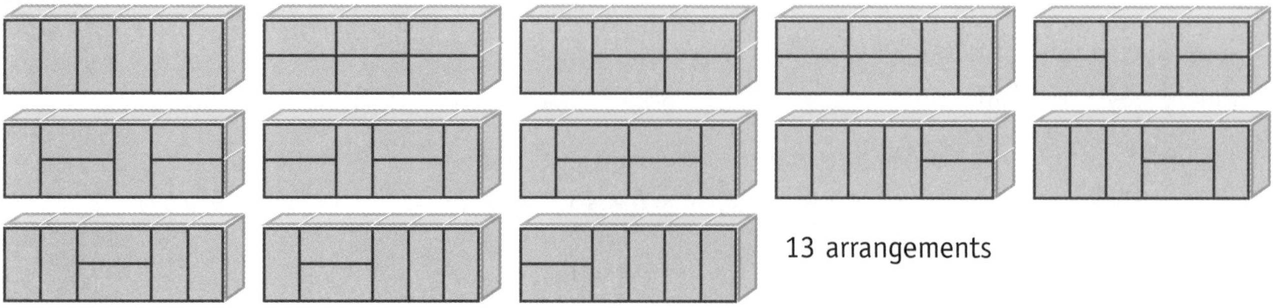

13 arrangements

GRID PATTERNS

(shading started on the first square, number 1)

2s   3s 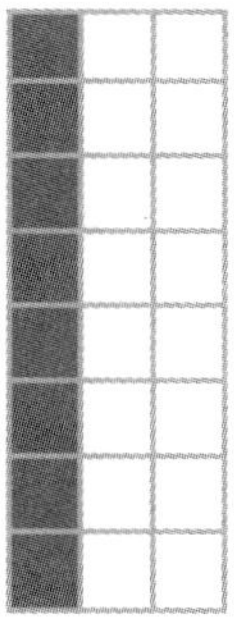  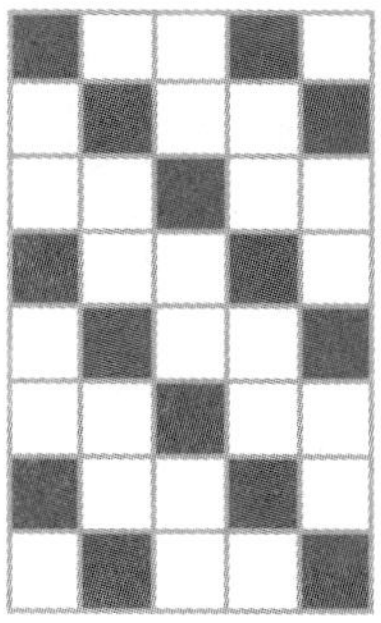   4s

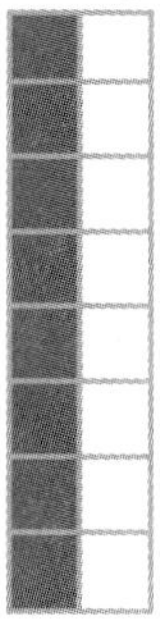

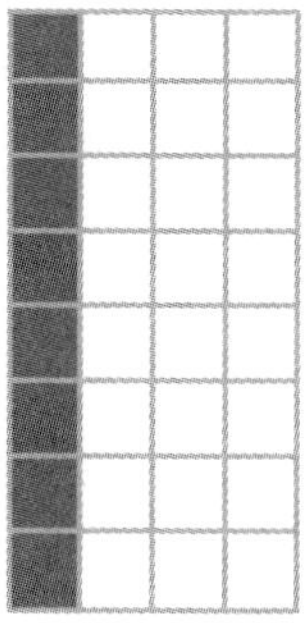

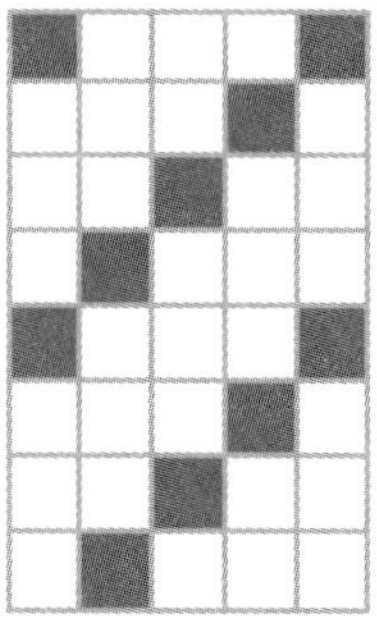

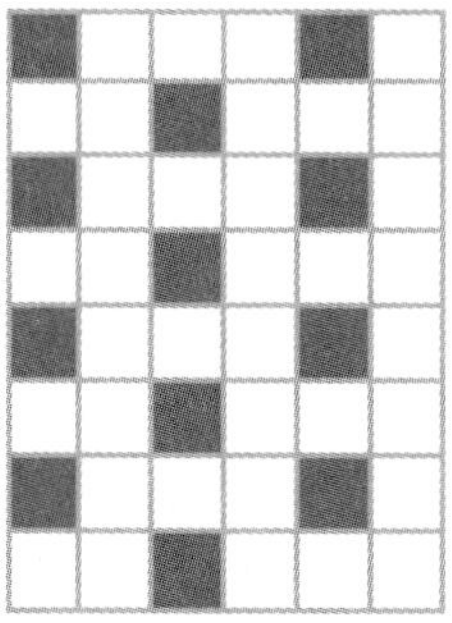

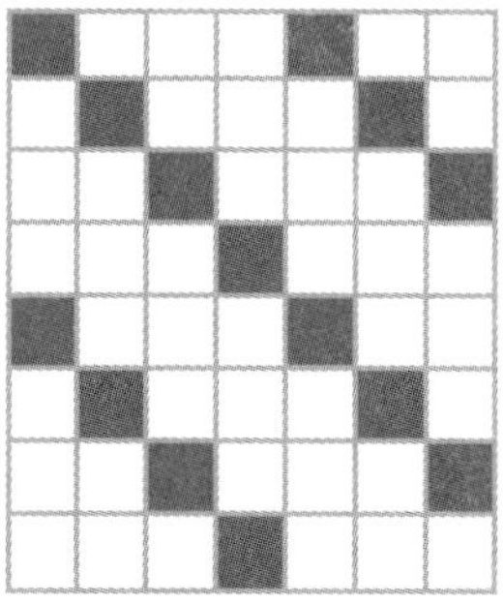

5s

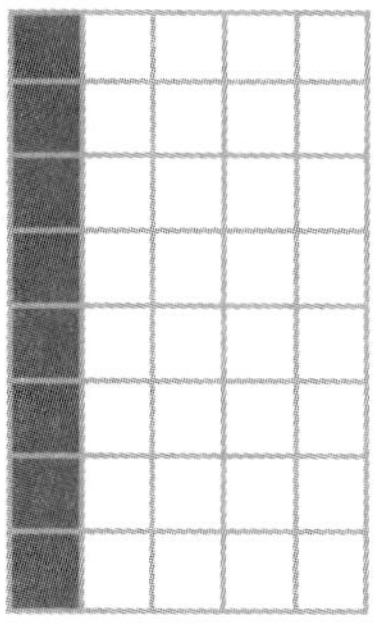

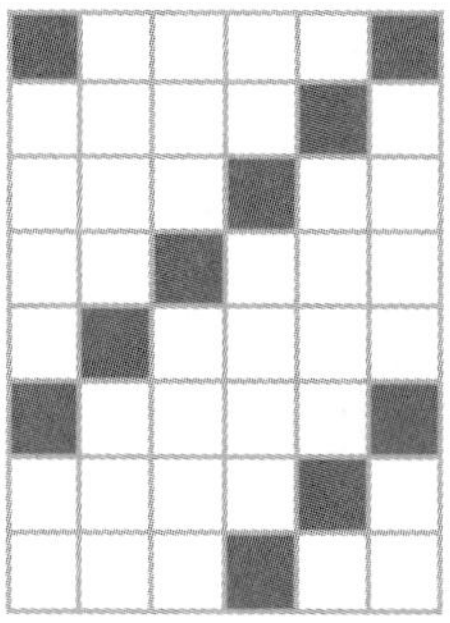

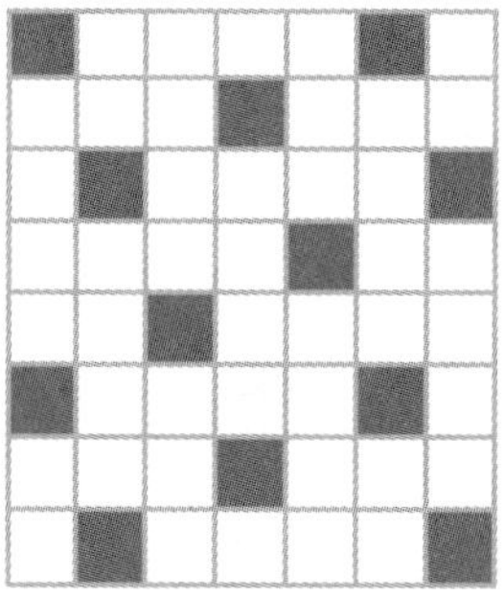

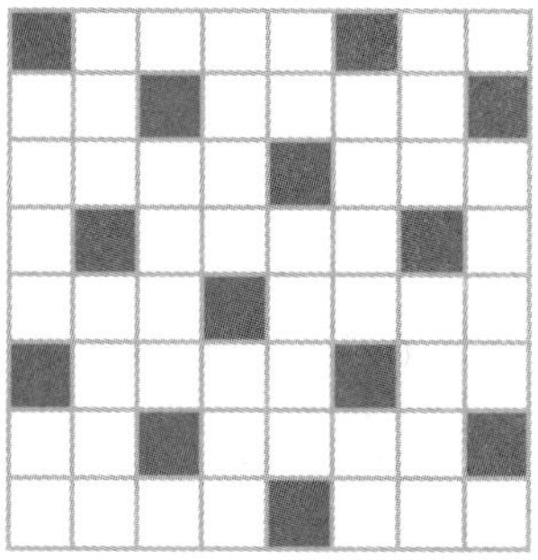

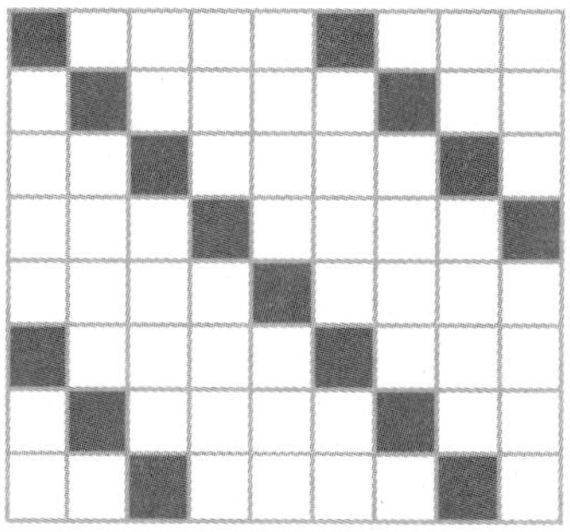

6s

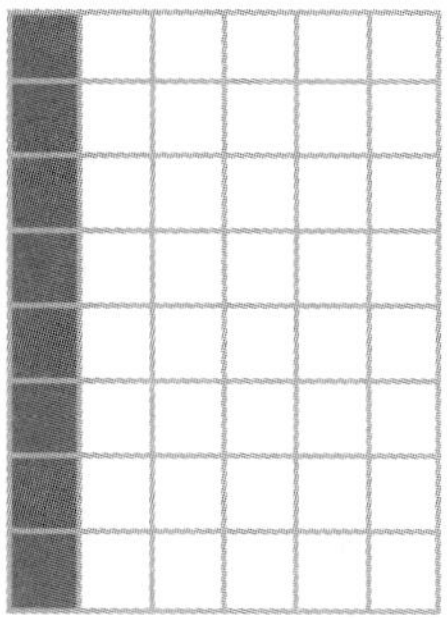

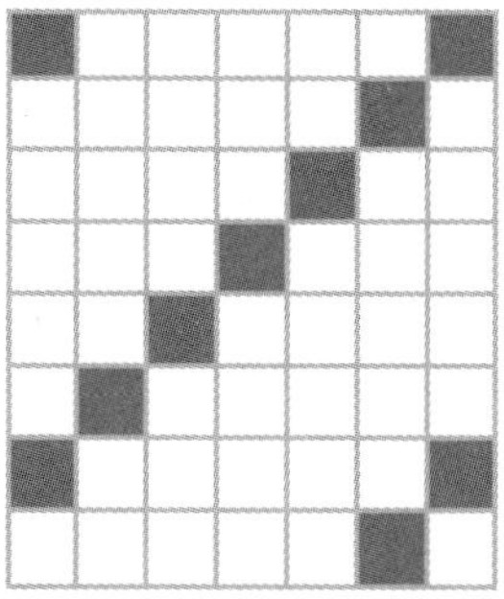

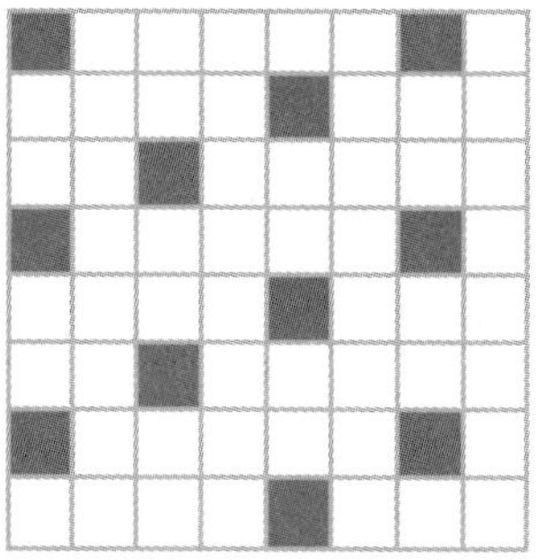

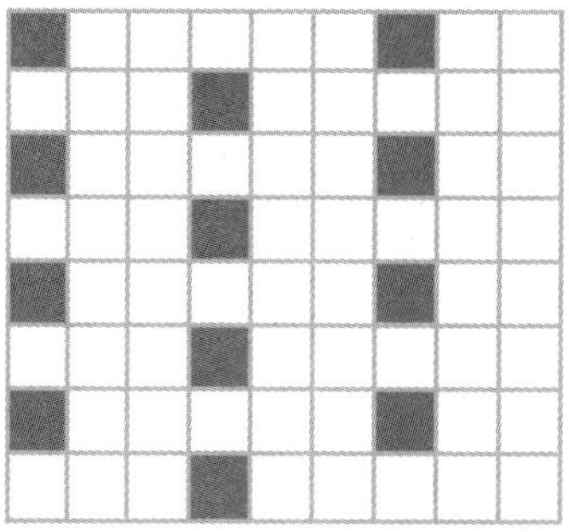

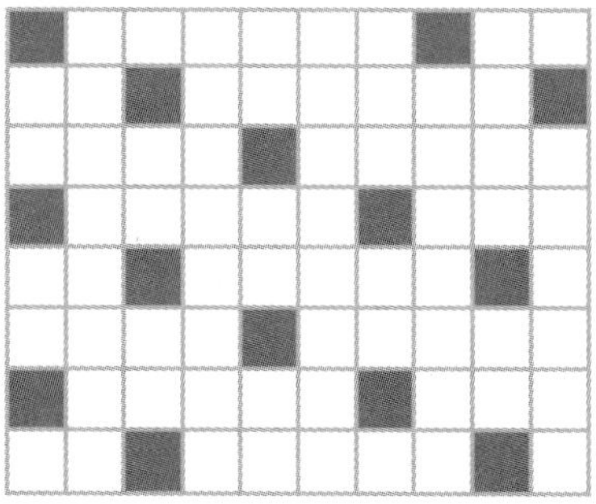

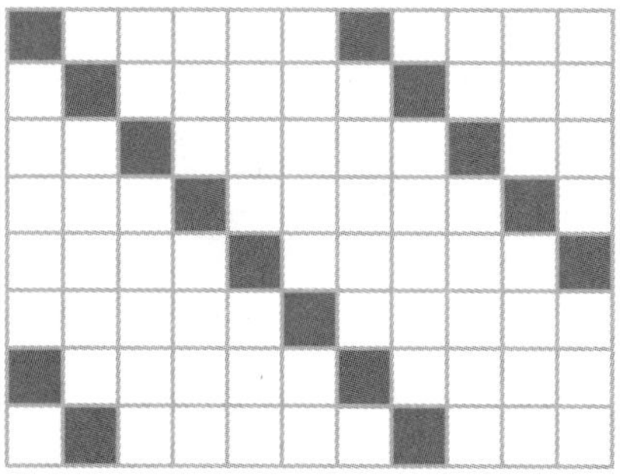

SYMMETRICAL SHAPES

Using two shapes to make shapes with line symmetry

Using two shapes to make shapes with rotational symmetry

Using three shapes to make shapes with line symmetry
(Some of these shapes can be made in more than one way.)

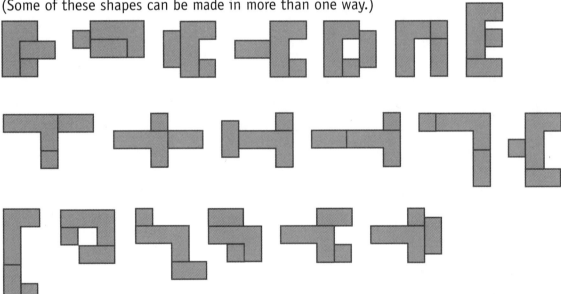

Using three shapes to make shapes with rotational symmetry

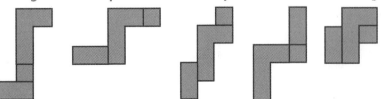

PENTOMINOES

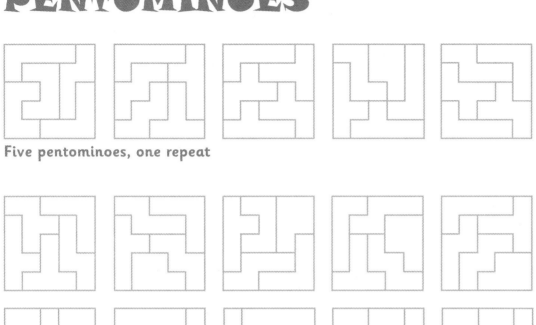

Five pentominoes, one repeat

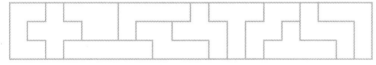

Five pentominoes, all different

3 × 20 rectangle

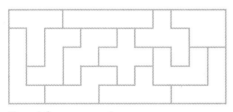

5 × 12 rectangle

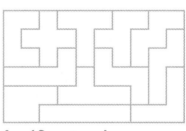

6 × 10 rectangle

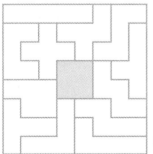

8 × 8 square

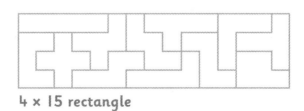

4 × 15 rectangle

FOUR BY FOUR GRIDS

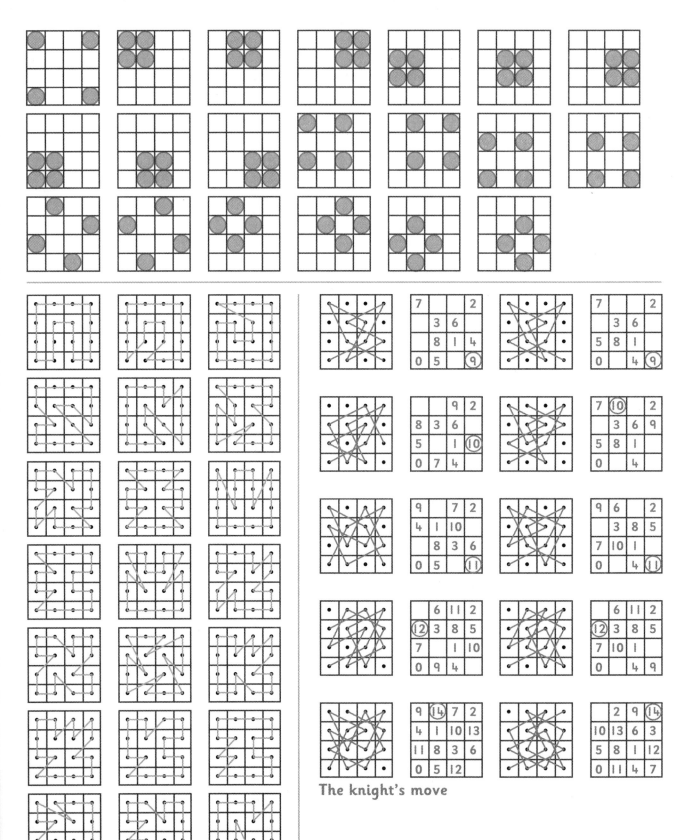

The knight's move

MAKE TWENTY

16 can be made using (1, 7, 8), (2, 6, 8), (3, 5, 8) and (4, 5, 7).
18 can be made using (1, 2, 7, 8), (1, 3, 6, 8), (1, 4, 5, 8), (1, 4, 6, 7),
(2, 3, 5, 8), (2, 3, 6, 7), (2, 4, 5, 7) and (3, 4, 5, 6).

```
10 = 1 2 3 4
11 = 1 2 3   5
12 = 1 2 3       6
13 = 1 2 3         7
14 = 1 2 3           8
15 =   2 3 4   6
16 =   2 3 4       7
17 =   2 3 4         8
18 =     3 4 5 6
19 =     3 4 5   7
20 =     3 4 5       8
21 =     3 4   6   8
22 =       4 5 6 7
23 =       4 5 6   8
24 =       4 5   7 8
25 =       4   6 7 8
26 =         5 6 7 8
```

If we create 2-D shapes with areas 1 to 8 we can fit four of these into a 5 × 4
rectangle in six ways. This gives another way of illustrating solutions to the
'Make twenty' problem.

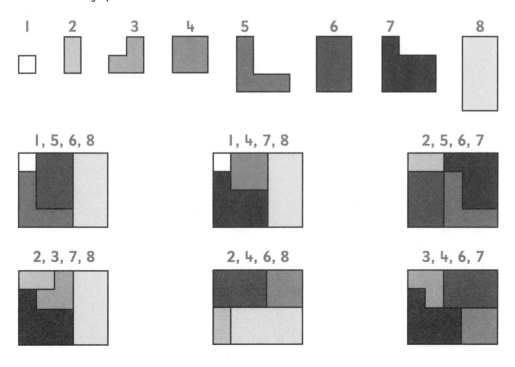

THREE RINGS

For 1, 1, 1, 2, 2, 2, 3, 3, 3 there are three possibilities: (3, 3), (1, 2, 3), (1, 1, 2, 2); (3, 3), (1, 1, 1, 3), (2, 2, 2) and (1, 2, 3), (1, 2, 3), (1, 2, 3).

Starting at 1 and adding consecutive numbers gives the triangle numbers, and 45 = 1 + 2 + 3 + 4 + 5 + 6 + 7 + 8 + 9 is a multiple of 3, so it can be split into 3 equal groupings with total 15. Many of the triangle numbers are multiples of 3, so for any of these 'special' triangle numbers it should be possible to split them into three groups with equal totals. For example: 1, 2, 3, 4, 5 makes 15 which splits into the three groups (5), (4, 1) and (2, 3). There is only one possible grouping here, and 15 is the smallest triangle number whose consecutive number components will break into three groups.

The next triangle multiple of 3 is 21 and this splits into three groups totalling 7 in just one way: (6, 1), (5, 2) and (4, 3).

Then 36 splits into three groups totalling 12 in three ways: (8, 4), (7, 5), (6, 3, 2, 1); (8, 4), (7, 3, 2), (6, 5, 1) and (8, 3, 1), (7, 5), (6, 4, 2).

The number 66 can be partitioned into three groups totalling 22 in lots of different ways. The table (left) is a possible starting point where the largest numbers are placed in the first group.

11, 10, 1	9, 8, 5	7, 6, 4, 3, 2
11, 10, 1	9, 8, 3, 2	7, 6, 5, 4
11, 10, 1	9, 7, 6	8, 5, 4, 3, 2
11, 10, 1	9, 7, 4, 2	8, 6, 5, 3
11, 10, 1	9, 6, 5, 2	8, 7, 4, 3
11, 10, 1	9, 6, 4, 3	8, 7, 5, 2
11, 9, 2	10, 8, 4	7, 6, 5, 3, 1
11, 9, 2	10, 8, 3, 1	7, 6, 5, 4
11, 9, 2	10, 7, 5	8, 6, 4, 3, 1
11, 9, 2	10, 7, 4, 1	8, 6, 5, 3
11, 9, 2	10, 6, 5, 1	8, 7, 4, 3
11, 9, 2	10, 5, 4, 3	8, 7, 5, 1
11, 8, 3	10, 9, 2, 1	7, 6, 5, 4
11, 8, 3	10, 7, 5	9, 6, 4, 2, 1
11, 8, 3	10, 7, 4, 1	9, 6, 5, 2
11, 8, 3	10, 6, 5, 1	9, 7, 4, 2
11, 8, 3	10, 6, 4, 2	9, 7, 5, 1
11, 8, 3	10, 5, 4, 2, 1	9, 7, 6
11, 7, 4	10, 9, 3	8, 6, 5, 2, 1
11, 7, 4	10, 9, 2, 1	8, 6, 5, 3
11, 7, 4	10, 8, 3, 1	9, 6, 5, 2
11, 7, 4	10, 6, 5, 1	9, 8, 3, 2
11, 7, 4	10, 6, 3, 2, 1	9, 8, 5
11, 6, 5	10, 9, 3	8, 7, 4, 2, 1
11, 6, 5	10, 9, 2, 1	8, 7, 4, 3
11, 6, 5	10, 8, 4	9, 7, 3, 2, 1
11, 6, 5	10, 8, 3, 1	9, 7, 4, 2
11, 6, 5	10, 7, 3, 2	9, 8, 4, 1

▶ Can you find any more?

CROSSOVER POLYGONS

There are 12 distinct shapes with five points:

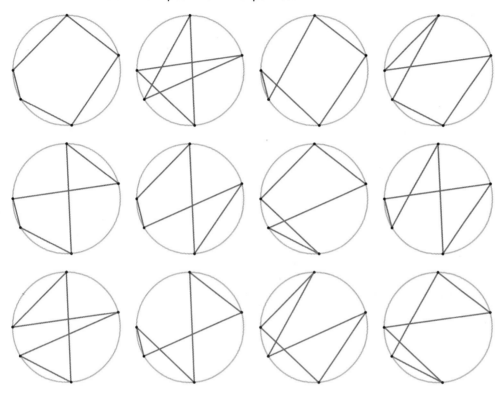

There are lots of possibilities with six points. These are 12 basic outlines, many of which can be rotated to appear differently.

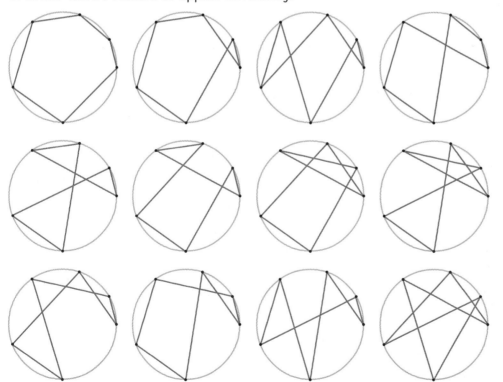

SQUARE BORDERS

All these shapes have a border of 20 squares.

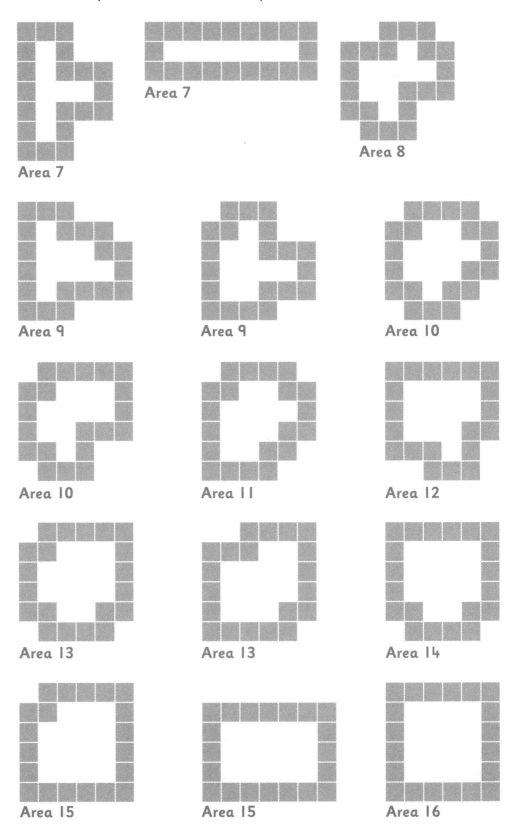

Area 7

Area 7

Area 8

Area 9

Area 9

Area 10

Area 10

Area 11

Area 12

Area 13

Area 13

Area 14

Area 15

Area 15

Area 16

PYRAMIDS

Each arrangement of four numbers gives four solutions with the same total number.

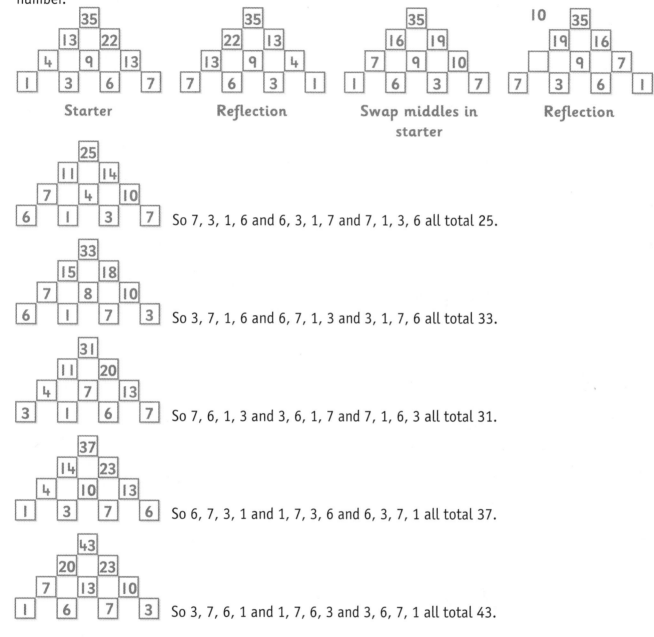

| Starter | Reflection | Swap middles in starter | Reflection |

So 7, 3, 1, 6 and 6, 3, 1, 7 and 7, 1, 3, 6 all total 25.

So 3, 7, 1, 6 and 6, 7, 1, 3 and 3, 1, 7, 6 all total 33.

So 7, 6, 1, 3 and 3, 6, 1, 7 and 7, 1, 6, 3 all total 31.

So 6, 7, 3, 1 and 1, 7, 3, 6 and 6, 3, 7, 1 all total 37.

So 3, 7, 6, 1 and 1, 7, 6, 3 and 3, 6, 7, 1 all total 43.

In general there are six distinct solutions.
The lowest total is given when the lowest numbers occupy the middle positions (6, 1, 3, 7).
The highest total is given when the highest numbers occupy the middle positions (1, 6, 7, 3).
Starters 1, 2, 3, 4 give totals 16, 18, 20 (twice), 22, 24.
For five starter numbers there will be 120 arrangements with 30 distinct solutions.

HEXOMINO CUBES

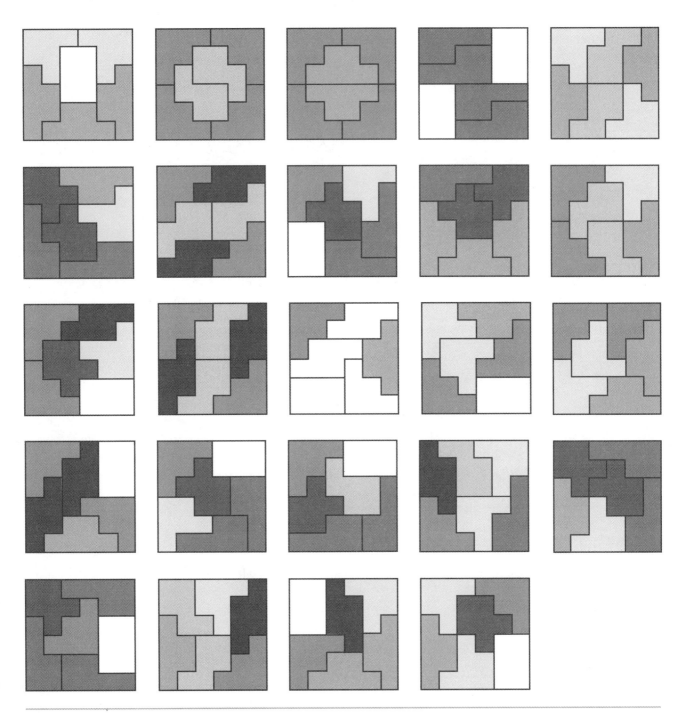

Expert solutions

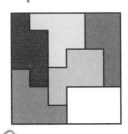 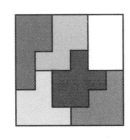

Are there only two solutions with
6 different pieces?

TWELVE STICKS: 1

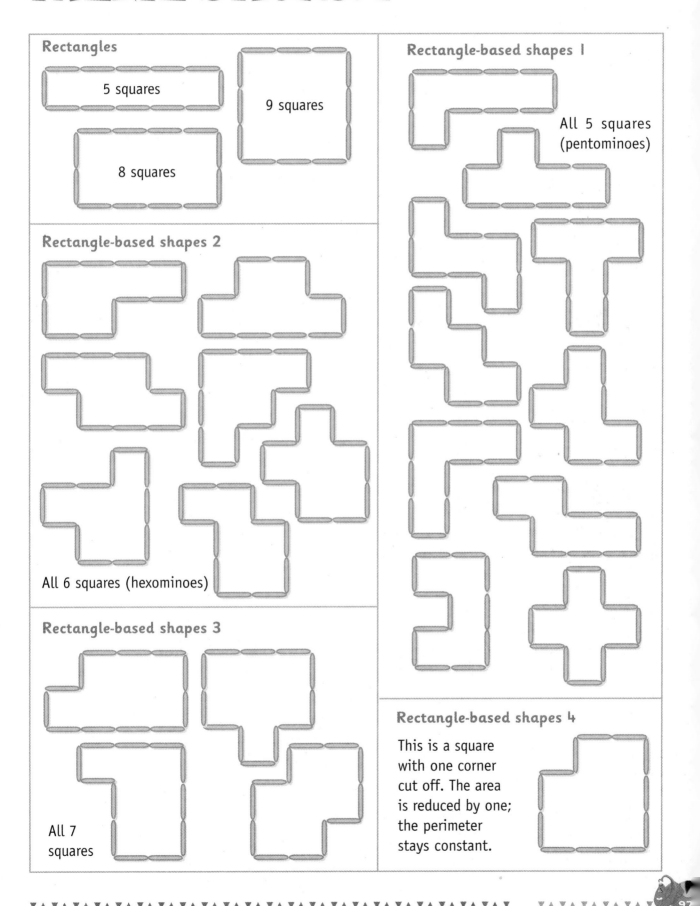

Rectangles

5 squares

9 squares

8 squares

Rectangle-based shapes 1

All 5 squares (pentominoes)

Rectangle-based shapes 2

All 6 squares (hexominoes)

Rectangle-based shapes 3

All 7 squares

Rectangle-based shapes 4

This is a square with one corner cut off. The area is reduced by one; the perimeter stays constant.

TWELVE STICKS: 2

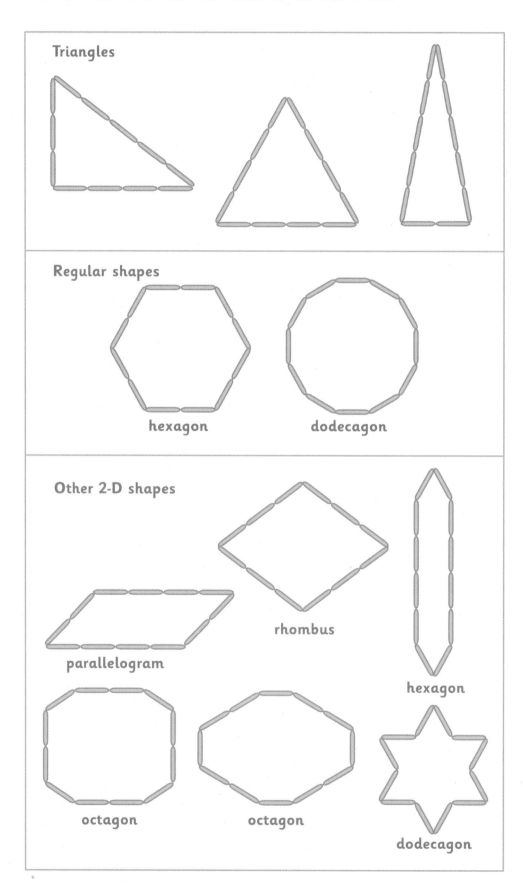

Triangles

Regular shapes

hexagon

dodecagon

Other 2-D shapes

rhombus

parallelogram

hexagon

octagon

octagon

dodecagon

SEVEN DIGITS

Possible solutions:

4 + 4 = 8

2 × 4 = 8

4 + 5 = 9

4 + 8 = 12

4 + 4 + 1 = 9

(2 × 4) + 1 = 9

8 = 5 + 4 −1

12 = 8 + 9 − 5

48 ÷ 12 = 4

24 = 8 × (4 − 1)

(4 + 2) × 9 = 54

(4 × 8) − 9 + 1 = 24

4 + 5 + 8 = (2 × 4) + 9

1 = (2 × 8) + 44 − 59

2 = (4 × 8) + 5 + 1 − (4 × 9)

4 = (94 − 85 − 1) ÷ 2

5 = 81 − (4 × 9 × 2) − 4

8 = (5 × 2) − (9 + 1) + 4 + 4

9 = (5 ÷ 8) × (4 × 4) − 2 + 1

12 = 9 + 8 + 4 − (5 + 4)

14 = (4 × 2) + (9 − 8) + 5

15 = 8 × (4 ÷ 4) + 9 − 2

18 = 9 + 5 − 4 + (2 × 4)

19 = (2 × 8) + 4 + 4 − 5

21 = (9 − 8) × 4 × 4 + 5

24 = (9 × 8) ÷ 4 + 5 + 1

25 = (4 + 4 + 8 + 9) × 1

28 = 1 + (4 × 9) − 4 − 5

29 = 4 (4 + 5) − 8 + 1

41 = (9 × 4) + 8 + 2 − 5

42 = (9 × 5) − 1 − (8 ÷ 4)

44 = (1 + 5) × 9 − 2 − 8

45 = (4 × 2 × 8) − 19

48 = (9 − 5) × (1 + 2) × 4

49 = [8 + 4 − (5 × 1)] ^{2}

51 = (5 × 8) + 9 + (2 × 1)

52 = (8 × 9) − 4 (1 + 4)

54 = (2 × 4 × 8) − (9 + 1)

58 = (9 + 4 + 1) × 4 + 2

59 = (8 × 4 × 2) − (4 + 1)

81 = 95 − (4 × 4) + 2

82 = (9 × 5) + 41 − 4

84 = 92 + 1 − 4 − 5

85 = 129 − 44

89 = (4 ÷ 2) × 45 − 1

91 = 84 + 5 + (4 ÷ 2)

92 = 45 + 48 − 1

94 = (84 × 1) + (2 × 5)

95 = (2 × 44) + 8 − 1

98 = 2 (44 + 5) × 1

TIMES-TABLE SUMS

A spreadsheet was used to calculate these totals.

totals decrease   **totals increase**

9	18	2	6	3			1	9	9	18	2	
36		10		18			5		54		14	
4	20	5	30	6	138		5	30	6	42	7	155
28		40		6	138		15		48		28	164
7	56	8	8	1	**276**		3	24	8	32	4	**319**

1	8	8	24	3			1	2	2	6	3	
4		40		18			4		10		18	
4	20	5	30	6	114		4	20	5	30	6	186
28		10		54	154		28		40		54	154
7	14	2	18	9	**268**		7	56	8	72	9	**340**

6	12	2	14	7			1	5	5	15	3	
30		2		28			7		45		18	
5	5	1	4	4	86		7	63	9	54	6	185
40		3		36	139		14		72		24	180
8	24	3	27	9	**225**		2	16	8	32	4	**365**

9	27	3	24	8			1	5	5	10	2	
36		15		16			7		45		12	
4	20	5	10	2	94		7	63	9	54	6	188
28		5		12	112		21		72		24	181
7	7	1	6	6	**206**		3	24	8	32	4	**369**

9	18	2	16	8			1	5	5	10	2	
9		10		24			6		45		14	
1	5	5	15	3	106		6	54	9	63	7	188
7		20		18	88		18		72		28	183
7	28	4	24	6	**194**		3	24	8	32	4	**371**

9	9	1	8	8			1	4	4	8	2	
18		5		24			5		36		14	
2	10	5	15	3	94		5	45	9	63	7	192
14		20		18	99		15		72		42	184
7	28	4	24	6	**193**		3	24	8	48	6	**376**

FOUR SQUARE PUZZLE

Fill each rectangle from one set of pieces.

6 × 4

8 × 3

8 × 4

7 × 4

9 × 4

6 × 6

FOUR BY FOUR MAGIC SQUARES

Find four numbers making 34.

16	3	2	13
5	10	11	8
9	6	7	12
4	15	14	1

16	3	2	13
5	10	11	8
9	6	7	12
4	15	14	1

16	3	2	13
5	10	11	8
9	6	7	12
4	15	14	1

16	3	2	13
5	10	11	8
9	6	7	12
4	15	14	1

16	3	2	13
5	10	11	8
9	6	7	12
4	15	14	1

16	3	2	13
5	10	11	8
9	6	7	12
4	15	14	1

16	3	2	13
5	10	11	8
9	6	7	12
4	15	14	1

16	3	2	13
5	10	11	8
9	6	7	12
4	15	14	1

16	3	2	13
5	10	11	8
9	6	7	12
4	15	14	1

16	3	2	13
5	10	11	8
9	6	7	12
4	15	14	1

16	3	2	13
5	10	11	8
9	6	7	12
4	15	14	1

16	3	2	13
5	10	11	8
9	6	7	12
4	15	14	1

16	3	2	13
5	10	11	8
9	6	7	12
4	15	14	1

16	3	2	13
5	10	11	8
9	6	7	12
4	15	14	1

16	3	2	13
5	10	11	8
9	6	7	12
4	15	14	1

16	3	2	13
5	10	11	8
9	6	7	12
4	15	14	1

16	3	2	13
5	10	11	8
9	6	7	12
4	15	14	1

16	3	2	13
5	10	11	8
9	6	7	12
4	15	14	1

16	3	2	13
5	10	11	8
9	6	7	12
4	15	14	1

16	3	2	13
5	10	11	8
9	6	7	12
4	15	14	1

MAGIC SQUARES

TWO NUMBERS

Examples of product problems with answers below in the same order. All solutions are less than 30.

Sum 19 Product 88	Sum 23 Product 126	Sum 28 Product 195	Sum 36 Product 203	Sum 37 Product 312	Sum 53 Product 702

Difference 4 Product 96	Difference 3 Product 154	Difference 10 Product 171	Difference 7 Product 294	Difference 5 Product 374	Difference 7 Product 588

Consecutive numbers Product 56	Consecutive numbers Product 156	Consecutive numbers Product 306	Consecutive numbers Product 420	Consecutive numbers Product 600	Consecutive numbers Product 812

Prime numbers Product 91	Prime numbers Product 187	Prime numbers Product 161	Prime numbers Product 323	Prime numbers Product 299	Prime numbers Product 667

8, 11	9, 14	13, 15	7, 29	13, 24	26, 27
8, 12	11, 14	9, 19	14, 21	17, 22	21, 28
7, 8	12, 13	17, 18	20, 21	24, 25	28, 29
7, 13	11, 17	7, 23	17, 19	13, 23	23, 29

DRAWING ON A PC

USING DRAW IN WORD TO CREATE, MOVE, COPY AND PASTE 2-D SHAPES

1. Open the Draw toolbar from View/Toolbars in the main menu.

2. Click on and OK the Grid/Snap to grid command from the Draw commands (no visual grid appears).

3. Use Autoshapes/Lines/ to access the Freeform tool.

4. Click the mouse, let go, move and click each point of your shape, returning to the start. Double click to end.

5. Click on the completed shape to Cut/Copy and Paste anywhere on the grid.

6. Click on the shape and use Fill to colour or shade your shapes.

7. Click on the shape and use 'Rotate or Flip' in the Draw menu to transform your shape.

EXAMPLE

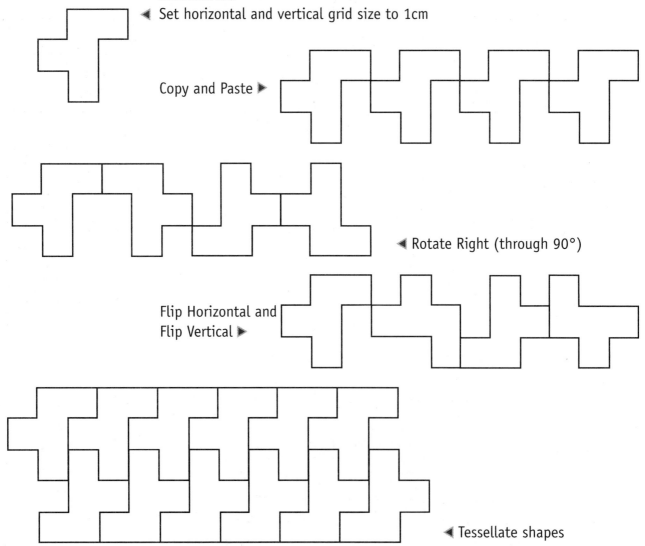

◀ Set horizontal and vertical grid size to 1cm

Copy and Paste ▶

◀ Rotate Right (through 90°)

Flip Horizontal and Flip Vertical ▶

◀ Tessellate shapes

FORTY-THREE

43 is not a square number.
$(7 \times 7) - 6$ or $(6 \times 6) + 7$
$1^2 + 2^2 + 2^2 + 3^2 + 3^2 + 4^2$

Two rectangles:
$(4 \times 7) + (3 \times 5)$
or
$(2 \times 11) + (3 \times 7)$
or
$(2 \times 8) + (3 \times 9)$

43 is not a rectangle number.
43 is a prime number

Double 21 then add one more

17 + 26
18 + 25
19 + 24
20 + 23
21 + 22

43% is less than half.

43 is less than fifty.
$43 < 50$

What do we want children to know about 43?

$(6 \times 5) + (4 \times 3) + 2 - 1$

4 tens and 3 units

10 more than 33
10 less than 53

One more than 42
Exactly half of 86
57 less than 100

129 divided by 3
172 divided by 4
215 divided by 5
258 divided by 6

It is an odd number.

The forty-third ball is the first ball of the eighth over in a game of cricket.

We write it as 'forty three'.

$4 \times 9 + 7$
$5 \times 8 + 3$
$6 \times 7 + 1$
$7 \times 6 + 1$
$8 \times 5 + 3$
$9 \times 4 + 7$

43 centimetres: less than half a metre
43 days: roughly school summer holiday
43 minutes: almost three-quarters of an hour
43 litres: a large petrol tank in a car
43 kilometres: about twenty-seven miles
43 seconds: running four hundred metres very quickly

60 – 17
59 – 16
58 – 15
57 – 14
56 – 13

PYRAMIDS SPREADSHEET

Enter the four bottom numbers in cells ▶
A4, B4, C4 and D4.

	A	B	C	D
1				
2				
3				
4	1	3	6	7

Click on cell A3, enter the formula ▶
'=A4+B4' to add 1 and 3 together. Type
in '=', then click on the relevant cells
with a '+' sign in between. The
computer will write the formula into
cell A3. The result places '4' in A3:

	A	B	C	D
1				
2				
3	4			
4	1	3	6	7

Copy and paste this formula into B3, ▶
C3, A2, B2 and A1. This completes the
pyramid of numbers:

	A	B	C	D
1	35			
2	13	22		
3	4	9	13	
4	1	3	6	7

The cell contents will be these formulae ▶

	A	B	C	D
1	=A2+B2			
2	=A3+B3	=B3+C3		
3	=A4+B4	=B4+C4	=C4+D4	
4	1	3	6	7

Copy and paste the completed pyramid, then change the order of the bottom
numbers. The values are recalculated and a new pyramid is created. In this way
a set of pyramids is produced on the spreadsheet page.

HEXOMINO CHALLENGE

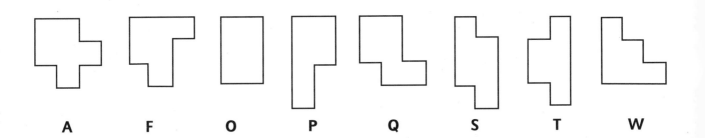

A   F   O   P   Q   S   T   W

Fill the squares with six shapes. Repeats are allowed where there is a choice.

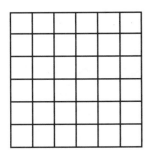

Any six

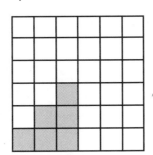

Five others

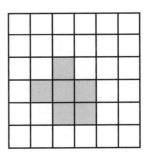

Five others

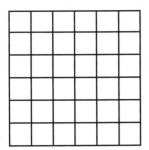

AFOSWW

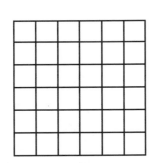

FPPQQT

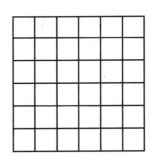

APPQQ and two others

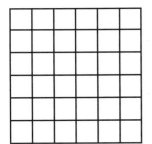

FFPQQT

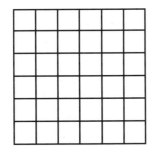

FFOTWW

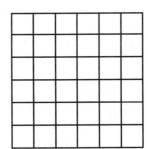

AFOP and two others

TIMES-TABLE SUM

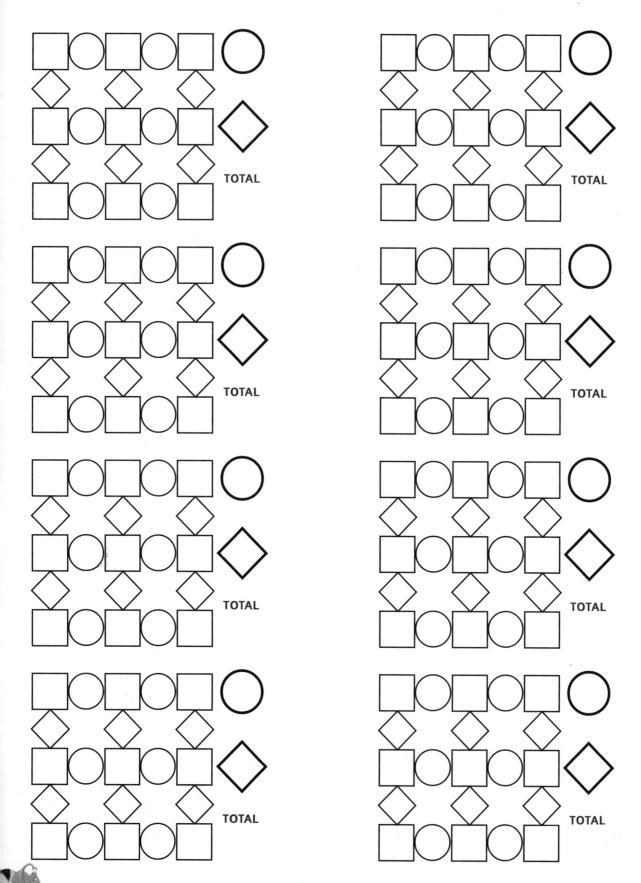

TIMES-TABLE SPREADSHEET

	A	B	C	D	E	F
1	1	=A1*C1	2		3	
2						
3	4		5		6	
4						
5	7		8		9	

1. Enter digits 1–9 in cells A1, C1, E1, A3, C3, E3, A5, C5 and E5.

2. Enter the formula '=A1*C1' in cell B1 to calculate the product.

3. Copy and paste this formula into D1, B3, D3, B5 and D5.

	A	B	C	D	E	F
1	1	2	2	6	3	
2	=A1*A3					
3	4	20	5	30	6	
4						
5	7	56	8	72	9	

4. Enter the formula '=A1*A3' in cell A2.

5. Copy and paste this formula into C2, E2, A4, C4 and E4.

	A	B	C	D	E	F
1	1	2	2	6	3	
2	4		10		18	
3	4	20	5	30	6	186
4	28		40		54	
5	7	56	8	72	9	

6. Enter the formula '=B1+D1+B3+D3+B5+D5' in cell F3 to calculate the sum of the horizontal products.

7. Enter the formula '=A2+C2+E2+A4+C4+E4' in cell F4 to calculate the sum of the vertical products.

	A	B	C	D	E	F
1	1	2	2	6	3	
2	4		10		18	
3	4	20	5	30	6	186
4	28		40		54	154
5	7	56	8	72	9	340

8. Enter the formula '=F3+F4' in cell F5 to calculate the total sum.

Copy and paste the spreadsheet, then change the digits around to create a different total sum.

NUMBER PROPERTIES

1 S T	2 P	3 T P	4 S T	5 P	6 T	7 P	8	9 S T	10 T
11 P	12	13 P	14	15 T	16 S	17 P	18	19 P	20
21 T	22	23 P	24	25 S	26	27	28 T	29 P	30
31 P	32	33	34	35	36 S T	37 P	38	39	40
41 P	42	43 P	44	45 T	46	47 P	48	49 S	50
51	52	53 P	54	55 T	56	57	58	59 P	60
61 P	62	63	64 S	65	66 T	67 P	68	69	70
71 P	72	73 P	74	75	76	77	78 T	79 P	80
81 S	82	83 P	84	85	86	87	88	89 P	90
91 T	92	93	94	95	96	97 P	98	99	100 S

The numbers 1–100 contain:

10 square numbers

13 triangle numbers

25 prime numbers

All numbers that are not prime are rectangular. Their factors (excluding one and the number itself) are:

1 1
4 2
6 2, 3
8 2, 4
9 3
10 2, 5
12 2, 3, 4, 6
14 2, 7
15 3, 5
16 2, 4, 8
18 2, 3, 6, 9
20 2, 4, 5, 10
21 3, 7
22 2, 11
24 2, 3, 4, 6, 8, 12
25 5
26 2, 13
27 3, 9
28 2, 4, 7, 14
30 2, 3, 5, 6, 10, 15
32 2, 4, 8, 16

33 3, 11
34 2, 17
35 5, 7
36 2, 3, 4, 6, 9, 12, 18
38 2, 19
39 3, 13
40 2, 4, 5, 8, 10, 20
42 2, 3, 6, 7, 14, 21
44 2, 4, 11, 22
45 3, 5, 9, 15
46 2, 23
48 2, 3, 4, 6, 8, 12, 16, 24
49 7
50 2, 5, 10, 25
51 3, 17
52 2, 4, 13, 26
54 2, 3, 6, 9, 18, 27
55 5, 11
56 2, 4, 7, 8, 14, 28

57 3, 19
58 2, 29
60 2, 3, 4, 5, 6, 10, 12, 15, 20, 30
62 2, 31
63 3, 7, 9, 21
64 2, 4, 8, 16, 32
65 5, 13
66 2, 3, 6, 11, 22, 33
68 2, 4, 17, 34
69 3, 23
70 2, 5, 7, 10, 14, 35
72 2, 3, 4, 6, 8, 9, 12, 18, 24, 36
74 2, 37
75 3, 5, 15, 25
76 2, 4, 19, 38
77 7, 11
78 2, 3, 6, 13, 26, 39
80 2, 4, 5, 8, 10, 16, 20, 40

81 3, 9, 27
82 2, 41
84 2, 3, 4, 6, 7, 12, 14, 21, 28, 42
85 5, 17
86 2, 43
87 3, 29
88 2, 4, 8, 11, 22, 44
90 2, 3, 5, 6, 9, 10, 15, 18, 30, 45
91 7, 13
92 2, 4, 23, 46
93 3, 31
94 2, 47
95 5, 19
96 2, 3, 4, 6, 8, 12, 16, 24, 32, 48
98 2, 7, 14, 49
99 3, 9, 11, 33
100 2, 4, 5, 10, 20, 25, 50

GLOSSARY

Area is a measure of the size of a surface of a 2-D shape.

Border is an area with constant width around the boundary of a 2-D shape.

Congruence: two 2-D shapes are congruent if one fits exactly on top of the other.

Decametre is a length of 10m. There are 100 decametres in a kilometre.
Decimetre is a length of 10cm (one orange Cuisenaire rod). There are ten decimetres in a metre.

a rectangle is equiangular

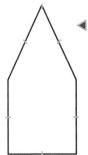

Equiangular 2-D shapes have all their angles the same. ▶
◀ **Equilateral** 2-D shapes have all their sides the same.

Factors of a rectangle number are numbers whose product is the value of the rectangle number.
Fibonacci sequence is a number pattern in which each number is the sum of the previous two numbers. The sequence 0, 1, 1, 2, 3, 5, 8, 13, 21, ... is found to occur widely in nature, but any two start numbers can generate a Fibonacci-type sequence: 4, 3, 7, 10, 17, 27, 44, ...

this pentagon is equilateral

Knight's move in chess consists of travelling two squares ▶ forward or backwards and one square left or right, or one square left or right and two squares forward or backwards. The move is represented as a path from the start square to the finish square.

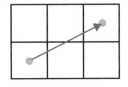

Line symmetry: a 2-D shape has one line of symmetry if it can be folded across a line so that one half of the shape covers the other exactly. Shapes with more than one line of symmetry have more than one fold line. ▶

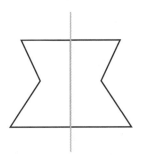

Multiples of a number are times-table values into which the number divides exactly.

Number line is an arrangement of numbers in order, positive, negative and zero where each number is aligned to a marker. Scales are sections of number lines that we use for measurement.
Number track is an arrangement of numbers in order, where each number occupies a space.

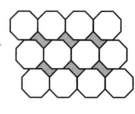

Packing is a way of filling space in a repeating pattern ▶ with no gaps where more than one 2-D shape is used.

Perimeter is the length of the boundary around a 2-D shape.

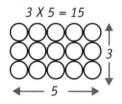

a cross-over polygon

◀ **Polygons** are 2-D shapes bounded only by straight lines that form one continuous path. In a crossover polygon, the straight lines that generate the shape intersect or cross over.

Polyominoes are arrangements of squares joined edge to edge. Some have special names, domino (two squares), tetromino (four squares), pentomino (five squares), hexomino (six squares).

Prime numbers are not rectangle numbers. Their pattern of dots is a rectangle with width one.

3 X 5 = 15
3
5

◀ **Rectangle numbers** can be represented as a rectangular pattern of dots, where the rectangle has length and width bigger than one. The length and width are a pair of numbers called factors.

Regular 2-D shapes have all their sides and angles the ▶ same.

Rotational symmetry: a 2-D shape has rotational symmetry of order 2 if the whole shape rotated about the centre fits onto its original position in half a turn.

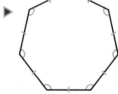

a regular heptagon

Similarity: two 2-D shapes are similar one is an enlargement of the other.

Square numbers are special rectangle numbers that have a square pattern of dots.

Tangrams are 2-D shapes cut into pieces that can be rearranged to make other recognisable 2-D shapes or pictures.

◀ **Transformation** in geometry is the effect of movement on a set of points or shapes. Examples are:

▲ *Rotation,* or turn through an angle about a fixed point.

▲ *Reflection,* or flip over a fixed line.

▲ *Translation,* or slide along a straight path. ▶

▲ *Enlargement* increases or decreases the size of a shape, keeping the proportions the same.

rotation

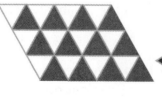

reflection

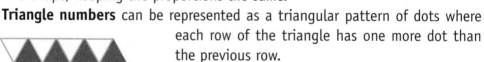

translation

Triangle numbers can be represented as a triangular pattern of dots where each row of the triangle has one more dot than the previous row.

Tessellation: a way of filling space with identical ◀ 2-D shapes in a repeating pattern with no gaps.

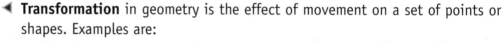

INVESTIGATING HIST○RY

MEDIEVAL BRITAIN 1066–1500

Martyn Whittock

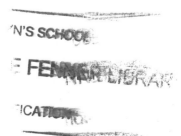

Hodder & Stoughton

A MEMBER OF THE HODDER HEADLINE GROUP

In memory of William Wyttok, burgess of Langport, Somerset, in AD 1327. And for Thomas and Adam Whittock, whose ancestors were Medieval citizens of Somerset.

Acknowledgements

The publishers would like to thank the following individuals, institutions and companies for permission to reproduce copyright illustrations in this book:

© Actionplus, page 80 top and bottom; © Aerofilms Limited, Borehamwood, page 62; Allstar/Cinetext Collection, page 79 top; Victor G. Ambrus, page 52; © Neil Beer/Corbis, page 4; Bowberry House Design, page 78 background; Très Riches Heures de Duc de Berry 1405–1415 painted by the Limburg Brothers Chateâu de Chantilly, France, Victoria & Albert Museum, London/Bridgeman Art Library, page 43 right; © Mike Brill, page 63; Bristol Records Office, pages 64, 65; © The British Library (Additional Charter 11296), page 72 left; © The British Library, page 54; © The British Library Chattrell Psalter col. 170, page 10 bottom; © The British Library, Cott. Nero. D.ii, f177. Det, page 12; © The British Library K17538, page 22; © The British Library Lutteral Psalter Add 42130 fl111v), page 42 left; © The British Library, Roy 20 CVII fol. V, page 11 top right; © The British Library (Royal ms 18.E.I. fo.165v), page 76; © CADW Welsh Historic Monuments, page 38 top; © CADW Photographic Library Collections, page 37 centre; Chester Archaeology, page 39; Collections/Colin Underhill page 38 (bottom); Corel, page 35 top; © Corpus Christi College, Oxford, page 68; © Myron Jay Dorf/Corbis, page 35 bottom; Durham Chapter Library/Copyright of Durham Cathedral, page 72 right; © English Heritage Photo Library/Jonathan Bailly, page 56; © English Heritage Photo Library/Ivan Lapper, page 17; © English Heritage Photo Library/Jeremy Richards, page 14; The Ronald Grant Archive, pages 78 top, 78 bottom, 79 bottom; © Sonia Halliday Photographs, page 11 bottom right; © HM Queen, page 25; Hodder & Stoughton Educational, page 36 top; Hodder & Stoughton Educational and Colin Taylor Productions, pages 6 and 7 (faces); House of Commons Public Information Office Photographic Collection, page 24; © Peter Knowles Photography, page 37 top; Lansmuseet Varberg, Sweden, pages 5, 6, 7; The Wilton Diptych/National Gallery Picture Library, London, page 10 top right; PA Photos/Owen Humphreys, page 57 right; Public Records Office, London, pages 18, 72 (top); Reuters/Pool/Adrian Dennis, page 27; Dr Charlotte Roberts, pages 48, 49, 50; The Royal Collection © HM Queen Elizabeth I (The Wriothesley Garter Book), page 10 left; Royal Library, Brussels, page 11 middle; © Setboun/Corbis, page 89; © Paul A. Souders/Corbis, page 40; © Ted Spiegel/Corbis, page 36; © A & J Verkaik/Corbis, page 40 top; © Adam Woolfit/Corbis, page 57 (left); www.castlewales.com/stclears.html, page 37 bottom.

The publishers would also like to thank the following for permission to reproduce material in this book: Canterbury Archaeological Trust for permission to redraw a perspective view of St John's Hospital by John Bowen on page 51; Carnegie Publishing for the extract from Bristol: A People's History by Peter Aughton (Carnegie Publishing, 2000); the Guardian for the extract from 'Support the Auld Enemy' by Kirsty Scott (25 February 2002) © Guardian; Kent Education website for extracts from their website; Extract from A History of Britain Volume 1 by Simon Schama reproduced with the permission of BBC Worldwide Limited. Copyright © Simon Schama 2000.

Chris Rothero (Beehive Illustration) and Richard Morris for artworks.
Every effort has been made to trace and acknowledge ownership of copyright. The publishers will be glad to make suitable arrangements with any copyright holders whom it has not been possible to contact.
References to Codicote, in Chapter 6, are based on research found in:
Michael Wood, Domesday, A Search for the Roots of England (BBC Publications,1986).

Orders: please contact Bookpoint Ltd, 130 Milton Park, Abingdon, Oxon OX14 4SB. Telephone: (44) 01235 827720. Fax: (44) 01235 400454. Lines are open from 9.00 – 6.00, Monday to Saturday, with a 24 hour message answering service. You can also order through our website www.hodderheadline.co.uk.

British Library Cataloguing in Publication Data
A catalogue record for this title is available from the British Library

ISBN 0 340 86904 6

First Published 2003
Impression number   10 9 8 7 6 5 4 3 2
Year   2009 2008 2007 2006 2005 2004

Copyright © 2003 Martyn Whittock

Cover photo from Très Riches heures by the Limbourg Brothers, Châteaux de Chantilly/Bridgeman Art Library.
Layout by Lorraine Inglis Design.
Printed in Italy for Hodder & Stoughton Educational, a division of Hodder Headline, 338 Euston Road, London NW1 3BH.

CONTENTS

INTRODUCTION
His-story... Her-story... Your-story...

You are history!

History is all around you. It is wherever you look: re-released pop songs, rediscovered fashions, houses and churches, tools and **technology**. All the things you see and use were first made in the past. Each one of them was first made at a particular time. And different things going on at that time affected *why* and *how* it was made.

And what about the things inside your mind? Your beliefs and values – the things you think 'good' and 'bad' – are all built on the ideas of people who came before you. Now you are adding to them. You are part of what people in the future will call History. You are History! You are connected to the *past* and to the *future*.

People like me?

People in the past were people too – just like you. They tried to make sense of their world. Just like you. But they were different too. Their world was different. Some of their ideas and beliefs, tools and skills were very different to yours. And people in different periods of history were different in different ways. And then – just like now – life was different for rich people and poor people. So, the past is a detective puzzle. It is a great collection of clues, telling you about people's lives.

1970s back in fashion

Historic moment in space exploration

The Millennium – 2000 years of Christianity

Million pounds needed to save historic castle

Ancient quarrels claim new victims in Middle East

New technology starts a new Industrial Revolution

Worst slaughter of civillians since Nazi Germany

'Pop Classics' DVDs for sale

Black Britons celebrate Black contribution to British culture

Meet a face from the past

Sometimes history stares us right in the face!

Body from the bog!

This is the head of a man from Bocksten in Western Sweden. He died in about AD 1350. He lived in a time we call the Middle Ages, or the Medieval period of History. His body was found in 1936. The acid soil in the peat preserved his hair and his clothes. In fact his clothes are the best preserved Medieval clothes in the whole of Europe. He is not just a pile of bones – he is a person from the past.

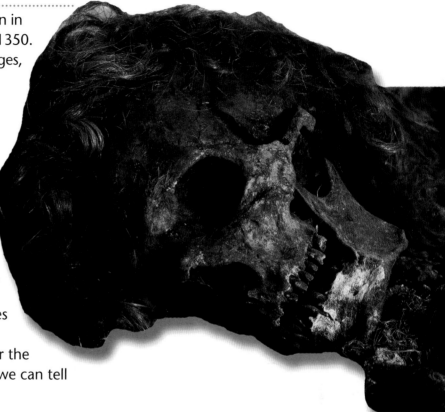

Putting flesh on the bones

The man from Bocksten was so well preserved it is possible to make clothes that are exactly the same as those he was wearing over 650 years ago! Over the next two pages we will see just what we can tell about his life ... and his murder!

We will look at:

- The clues preserved in the **peat bog**.
- What these clues might tell us.

GET HISTORIC

1. Think of any five important dates that you can remember from your own life. Say why each one of them is important to you. These are part of your personal history. Write them down in chronological order. This means, in the order in which they happened.

2. Now think of any five important dates from the past, before you were born. Say why you think each one of these is important. Write them down in chronological order.

Murder Investigation
Joining the history squad

Historians act like detectives as they find out about people in the past. They look at the clues. When this evidence comes from the time they are studying, it is called a Primary Source. Some Primary Sources are objects and buildings. Others are the words, recorded in some way, by people in the past. Just like the words of modern people, some of these can be trusted, some cannot. They are not all *reliable*. But they are all *useful* for finding out about the ideas of different people.

Historians then try to make sense of each clue. The answers historians come to are called Secondary Sources. Secondary Sources on these pages are in the historians' speech bubbles.

Different historians sometimes come to different conclusions, or **interpretations**. Some interpretations may be more reliable than others. This makes History very exciting. You always have to ask questions: Can I trust this piece of evidence? Why was it created? What can it tell me?

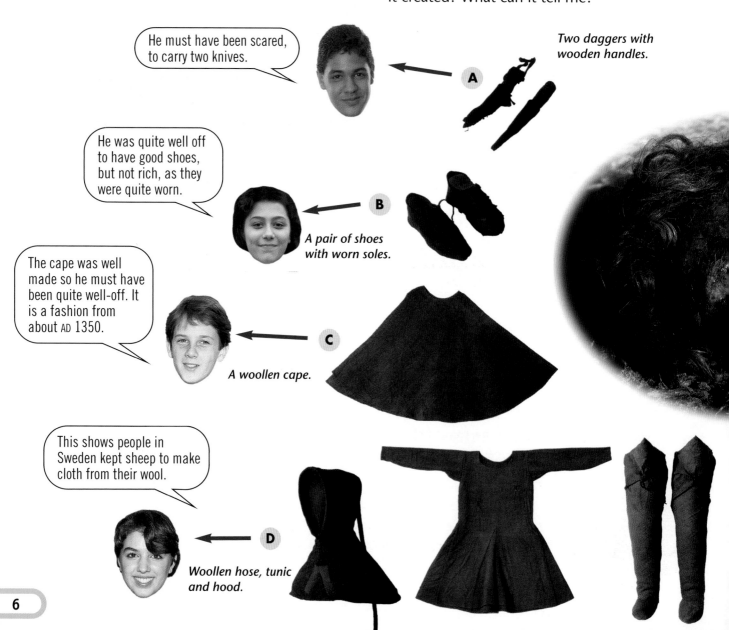

He must have been scared, to carry two knives.

Two daggers with wooden handles.

A

He was quite well off to have good shoes, but not rich, as they were quite worn.

B

A pair of shoes with worn soles.

The cape was well made so he must have been quite well-off. It is a fashion from about AD 1350.

C

A woollen cape.

This shows people in Sweden kept sheep to make cloth from their wool.

D

Woollen hose, tunic and hood.

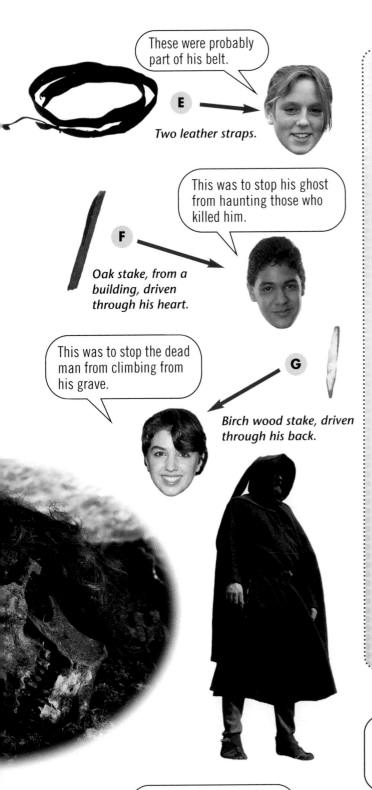

These were probably part of his belt.

E

Two leather straps.

This was to stop his ghost from haunting those who killed him.

F

Oak stake, from a building, driven through his heart.

This was to stop the dead man from climbing from his grave.

G

Birch wood stake, driven through his back.

MURDER SQUAD!

1. Write a 'Police Murder Report' on the dead man from Bocksten. Mention what you can discover and what clues helped you. Write these in seven paragraphs to cover:
   - his age
   - when he might have died
   - how he died
   - why he might have been killed
   - beliefs of people at the time
   - clothes he was wearing
   - how well-off he was

2. Now read out your Report to a neighbour. Get them to underline in two colours:
   - things they are *sure* are correct
   - things that *may not* be correct
   - get them to tell you why they are less sure about some things in your Report? What does this tell you about finding out about the past?

3. Look at Labels A, F and I. Think of three completely different interpretations which might also fit these clues. Be as imaginative as you like!

4. What have you learned so far?
   - Explain what you know about Primary Sources. 'A Primary Source is ...'
   - Explain what you know about Secondary Sources. 'A Secondary Source is ...'

He was murdered with a blow to his head. He was probably a servant of the Danish king, who was attacking Sweden at this time. The local people must have murdered him because of this.

These show he was about 35 years old.

H

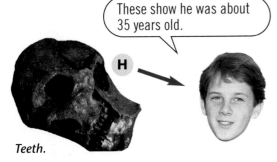

Teeth.

I

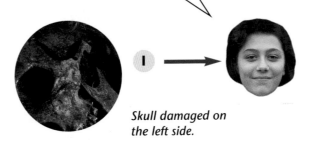

Skull damaged on the left side.

CHAPTER 1

The Middle Ages
Stuck in the middle?

This book is about people in the *Medieval* period of History, or *Middle Ages*. Historians use that name for the time between about AD 1066 and 1500. Some think it really starts in Anglo-Saxon times after the end of Roman Britain in AD 410. It is an odd name.

You might be thinking:
'What's it in the 'middle' of?'
This is a good question. The answer is:
'It comes between the Roman Empire and the Ancient World *and* the start of the early Modern World.'
The name was made up by later people. No one at the time used it! No one in the Middle Ages thought they were 'stuck in the middle'. They just thought that they were modern, up-to-date – just as people of any time do!

Getting an overview

Lots of things in our world today are built on things people in the Middle Ages did ... or said ... or believed ... The ideas around the map show how Britain became more connected with the wider world during the Middle Ages. In this book we will investigate the reasons why the Middle Ages were so important – and not just 'stuck in the middle'!

A more connected world?

Britain has always been connected with the wider world. During the Middle Ages these connections changed and developed.

THINK ABOUT IT

1. Look at some of the 'connections' between Britain and the wider world. Have you ever heard of any of these before? List any you have already heard of. Explain what you already know about them.

2. When people today want to describe something as being horrible, they often say 'It's Medieval'. That means it is just like in the Middle Ages.
   Here are some examples:
   'Medieval savagery'
   A description of war crimes, in Bosnia, February, 2002.
   'Baby seals clubbed to death in scenes of Medieval cruelty'
   Animal Rights website, 2002.

   Read through each of the events connecting Britain with the wider world. Which of them make you realise this view of the Middle Ages is not completely accurate? Explain why they challenge the view that the Middle Ages were just a savage time.

The Norman Conquest in 1066 increased the connections between England and France.

The Christian Church gave a common religious belief to most people in Europe.

Christian knights from Western Europe travelled to the Middle East to fight Muslims for control of Jerusalem.

Arab ideas – some preserving Greek and Roman ones lost in Europe – about science, maths and medicine spread to Europe.

0   km   200

N

Increased trade linked Britain with countries as far away as China. This brought benefits and problems.

By 1500, sailors from Britain were joining other Europeans exploring America.

More trade encouraged the growth of towns.

By the end of the Middle Ages ideas were spread more easily by the invention of printed books.

The end of the Hundred Years War in 1453 meant England no longer ruled large parts of France.

During the Middle Ages, England conquered Wales and invaded Ireland and Scotland.

WHAT ARE THE BIG QUESTIONS ABOUT THE MIDDLE AGES?

A What impact did Christian beliefs have on people's lives?

B Who had the real power in the country?

Jesus, Virgin Mary and angels.

Picture of King Edward I and parliament.

C How much did the lives of ordinary people change?

Picture of labourers from the Luttrell Psalter

D How well did England get on with its neighbours?

Soldiers looting

Black Death grave diggers.

E Why could people not avoid killer diseases?

F How 'connected' was the Medieval world?

Muslim scientists

THINK ABOUT IT

Look at these important questions. Which of these questions are still important in your life today? Choose three and explain why they are still important questions to you. Here is one idea to get you started:

'In the Middle Ages people's lives were affected by wars and they still are. The ways wars are fought have changed but soldiers from Britain still sometimes fight in wars today and people argue about whether they should, or not. I think this is still important as wars affect peoples' lives in many different ways.'

CHAPTER 2

Power and Control
Who is in charge?

In this chapter you will:

- Decide which groups of people held power.
- Explore how much the Norman Conquest changed England.
- Examine how the power of different groups changed over time.
- Prepare a debate to decide 'Who really held the power?'

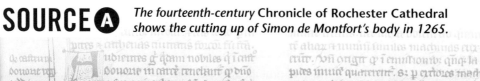

Latest news

Place: Evesham

Date: August 4, 1265.

Events: Simon de Montfort, leader of the revolt against King Henry III, defeated by royal army led by Edward, son of Henry III. Simon's body chopped apart after he was killed.

Background: Henry a weak ruler. Showed favouritism to unpopular friends from Poitou in France. Rebellion 1233 forced out favourites. 1236 Henry marries Eleanor of Provence. Power given to her relatives. Angers most powerful English landowners, called '**barons**'. Revolt forced Henry to agree to Provisions of Oxford (1258) which limit his power. Henry breaks agreement. Second Barons' Revolt (1264) led by powerful baron, Simon de Montfort. Simon captures Henry. Barons begin to resent Simon's power and fear chaos in country. Simon turns to less powerful country knights and calls them to parliament to help rule the country. Simon popular in country but lacks support from barons. Simon killed 1265.

SOURCE A

The fourteenth-century Chronicle of Rochester Cathedral *shows the cutting up of Simon de Montfort's body in 1265.*

What is going on?

Simon de Montfort led a revolt by powerful English landowners, called barons, who were angry that King Henry III was giving too much power to his French friends and relatives. But all the barons were descended from French families and spoke French not English. Simon himself was French and held land in France and England. He inherited land in England in 1231. He soon became a close friend of King Henry III. Simon only led the revolt after he had fallen out with the half-brothers of King Henry and lost a powerful job he had in lands the king owned in Gascony, in France. Simon also owed Henry a lot of money. Simon was a rich landowner who only called less

powerful knights to parliament when he was running short of friends.

After he died, many ordinary people started calling him a **saint** for trying to reduce the power of Henry's unpopular favourites. Many people had hoped Simon might improve their lives. Londoners wanted less interference by the king in the running of their city. Peasants hoped to reduce the power of landowners over their lives. Country knights hoped they would be consulted about new laws in parliament. In real life Simon had no plans to transform the country. He was no revolutionary.

Wait a minute ... I have a few questions!

- *How is it that French people held land in England?*
- *What is a baron?*
- *How did the barons get all this power?*
- *What is parliament?*
- *What does it do?*
- *How powerful is the king or queen?*
- *Who is really in charge?*

THINK ABOUT IT

1. Look at the questions on the right. Can you answer any of them? If you can, write a sentence as an answer to any you know something about.

2. Have you any other questions you think you would need to ask to decide who was really in charge in the Middle Ages? Write them down. We'll come back to them at the end of this chapter.

3. What different reasons did (a) Simon, (b) English barons, (c) ordinary people have for rebelling against King Henry III? Write a short paragraph for each. Start each paragraph with these words: '*The reasons for rebelling were* ...' End each paragraph with: 'This was different to other people's reasons for rebelling because ...'

STOP AND REFLECT: Write a paragraph explaining how Simon de Montfort's revolt shows that different groups of people might challenge the power of the king for different reasons.

What really changed at the Battle of Hastings?

SOURCE A

A modern artist's picture of the Battle of Hastings, 1066, in which the English King Harold and many leading English landowners were killed by William of Normandy and his invading Norman army.

SOURCE B

Was England like this in 1070?

'Charred stakes and burnt ground were all that was left of the village and manor, though a handful of twenty round hovels huddled together in a hollow below. Not all was destruction, however – there had been building too.

A huge stone structure had been begun on the highest point of the hill where it perched above a small natural cliff. The soldiers who had passed him were just crossing a bridge over the moat and more patrolled the crest of the bailey. Men and women laboured all round, carrying stones in huge sacks, mixing mortar, climbing ladders, hoisting larger, shaped rocks on rickety derricks [cranes] perched on a wooden frame of scaffolding.

There was a gallows at the gate. Eight bodies slowly turned in the rain or swung more sharply as a carrion crow or raven flapped onto a shoulder or perched on a head, so its heavy wedge of a grey beak could tear at a mouth or a neck.'

From The Last English King, *a historical novel written by a modern writer, Julian Rathbone, in 1997. A historical novel is fictional writing in which a writer uses historical events to explain their own view of people in the past.*

THINK ABOUT IT

1. The writer of Source B had his own view of whether the Norman Conquest was a good or bad thing. Read again carefully how he describes (a) what has happened to English homes, and (b) what has happened to English people, and (c) his description of what was being built by the Normans.

2. Which of the events in *Was 1066 a disaster for the English people?* might the writer of Source B have used as evidence to support his view.

What was 1066 all about?

In October 1066, William, Duke of Normandy in France, defeated the English King Harold II (Godwinson) at the Battle of Hastings in Sussex. Anglo-Saxon England was defeated and a new Norman king was on the throne. Earlier in September Harold had defeated another attempt to take his crown. This had been made by Harald Hardrada, king of Norway. At the Battle of Stamford Bridge, in Yorkshire, the Norwegian army had been defeated and Harald Hardrada had been killed. But for Harold Godwinson the success was not to last and he was killed at Hastings.

Harold Godwinson was not a royal prince. But his family had been very powerful under the last English king – Edward the Confessor – and Harold claimed that, before he died in January 1066, old King Edward had named Harold as the next king. Edward was married to Harold's sister, but they had no children. William of Normandy was furious. He claimed Edward had promised the crown to him. William also claimed that Harold had promised to support William's claim when Harold had visited Normandy in about 1064. William collected an army and invaded England. At Hastings he made himself ruler of both Normandy and England. By the time William died, in 1087, England had experienced huge changes.

Was 1066 a disaster for English people?

Revolts crushed. Thousands killed.

Land taken from English and given to Normans barons, who fought for William.

Norman castles kept the English under control.

The English language was banned from government.

Normans pulled down and rebuilt English churches.

All bishops, except two, replaced by Normans.

Or were things more complicated?

English nobles reduced in numbers by the Battle of Stamford Bridge as well as the Battle of Hastings.

William accepted as King by the English in December 1066.

In 1066 William promised to rule England according to English laws and customs.

William's followers demanded land in England.

English revolts (in 1067, 1068, 1069, 1070, 1075) against William.

Normans fought back to stay in power: thousands killed, English leaders fled abroad, Normans seized their lands.

SOURCE ⊙

'If anyone desires to know what kind of man he was, or in what honour he was held, or how many lands he was lord over, then we shall write about him as we have known him, who have ourselves seen him and at one time lived in his court.

King William was a man of great wisdom and power. Though stern beyond measure to those who opposed his will, he was kind to those good men who loved God. During his reign was built the great cathedral at Canterbury and many others throughout England. He was so stern and relentless a man that no one dared to go against his will. Earls who resisted him, he held in prison. Bishops lost their positions. Rebellious **thanes** he cast into prison. Among other things we must not forget the good order he kept in the land, so that a man of any kind could travel safely throughout the country. No man dared to kill another. If a man attacked a woman he was **castrated**.

He ruled over England. Wales he controlled, and built castles there and held its people under his control. Scotland he controlled by his great strength. Normandy was his by right of birth. If he had lived only two more years he would have conquered Ireland by his clever actions, not by force.

We have written down these things about him, both good and evil, so that men may cherish the good and utterly avoid the evil.'

Written by an English monk in the **Anglo-Saxon Chronicle,** *probably at Canterbury in Kent, following William's death in 1087. It is an eyewitness account.*

SOURCE

An earth and wood castle (a motte and bailey) built by Normans to control England after revolts. This shows one being built at Pickering, Yorkshire. Later many were rebuilt in stone.

THINK ABOUT IT

1. Imagine you are William of Normandy. Write a short speech in which you defend yourself against the accusation that your victory at Hastings ruined life for English people. Mention other things responsible for problems, say how the way the English responded to your rule helped cause bigger changes than had happened after Hastings in 1066. How did these events change the way you ruled England?

2. Read carefully through Source C. Write down all the (a) positive and (b) negative things about the rule of King William.

3. Did this writer think he was a *strong* ruler? How did the writer decide a king was strong? Did this writer think he was a *good* ruler? How did the writer decide a king was good?

4. How similar/different is the view of the Norman Conquest in Source B compared with Source C? Pick out any areas in which they give a similar view. Pick out any areas in which they give a different view of the effects of the Conquest.

5. Which source is the most *useful* (tells you a lot) for trying to find out what life was like after the Norman Conquest? Explain how you decided.

6. Which source is the most *reliable* (likely to be true)? For each one: think about who wrote them ...; when they wrote them ...; how balanced they are (looking at both sides of a point of view) ...; the kind of writing they are examples of ...; whether this makes what they actually wrote more or less likely to be true. Then decide which is the most reliable in your opinion and explain why.

STOP AND REFLECT: Write a sentence to remind you how French landowners came to own land in England after the Norman Conquest. Write another sentence which describes the way a strong king ruled.

What can Domesday Book tell us?

What do we know?

Stored in the Public Records Office in London is an amazing book. There is nothing else like it in Europe. It is Domesday Book and it tells us who held what land in England twenty years after the Norman Conquest. But it is not just about land. It is about power! It tells us who was in charge and that is why we are going to look at what we can find out from this amazing document.

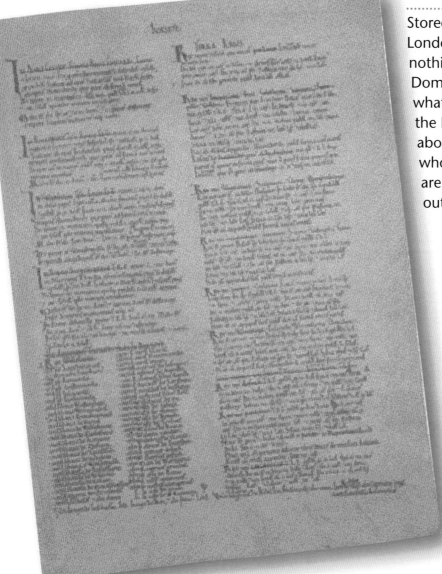

SOURCE Ⓐ

A page from Domesday Book. It was written between 1085 and 1086. It was written in Latin with many words shortened. The red lines are underlinings. In the eleventh century people put these lines through a word instead of below it.

SOURCE Ⓑ

'The king spent Christmas with his councillors at Gloucester and held his court there for five days. After this the king had much thought and very deep discussion about this country. How it was occupied and with what sort of people. Then he sent his men all over England into every **shire** and had them find out how much land there was in each shire, or what land and cattle the king himself had in the country, or what taxes he ought to have each year from each shire. Also he had a record made of how much land his archbishops had and his bishops and his abbots and his earls and what, or how much, everybody had who held land in England and how much money it was worth.'

From the **Anglo-Saxon Chronicle,** *written by an eyewitness to the events in 1086.*

SOURCE C

'The king's men made a survey of all England, of the lands in each shire, of what was held by each of his barons, their lands, their houses, their men both slave and free; the number of ploughs and horses and other animals; services and payments due from every estate. After these investigators came others who were sent to unfamiliar shires to check the first descriptions and to tell the king about anyone who had lied. And there was much trouble in the land because of the collecting of the royal taxes.'

Written by Robert, Bishop of Hereford, a friend of William the Conqueror.

SOURCE D

'They asked:

What is this manor called?

Who held it at the time of King Edward and now?

How big is it?

How many ploughs work on the lord's **demesne** land?

How many villagers, cottagers, slaves, freemen?

How much woodland, pasture?

How many mills, how many fisheries?

How much has been added to, or taken from, the estate?

How much it was worth and how much it is worth now?

All this was to be recorded three times: as it was in King Edward's time, as it was when King William gave it, as it is now. And it was noted whether more could be taxed from it than was being taken.'

The questions asked by the Domesday commissioners. This is recorded in a book called The Ely Inquest, *written about the same time as* Domesday Book.

THINK ABOUT IT

1. **Why did William do it?** Look carefully at Sources B, C and D. Skim through each to get an idea of what it is about. Then scan it for anything you can find about *why* King William ordered this survey to be carried out. Write down any key words which you spot which tell you about this. What is the one reason that all three sources agree on?

2. Why was this reason so important to a king's power?

3. Why is it still important for governments today?

4. List five different areas of life a modern government spends money on. Choose areas which affect your life or that of your family.

5. From what you can see here about Domesday Book, how well organised do you think King William's royal power was?

STOP AND REFLECT: Write a paragraph explaining why Domesday Book is such a valuable piece of evidence.

What does Domesday Book tell us about ownership of land?

Who controlled what land?

17% King and royal family.

26% Bishops and abbots.

54% Barons or tenants-in-chief.

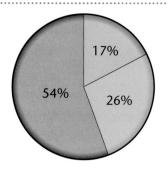

Power of the barons

▸ 12 leading barons held 25% of England.

▸ All leading landowners, except one, were French. The exception – Thorkill of Arden – had supported William the Conqueror.

▸ Almost all landowners were men. The only woman holding a large area of land was Judith, Countess of Northumbria and Huntingdon, niece of William the Conqueror.

▸ Barons' land was scattered about England not grouped into regions like it had been before 1066. 14 barons held land north of the River Trent *and* south of the River Thames.

▸ Barons had to provide knights to fight for the king when he called. Barons gave some of their land to their knights. Money from this land supported the knights, paid for their horses, armour and a comfortable lifestyle. Under the knights the ordinary people in the village did all the work. This was called the **Feudal System**.

THINK ABOUT IT

1. Who were the three most powerful types of people in Norman England?

2. Think of one reason why William rewarded the Church so well.

3. Why might William have rewarded his chief supporters (barons or tenants-in-chief) so well?

4. What do Sources B and C (on pages 18 and 19) tell you about how William tried to control even these powerful people? Why was it so important for him to be able to do this?

STOP AND REFLECT: What does Domesday Book tell us about (a) who the most powerful people were in the eleventh century, (b) the power of the king and (c) the way organisation of power changed after 1066?

Why was Thomas Becket murdered?

Who is in charge? The King or the Church?

What would happen today if a vicar, priest, rabbi, imam, or any other religious leader broke the law? The answer is: they would be arrested and brought to court like anyone else. In the Middle Ages things were more complicated. The Christian Church was very powerful and most people in Western Europe were Christians. The Church had its own laws called 'Canon Law' and its own courts. Many leaders in the Church thought that if a member of the Church broke the law, they should not be tried in the royal courts. This could apply to lots of people, since anyone educated by the Church could claim to be a 'clerk in minor orders' and get this protection.

SOURCE Ⓐ

'In 1162 King Henry II persuaded his **Chancellor**, Thomas Becket, to become Archbishop of Canterbury, although Becket warned him that his chief loyalty would then be to the Church and not to the King. They disagreed about many matters concerning the relations between Church and **state**. One of the most important was whether **clergy** who had broken the law could be tried in the King's courts or whether they could appear only before the Church courts. Eventually in 1170 Becket was murdered by three of the King's knights and Henry was blamed.'

Written by Peter of Langtoft during the reign of King Edward II (1307–27). Edward II was a weak king and this led to trouble in the country. Peter admired strong rulers who brought law and order.

Power to the King?

Kings did not like this situation. It reduced their power. And it meant that some people guilty of very serious crimes got off with lighter sentences in the Church Courts. Kings also wanted to decide who got the top jobs in the Church. It was a way of rewarding their friends and making sure the Church did as the king said!

Power to the Church?

By the eleventh century many Church leaders were getting fed up with kings putting their friends into Church jobs. How could the Church improve the way it was run if many of its leaders were not really up to the job and more interested in pleasing the king? The answer was to reduce the control kings had over the Church.

King Henry II and Thomas Becket

In 1162 Thomas Becket, a close friend of the English king, Henry II, was given the top job in the English Church – Archbishop of Canterbury. But Becket changed. He no longer acted as the king's servant. Thomas tried to reduce Henry's power over the Church. He **excommunicated** other Church leaders who accepted Henry's control. The argument grew very bitter. Neither side would compromise. Henry wished Thomas was dead! On December 29,1170, royal knights, keen to please Henry, murdered Becket in Canterbury cathedral. To say sorry for the murder, Henry allowed the Pope more control over the English Church. But Henry still kept a lot of control over who got top jobs in the English Church. The balance of power between the Church and the King continued to be a difficult one. But mostly it was royal power which continued to grow.

SOURCE B

'A great disagreement arose between the king of England and Thomas, Archbishop of Canterbury, concerning the rights of the Church, which the king of the English was attempting to disturb and reduce. On the other hand the archbishop tried by every possible means to keep Church power and rights intact. For it was the king's wish that if priests, deacons, subdeacons, and other rulers of the Church should be caught committing theft, or murder, or arson, they should be taken before the king's judges, and punished like the **laity**. Against this the Archbishop of Canterbury urged, that if a **clerk** in **holy orders**, or any other ruler of the Church, should be charged upon any matter, he ought to be tried by members of the Church and in the Church court; and if he should be convicted, then he ought to be deprived of his rights, and that, when thus stripped of his office, if he should offend again, he ought to be tried by the king's judges.'

Written by Roger of Hoveden, a royal servant who wrote a History of England *in the early years of the thirteenth century. As a royal clerk he was well placed to gather information and opinions from members of the royal court, and he also included many documents, especially letters, into his history.*

SOURCE C

'He [Becket] said, "I am prepared to die for my Lord, so that in my blood the Church will gain freedom and peace; but in the name of Almighty God I forbid that you hurt my men, either cleric or layman, in any way." He bravely pushed one [of the knights] who was pursuing and drawing near to him; he called him a **pimp** saying, "Don't touch me, Rainaldus, you who owe me faith and obedience, you who foolishly follow your accomplices." On account of the insult the knight was suddenly set on fire with a terrible rage and, wielding a sword against the sacred head said, "I don't owe faith or obedience to you that is in opposition to the loyalty I owe my lord king."

The **martyr** gave himself and the cause of the Church to God, St Mary, and the blessed martyr St Denis. "For the name of Jesus and the protection of the Church I am ready to embrace death." But the third knight inflicted a grave wound on the fallen one; with this blow he shattered the sword on the stone and the top of his [Thomas'] head, which was large, separated from his head. The fifth placed his foot on the neck of the holy priest and precious martyr and (it is horrible to say) scattered the brains with the blood across the floor, calling to the rest, "We can leave this place, knights, he will not get up again."'

Written by Edward Grim. Grim was a friend of Becket's and was in Canterbury the night Becket was murdered. He was wounded by one of the knights who killed Becket.

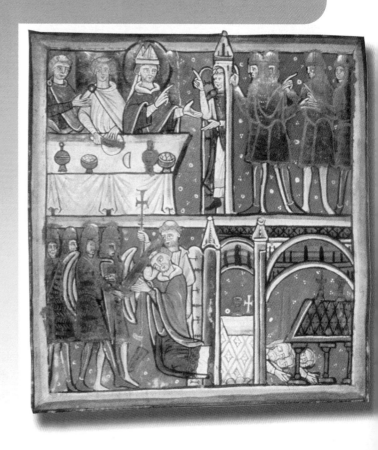

SOURCE D

'Finally, it was declared, in King Henry's presence, that during his reign more than a hundred murders had been committed by the clergy in England alone. The king became extremely angry and enacted laws, in the heat of his passion, against criminals in the Church. This showed his enthusiasm for public justice, though his anger caused him to go beyond what was needed. The bishops, however, were more concerned to maintain the freedoms or rights of the clergy than to correct and root out their crimes. They suppose that they serve God, and the Church, by protecting against the law those clergy, whom they either refuse or neglect to control as they should.

When the king brought in certain laws against the criminals within the Church, he believed that they would be agreed by the bishops. Therefore, having assembled them, to get their agreement by any means whatsoever, he so persuaded the whole of them with the exception of one, by promises, or terrified them with threats that they thought it best to agree to and obey the king. I say, with the exception of one, for the Archbishop of Canterbury was alone inflexible, and remained unshaken by every threat. Upon this, the king's anger increased against him, especially as the king thought him ungrateful for all the kindness the king had earlier shown him. The archbishop argued that, having finished his royal duties, he had been completely transferred to the Church by the king in whose service he had once worked.'

Written by William of Newburgh in about 1200. William, writing a generation after the murder, was more willing to look at both sides in the quarrel than earlier writers. These had usually taken Becket's side.

SOURCE E

A picture of the murder painted in about 1180. At the top the knights arrive. At the bottom they kill Becket. Later they beg God to forgive them for the crime.

THINK ABOUT IT

1. Select and combine information from Sources A–D, in order to give:

   (a) the knights' reasons for opposing Becket.

   (b) Becket's reasons for opposing Henry II. To do this: skim through each source to get its general meaning. Then scan it, noting any key words which help answer the question. Record answers using spidergrams to collect ideas.

2. Which of these sources do you think is most useful for trying to decide what happened on the night of the murder (the actual events). Explain your decision.

3. Different people have different ideas about the meaning of events in the past depending on their own values and ideas. This is true of people in the past *and* modern historians.

   (a) Which source do you think is most *in favour* of Becket? Can you suggest any reasons why? (b) Which source is most *critical* of Becket? Can you suggest any reasons why?

4. Which source do you think is most reliable for deciding why the murder happened? Explain why you came to this conclusion and why, in your opinion, it is the best one for deciding the motives of both sides in this quarrel.

STOP AND REFLECT: Who had more power – the king or leaders of the Church? Explain the way they sometimes competed for control.

How powerful was Parliament?

Parliament. The House of Commons, meeting to make new laws.

Talk, talk ...

Parliament comes from a French word, *'parler'*, meaning 'to talk'. Since before the Norman Conquest kings have met with the most powerful people in the country. They did this to get advice and get their plans agreed by people whose support they needed. The idea of Domesday Book started when King William I met with his supporters, in 1085, to talk about who held what land in England. The people who came to these royal councils were the barons and Church leaders. These were the **Lords**.

Spend, spend ...

Kings in the Middle Ages lived on money from their royal lands. Often, though, they needed more! This was usually because they were fighting wars. During the thirteenth century wars in France and then in Wales and Scotland cost a lot. More meetings of the royal council were needed to agree to new taxes. From 1240 these began to be given the name 'parliaments'. These started to include more than just the barons. The growth of trade and towns had meant that merchants and townspeople had more money. These were called the **Commons**. Kings needed their agreement to raise new taxes; kings needed their money!

In 1265 Simon de Montfort, a former friend of King Henry III, was leading a rebellion against the king. He needed to increase his support and called the Commons to parliament. Simon was killed, but the idea continued. By the fourteenth century, more wars with France meant kings needed even more money. Parliament was here to stay!

THINK ABOUT IT

1. Imagine a person from another country wanted to find out about our Parliament today.

    a) In a small group write down some of the questions they might ask.

    b) Swap these questions with another group. See if they can answer your questions. See if you can answer theirs. Any you cannot answer – research to find the answer.

2. Make a spidergram of reasons why it is important that we have Parliament today. Think about things like laws, schools, hospitals, and our relations with other countries.

THINK ABOUT IT

3. The person who drew Source A was showing how they thought power should be organised. Look at it carefully and explain how the artist showed:

   - The power of England compared with Scotland and Wales.
   - The power of the king compared with other groups in the country.
   - Which other groups shared some power with the king.

4. Which group was missed out from this picture? Why were the 'missing people' actually very important?

SOURCE Ⓐ

A picture of what parliament looked like in 1270. At the top is King Edward I of England. Below him are Alexander, king of Scots and Llewelyn, prince of Wales. On the right are the barons. On the left are Church leaders. In the middle are royal judges. This picture was actually made in the fifteenth century and shows the artist's opinion of how government power was organised in the Middle Ages.

Listen to us!

SOURCE B

War with France is going badly!

War is costing a lot!

Taxes are too high!

Too much crime!

The king's advisers are corrupt!

Not enough freedom to trade!

Poor quality coins!

The MPs are restless!

By 1376 parliament was getting more aware of its power. And it was getting annoyed. That year parliament elected a Speaker (a kind of chairperson) named Sir Peter de la Mare. He took the complaints of parliament to the royal court. He got results. Royal advisers accused by the Commons of being corrupt were **tried** by the Lords. New advisers were chosen for the king. There were no new taxes that year!

But ...

Though there were hard bargains, parliament mostly co-operated with the king. There were few conflicts. Parliament only met for a few weeks a year. For the rest of the year the king ignored the Commons! There were lots of *discussions* in parliament but most big *decisions* were made elsewhere – by the king and his close supporters.

THINK ABOUT IT

Imagine you are Sir Peter de la Mare. Write the speech you will deliver to the king.

- Remember it needs to be a structured piece of formal writing. It is going to be addressed to a king. It will need to use proper sentences, correct language and terms (e.g. 'Your majesty', 'Your highness'), respectful language (e.g. 'we ask you to consider').

- Identify your complaints (Source B). Decide in which order to present them – the most important first. Use explanatory connectives to make it clear why these are problems (e.g . 'This worries us because ...' 'This problem damages the country as it ...')

- Link your complaints with connective words showing the flow of your argument (e.g. 'As well as this ...' 'We are not only concerned with this but also ...' 'Another concern ...'). Some may be contrasting connectives (e.g. 'Though not as serious there is another problem ...')

- Include a conclusion, which makes it clear how you want things to change.

STOP AND REFLECT: Why was the growth of parliament important? Why did royal power continue to be more important than parliament power?

SOURCE C

A modern 'Speaker' of the House of Commons, Michael Martin. The Speaker acts as a chairperson and keeps order in debates and decides how debates should be run. The Speaker decides who can speak. The Speaker does not vote, unless a vote is tied.

This program has performed an illegal operation and will be shutdown

'System Crash ...' Why did Government sometimes fail?

You are working on your computer. Everything is going fine. But then you open one window too many. Or you overload the system in some way. Suddenly the computer crashes. Aagghh!

Well, power in the Middle Ages was part of a system of government. Often it worked. This was how it was meant to work: at the top was a strong king, ruling justly. His barons controlled the country and were loyal to him. They fought for him.

The Church controlled what people believed, although the king tried to influence its decisions. Needing money and support for wars, kings began to call parliaments so that less powerful people would agree to taxes and sort out problems peacefully.

It was a system and, although it changed over time, it generally worked. But at times it crashed. Things went wrong. The system went down. Why? Here are some examples.

CRASH!!! MATILDA

1135 Henry I dies without a son. Many barons will not accept his daughter, Matilda.

Other barons in England support her cousin Stephen.

Stephen's brother a powerful Church leader in England.

1136–53 Civil War. Different barons support each side. Law and order broke down.

CRASH!!! KING JOHN

1204 King John defeated in wars in France.

1207 John falls out with Pope over next Archbishop of Canterbury.

1214 Short of money, John tries to force it from barons.

1215 Barons rebel. Force John to agree to *Magna Carta* – limits his power and increases rights of the barons.

CRASH!!! HENRY III AND SIMON DE MONTFORT

Henry III a weak ruler. Shows favouritism to unpopular friends.

1233 English barons rebel. Force out favourites.

1236 Henry marries. Power given to wife's relatives. Angers English barons.

1258 Provisions of Oxford. Barons limit Henry's power.

1264 Second Barons' Revolt, led by Simon de Montfort.

Many barons abandon Simon, fearing he is getting too powerful.

1265 Simon killed.

CRASH!!! RICHARD II

1383 Despite heavy taxes to pay for soldiers, English fail in war against France.

1384 The young king and his friends fall out with powerful barons.

1388 Private armies grow up around the king and the barons. Law and order breaks down.

Parliament accuses Richard of bad government.

1398 Richard **banishes** a baron, Henry of Bolingbroke, who returns and overthrows him in 1399.

CRASH!!! THE WARS OF THE ROSES

Henry VI defeated in wars against French.

Henry VI was a weak king and was mentally ill.

The Royal family was divided between rival families of Lancaster and York.

Barons take different sides.

1455–85 The Wars of the Roses. Lancaster wins and Henry VII claims the throne.

STOP AND REFLECT: Which do you think was the most important reason why the system of government in the Middle Ages sometimes 'crashed'?

THINK ABOUT IT

1. In your own words, explain how the system of government in the Middle Ages was supposed to work. You should include in your answer: *king, barons, Church, parliament.*

2. Look at each one of the times when the system 'crashed'. For each 'crash' explain:
   a) what went wrong, and
   b) how this differed from the way the system was supposed to work.

   For each one, use these sentence starters to help you:
   a) 'Government broke down because ...'
   b) 'This was different to how government was meant to work, in these ways ...'

Pulling it Together

Who really held the power in the Middle Ages?

You are going to work in small groups to take part in a debate on who you think really held power in the Middle Ages.

Stage 1   Getting your thoughts together

(a) Skim back through this chapter.

(b) Re-read the **Stop and reflect** notes you made.

(c) Decide about the impact of the Norman Conquest and how it changed England.

(d) In a small group, analyse the different 'power groups': *king, barons, Church, parliament.* Select and put together information from different parts of this chapter. Collect information to answer these questions: Why were they powerful? What power did they have? How did different areas of their power work together to make them important? What limited their power? What/who challenged their power? Did their power change over time? How did their power compare with that of the other 'power groups'.

Stage 2   Planning your presentation

Your teacher will give you the name of *one* of the 'power groups'. It is your job to say that this group held a lot of power and why you think this power was more important than the power held by the other groups. This type of presentation involves **persuasion**:

(a) Argue the case for your group.

(b) Compare 'your group' with the other groups, explaining why they might seem more important but are not (e.g. 'Some imagine that ...' 'It might seem as if ...').

(c) Use longer sentences to outline facts. Then short sentences to sum up and emphasise your viewpoint.

(d) Use connectives related to logic (e.g. 'this shows ...', 'because ...', 'in fact ...').

(e) Think up a catchy slogan to sum-up your viewpoint.

(f) Use value judgement words (e.g. 'obviously ...', 'crucial ...').

(g) Use strong adjectives for effect (e.g. 'majestic', 'holy', 'brave'). At the end of the presentation have a conclusion which sums up your main points.

Stage 3   Review

After each group has made its presentation, discuss which group was most persuasive and analyse why.

Then discuss what you actually think. After all, you might not have been arguing for the group you would have chosen yourself as the most powerful.

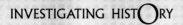

CHAPTER 3

Gerald's Journey

How Christian was the Church in the Middle Ages?

In this chapter you will:

- Explore why events in the Middle East caused such excitement in Britain.
- Examine different aspects of the Christian Church in the Middle Ages.
- Construct a documentary.
- Decide how Christian the Church was in the Middle Ages, on the basis of your exploration of the evidence from 'Gerald's Journey ...'

Introducing Gerald of Wales

I was born at the castle of Manorbier in Wales in 1145. My father's family were Norman. Norman lords began to invade Wales from 1067. Some parts of Wales came under their control. My mother was from a Welsh royal family.

A

I became a monk at Gloucester. By 1188 I was Archdeacon of Brecon. I had hoped to become Bishop of St David's but King Henry II of England would not allow it.

B

I was keen to improve the way the Church was run. I made sure people paid their tithes. I got rid of priests who lived with women. I did what I could to stop people who were not priests running local churches.

C

In 1185, I went with the army of Prince John of England on his invasion of Ireland.

D

In the Middle East, Christian knights on the First Crusade (1095–9) captured Jerusalem from Muslim rulers and set up Christian Crusader Kingdoms. Jerusalem is a holy place because it was where Jesus died and was raised from the dead. A Second Crusade (1147–8) failed to defeat the Muslims. Then in 1187 Jerusalem was recaptured by Muslims. I joined Baldwin, Archbishop of Canterbury, in his journey around Wales encouraging people to go on a Third Crusade to the Middle East. We called this 'taking the Cross'.

E

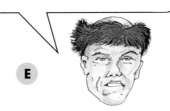

THINK ABOUT IT

1. Write a short biography of Gerald. A biography is a story of a person's life. It includes information like: where they were born, who their family were, jobs they did, their beliefs, etc.
2. What other things would you need to know about him in order to write a more detailed story of his life? Make a list of these things.

Gerald's journey round Wales, March–April, 1188.

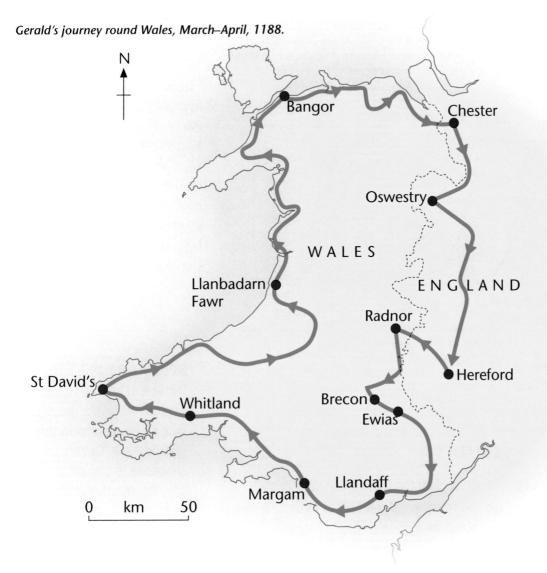

What was the Church like in the Middle Ages?

The Medieval Christian Church

*Many thought the holiest lives were lived away from the world in **monasteries**: own nothing, no marriage, strict rules, worshipping God. Cistercian monks and nuns were especially keen to live in wild and lonely places.*

*Services in local churches were led by parish priests. Priests were not allowed to marry. Priests called **bishops** led all the churches in a wide area. Above bishops were **archbishops**. The Church in Wales was controlled by the English Archbishop of Canterbury.*

*The Church taught people what was right and wrong. People paid a **tithe** (tenth) of all they had to support the Church. They also paid the local priest for marriage and funeral services. The Church helped the poor and the sick.*

The Church controlled all education. The language it used was Latin.

Christendom

In the Middle Ages virtually everyone in Britain and in Western Europe was a Christian. The Christian Church in Britain was part of the Roman Catholic Church. Its leader was the Pope in Rome. In south-eastern Europe and the Middle East many Christians were part of the Orthodox Church. Its leader was the Patriarch in Constantinople.

There were also many Jews living in Christian countries. Parts of Spain, southern Italy and the Middle East were Muslim. In some areas Christians and Muslims lived together in peace, but in other areas there was fear, mistrust and war between them.

THINK ABOUT IT

Describe the Christian Church at the time of Gerald. Explain how it was organised and run, the different kinds of church men and women, how it affected the lives of ordinary people.

STOP AND REFLECT:

Write a sentence to explain why the Church was so important in the Middle Ages. Write a sentence to explain why events in the Middle East were so important to Christians.

Postcards from Gerald's journey in 1188

Here are some of the places that Gerald visited. He recorded his experiences in a kind of diary dedicated to William, Bishop of Ely. Here is what Gerald might have written if postcards had been invented in 1188.

'Croeso i Gymru',
'Welcome to Wales'

Dear William,

In this very year God in his judgement, which is never unjust but sometimes difficult to understand, permitted Saladin, the leader of the Egyptians and of the men of Damascus, to win a victory in pitched battle and to seize the kingdom of Jerusalem. Soon after Ash Wednesday, Baldwin, Archbishop of Canterbury, reached Radnor. In Radnor Baldwin was met by Rhys ap Gruffydd, Prince of South Wales and by other nobles from these parts.
The Archbishop gave a public sermon on the taking of the Cross and this was explained to the Welsh by an interpreter. I was the first to stand up. I threw myself at the holy man's feet and took the sign of the Cross. It was the urgent command given by the king [of England] which inspired me to give this example to others. Tomorrow we continue our journey further into Wales.

Best wishes,
Gerald

Postcard 1

Dear William,

We crossed the River Wye and made our way to Brecon. In this same neighbourhood a boy tried to steal some young pigeons from a nest in St David's church in Llanfaes. His hand stuck to the stone on which he was leaning. This was a miraculous punishment inflicted by St David, who was protecting the birds of his own church. For three days and nights the boy, accompanied by his parents and his friends, offered **vigils**, **fasts** and prayers at the church altar. On the third day, by God's intervention, the power which held his hand was loosened and he was released from the miraculous force, which had kept him fixed to the stone. The stone is preserved to this day among the relics of the church, with the marks of the boy's fingers pressed into the flint as though in wax and clearly visible.

Best wishes,
Gerald

Greetings from Brecon

Postcard 2

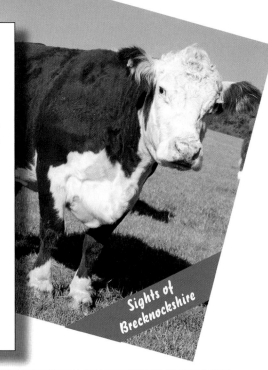

Sights of Brecknockshire

Dear William,

We are still having an interesting time around Brecon. Have heard about an amazing event. A certain knight, named Gilbert Hagurnell, after long being in pain, which lasted for three years, finally had the most severe pains like a woman about to give birth. Finally he gave birth to a calf! This event was witnessed by a large crowd of onlookers. Perhaps it was the sign that something terrible is to happen in the future. It was more probable that he was being punished for some unnatural sin he had committed. This county of Brecknock is divided into three areas, called 'cantrefs'. The first Norman to capture it from the Welsh was Bernard de Neufmarche.

Best wishes,
Gerald.

Postcard 3

Away from it all at Ewias!

Dear William,

Finally reached the monastery at Ewias. The deep valley of Ewias is shut in on all sides by a circle of high mountains. The valley is just three arrow shots wide. In the valley is the abbey of St John the Baptist. It is roofed with sheets of lead and built of squared stones. The church is built on the very spot where once there stood the humble chapel of St David the Archbishop, which was covered with woodland moss and ivy. It is a site most suited for being religious and better chosen for holy living and discipline than any other monastery in the whole island of Britain. It was started by two hermits wanting solitude and was far away from the bustle of everyday life. They built it on the banks of the River Honddu, in a secret place, where that river flows along the valley.

Best wishes,
Gerald.

Postcard 4

THINK ABOUT IT

1. **What events in the Middle East had angered and saddened Gerald? Why did Gerald feel this way about these events?**

2. **What can you discover in these postcards about:**
   - **Beliefs about the holiness of Church buildings.**
   - **Beliefs about the power of God.**
   - **Beliefs about how best to live holy lives.**

You're always made Welcome at Margam

Dear William,

We preached about the Crusade at Llandaff. The English stood on one side and the Welsh on the other. And from each nation many took the Cross. Next morning we set off for the fine Cistercian monastery at Margam. Of all the abbeys belonging to the Cistercians in Wales this was the one most famous for giving help to the sick and the poor. There is no limit to their kindness and hospitality, which never stops being given to those in need and to travellers. As a result, whenever famine threatens, God in his mercy protects Margam and their supplies actually increase! Recently there was a famine. A vast crowd of poor people came daily for help. When supplies ran out, a field nearby was found ready to be harvested a month or more earlier than it should be. So God in his kindness supplied the monks and the poor people.

Best wishes,
Gerald.

Postcard 5

Dear William,

While we were travelling from Carmarthen to the Cistercian monastery called Whitland, the Archbishop was told of how a young Welshman, who was coming to meet him, had been murdered. The Archbishop stopped, ordered the man's body to be wrapped in a cloak and prayed, giving the soul of the murdered young man to heaven. The next day twelve archers from the nearby castle of St Clears, who had killed the young man, were signed with the Cross at Whitland and made to go on Crusade as punishment for their crime. The people living in this area came from Flanders and were sent there by Henry I, king of the English to control the area. They are brave but hate the Welsh.

Best wishes,
Gerald.

Postcard 6

A hot reception awaits you at St Clears Castle

Dear William,

We've reached the cathedral at St David's. There was once an archbishop here but now he is only a bishop. Until the defeat of the Welsh, by King Henry I of England, this bishop of St David's had the power to make all other bishops in Wales. He in turn was chosen by other Welsh bishops. They were not controlled by another church. But after the Welsh were defeated by King Henry I, he ordered that all bishops of St David's should be made bishop at Canterbury in England. Today Canterbury has the support of the English king, great wealth, and is supported by many well-educated bishops and other churchmen. St David's has none of these things. And no one seems to care.

Yours, sadly,
Gerald.

St David's Cathedral.
Hoping for better days.

Postcard 7

A shocking time awaits you at Llanbadarn Fawr

Dear William,

We finally reached Llanbadarn Fawr and the next morning we attracted many people to the service of Christ — joining the Crusade. Strangely enough, like so many monasteries in Ireland and Wales, this one has an abbot who is not a churchman. He's an ordinary person! How has this wrong thing happened? Well, in the past church leaders allowed the most powerful local people to help run and protect the church. Over time these greedy people took over the running of the church. They only appoint priests who are members of their own families.

Yours, shocked,
Gerald.

Postcard 8

Dear William,

We spent the night at Bangor, the chief church in Gwynedd, where we were well entertained by the local bishop. The next morning **mass** was celebrated by the Archbishop before the high altar. On the right hand side of the altar stood Gwion, Bishop of Bangor. He was hard pressed by the Archbishop and a number of other people, forced rather than persuaded. In the end he had no choice but to take the Cross. This caused great concern to his flock, assembled in the church, for both men and women there wept and wailed very loudly.

Best wishes,
Gerald.

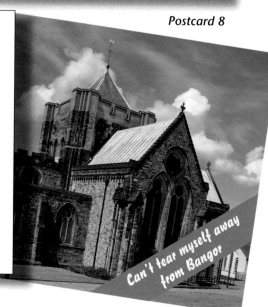

Can't tear myself away from Bangor

Postcard 9 ALLEYN'S SCHOOL LIBRARY

THINK ABOUT IT

1. Compare and contrast Postcards 5 and 8. This means, look at ways in which they are similar and different. Then write two sentences summing up Gerald's opinion of, firstly the monastery at Margam, then the monastery at Llanbadarn Fawr. This is called a précis. To do it you need to decide the most important points and opinions in a document and then choose the way to write these in the simplest and shortest way.

2. What evidence does Gerald put forward to support his good opinion of the monastery at Margam? Show how this information helps him show a positive view of Margam.

3. Read Postcards 6 and 7. Compare these. In what different ways do they give you evidence about ways in which the English had a negative impact on Welsh people?

4. How might King Henry I of England have used evidence like that in Postcard 8 to justify his forcing the Welsh church to come under the control of the English church? How might a Welsh person argue that this was not the right thing to do?

Dear William,

We crossed a ford over the River Dee, which the Welsh call Dwfr Dwy, and so came to Chester on the third day before Easter [April 14, 1188]. Chester boasts of being the burial-place of the Holy Roman Emperor Henry V. In the same way they claim that King Harold is buried here. He was the last of the Saxon kings in England. He was wounded in many places, losing his left eye through an arrow which penetrated it. But, although beaten, he escaped to these parts. The real identity of these two people, which before this had been kept secret, was only revealed when they made their last confession before they died.

Yours not totally convinced,
Gerald.

Postcard 10

Chester: hideaway of kings

Dear William,

We spent the night at Oswestry. It was here that King Henry II of England entered Powys but was forced to retreat because of a sudden and unexpected fall of rain. The previous day the leaders of the English army had burnt down certain Welsh churches, with their villages and churchyards. As a result, the sons of Owain Gwynedd swore they would never again spare any English churches. Owain stopped the argument: 'I do not agree,' he said. 'Unless we have God on our side we will never defeat the English. Let us instead promise God that we will show greater respect to all churches and holy places.' On the night which followed, the English army, as I have told you, learned what God's anger could bring.

Best wishes,
Gerald.

On the Welsh-English border

Postcard 11

Jerusalem

Dear William,

We finally completed our journey at Hereford. About three thousand men were signed with the Cross. All of them were skilled in the use of the spear and the arrow and only too keen to attack the enemies of our faith at the first opportunity. They were all sincerely and warmly committed to Christ's service. If only the Crusade itself had been carried out with such an urgency. By the judgement of God, which is sometimes hard to understand but never unjust, it was delayed because of the slowness of the Holy Roman Emperor, the disagreements between our own kings and the unexpected death of the King of Sicily. After his death our kings quarrelled over who was in control and so the faithful Christians beyond the sea were left surrounded by their enemies in their hour of need.

Yours in great disappointment,
Gerald.

Postcard 12

Pulling it Together

How Christian was the Church in the Middle Ages?

You are presenting a documentary (an accurate news account) telling the story of Gerald's Journey.

Your documentary will need to:

- Explain when and why he went on his journey.
- Outline the places he visited.
- Interview Gerald about what he did and why he did it.
- Interview some of the people he met and ask them to give their opinion on the events and how their lives were changed. Re-read the Postcards. Who will you choose to talk to?
- Involve expert witnesses giving their opinions on:
  - The Crusade. Why did it happen? How did it end up?
  - How the Church was organised in the Middle Ages.
  - What kind of impression Gerald's journey gives about how Christian Medieval Christianity was.

To find the information for this documentary you will need to think about what evidence Gerald's postcards tell you about the love and care offered by the Church and its message to people ... Concerns you might have about some Medieval Christian people's attitude towards people of other religions and towards Christians from other countries ... Concerns about rivalries between the Welsh and English Churches ... Concerns about strange superstitions and beliefs, which are nothing to do with Jesus, which seem to have got into Medieval Church beliefs.

Stage 1

Decide who is going to be:
- Interviewers, who will need to ask detailed questions of Gerald, people Gerald met, the Experts
- Gerald
- People he met
- Experts
- 'Link-people' who will introduce, set the scene, connect between different people
- Researchers looking for extra information

Stage 2

Bring your presentation together with group members presenting their information. Video it?

Finally — How Christian was Medieval Christianity?

Remember, Gerald's Journey cannot tell us all we need to know about the Christian Church in the Middle Ages. But we can get some idea of its impact on the lives of different people.

Write an essay to explain what you have learned.
- Start with an introduction saying why the Church had such an impact on people's lives.
- Include a paragraph telling how it was organised and changing.
- Include a paragraph telling how it had a positive impact on people's lives. Remember Christianity is about telling people about God's love, living lives of love like that of Jesus.
- Include a paragraph explaining why you might have concerns about how Christian some areas of Church life were in the Middle Ages.
- Conclude with saying, from what you have seen, how Christian the Medieval Church was.

41

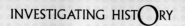

CHAPTER 4

The Diseased and Deadly Middle Ages!
Why was life so unhealthy?

In this chapter you will:

- Explore the link between trade and the Black Death.
- Investigate the connection between disease and dirt in towns in the Middle Ages.
- Decide why people in the Middle Ages found it hard to prevent disease.
- Decide how effective medicine was in the Middle Ages.
- Plan and present a presentation on 'Why was life so unhealthy in the Middle Ages?'

Dying in the Middle Ages

By the year AD 2021 it is thought that the average British man will live until he is 74 years old. The average woman will live to 80. This is called life expectancy.

In the Middle Ages things were very different. The average life expectancy for a man was only about 35 years.

For a women it was only about 25 years. This is like some of the poorest countries in the world today. In fact, in modern Sierra Leone – which has the lowest life expectancy in the world today – women live longer than in Britain in the Middle Ages.

Country	Life expectancy for men	Life expectancy for women
Britain by AD 2021?	74 years	80 years
Medieval Britain	35 years	25 years
Modern Burkina Faso	35.3 years	35.7 years
Modern Sierra Leone	25.8 years	26 years

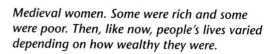

Medieval women. Some were rich and some were poor. Then, like now, people's lives varied depending on how wealthy they were.

How did the Black Death reach Britain from China?

In 1348 a deadly disease hit Britain. This fictional account (based on evidence from the time) is how someone living through this terrible time might have remembered it.

A Dorset Horror Story

'After Easter, 1348, sailors, coming into our port of Melcombe Regis brought the first terrible rumours. They said that far away, between China and Persia, rains of fire killed those living there. The foul smoke drifted westward, poisoning those who breathed it in.

By June it seemed the stories were not just sailors' tales. Sailors brought news that God had struck down our enemies the French with the plague. It seemed that travellers returning to Genoa in Italy from the eastern Mediterranean had brought the disease home. From there it had come, somehow, into France. We took it for a sign that God was on our side against the enemy. But then news came that the plague was loose in the Channel Islands – on English soil. We blamed the French for spreading the disease to us!

At the end of June a ship came in from Gascony, on its way back to Bristol. But it was carrying more than wine. Within days the plague was amongst us. Our neighbours started dying. At first, a fever burnt them up. Then came great, swelling boils in their armpits and groins. The pain was terrible. And if the boils burst a stinking, black poison poured out. People tried all kinds of cures but none stopped it. People stayed at home to avoid meeting others. But they died all the same.

In August, the Bishop of Bath and Wells ordered processions every Friday to beg God to turn away this terrible judgement against us but by then it was already in Bristol. So many priests are dead that the bishop has given permission to ordinary people to hear the **confessions** of their dying neighbours. Is this the end of the world?'

BLACK DEATH FACT FILE

- Started in Central Asia.

- First reached Britain in 1348.

- Not called the 'Black Death' until 1555.

- Possibly Bubonic Plague, though some other diseases are a possibility.

- If it was Bubonic Plague, it is spread when rats carry it in their blood and rat fleas bite people. A type of this disease can also be passed by coughing.

- It killed between a quarter and a third of the population of Western Europe.

- Last great outbreak in Britain was in 1665.

THINK ABOUT IT

Read the 'Dorset Horror Story'. In groups of three take the parts of:

   a) one of the sailors

   b) a plague victim

   c) the Bishop of Bath and Wells.

Think about this story as 'your person' might remember it. Think about their point of view. Then, *imagining you are that person*, write down how the disease has affected *you*, what/who you think might have caused it and how you have reacted to it. Then, read these imaginary accounts to each other. In what ways are they similar, or different? Try to explain why.

Why did trade spread disease?

SOURCE A

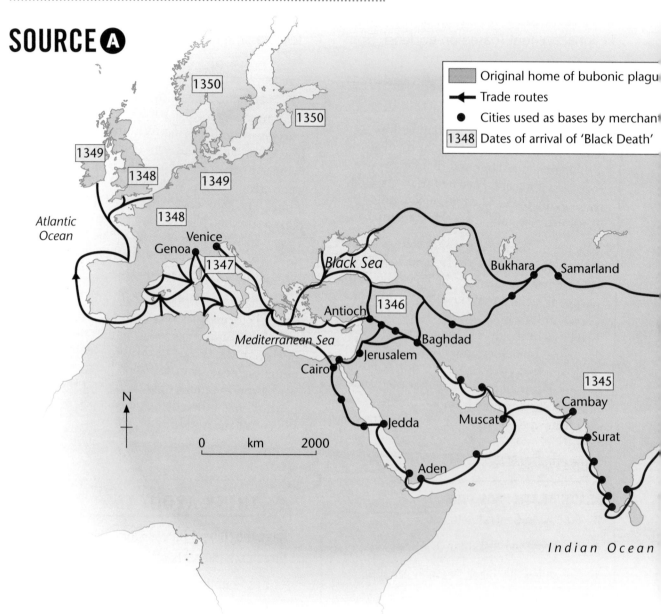

Legend:
- Original home of bubonic plagu[e]
- ← Trade routes
- • Cities used as bases by merchant[s]
- 1348 Dates of arrival of 'Black Death'

Map labels: 1350, 1350, 1349, 1348, 1349, 1348, 1347, 1346, 1345

Atlantic Ocean, Venice, Genoa, Black Sea, Bukhara, Samarland, Antioch, Baghdad, Mediterranean Sea, Jerusalem, Cairo, Jedda, Muscat, Cambay, Surat, Aden, Indian Ocean

N, 0 km 2000

Trade routes linking Asia with Europe in the Middle Ages.

SOURCE B

In this year, 1348, in Melcombe in the county of Dorset, a little before the feast of St John the Baptist, two ships, one of them from Bristol, came alongside. One of the sailors had brought with him from Gascony the seeds of the terrible pestilence, and through him the men of that town in Melcombe were the first in England to be infected.

From Grey Friar's **Chronicle** *(fourteenth century).*

SOURCE **C**

'The seventh year after it began, it came to England and first began in the towns and ports joining on the seacoasts, in Dorsetshire, where, as in other counties, it made the country quite empty of people, so that there were almost none left alive.

From there it passed into Devonshire and Somersetshire, even reaching Bristol and was so bad that men from Gloucestershire would not allow men from Bristol to have anything to do with them. But eventually it reached Gloucester and even Oxford and London. Finally it spread over all of England and so killed the people that hardly one in ten survived. In Bristol the plague raged so badly that the living were hardly able to bury the dead and at this time the grass grew several inches high in the High Street and in Broad Street.'

Geoffrey the Baker in the **Chronicle of England** *(fourteenth century).*

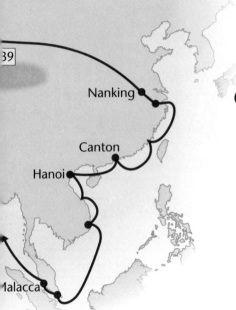

39

Nanking

Canton

Hanoi

Malacca

THINK ABOUT IT

'The way the world was becoming more "connected" in the Middle Ages helped bring the Black Death to Britain.'

1. Explain why this was so. Decide *where* the disease started. Suggest the *route* it may have followed to Britain, including *places* it may have passed through and *when*.

2. Our modern world is even more 'connected' due to easier travel. Carry out a research project, using the library or Internet, on the way in which this affects the spreading of modern diseases. Two to focus on could be Aids and Influenza ('flu').

STOP AND REFLECT: How did the increasing trade links between Europe and Asia help make the Middle Ages less healthy?

Why were towns such deadly places?

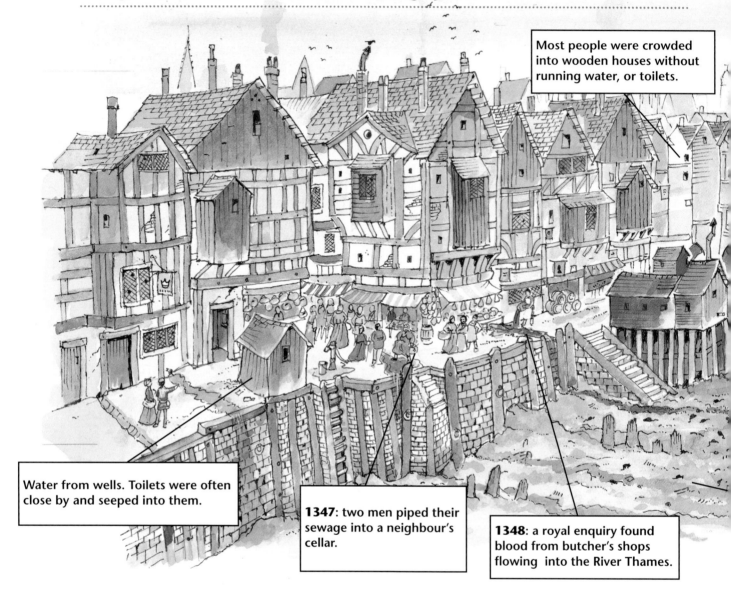

Most people were crowded into wooden houses without running water, or toilets.

Water from wells. Toilets were often close by and seeped into them.

1347: two men piped their sewage into a neighbour's cellar.

1348: a royal enquiry found blood from butcher's shops flowing into the River Thames.

Deadly dwellings

Towns and villages in the Middle Ages were dirty places. The reason people died in Britain in the Middle Ages as young as they do today in Less Economically Developed Countries (LEDCs) was because people in the Middle Ages often lived in the same conditions as people in LEDCs do today. Here is evidence about the state of London in the fourteenth century.

What a life!

The way people lived in the Middle Ages helped disease spread. Here are some horrible diseases and what causes them: Leprosy is a skin disease spread where lepers are crowded together. Dysentry, Diarrhoea and Typhoid are often caused by drinking dirty water. Bubonic Plague was caused by rat fleas biting people. Worms are caused by eating food infected by excrement of a person suffering from worms.

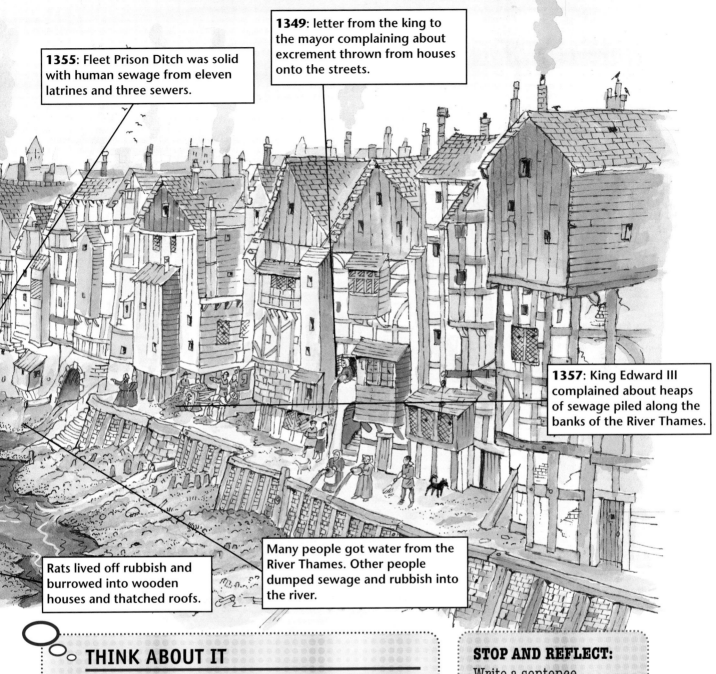

1349: letter from the king to the mayor complaining about excrement thrown from houses onto the streets.

1355: Fleet Prison Ditch was solid with human sewage from eleven latrines and three sewers.

1357: King Edward III complained about heaps of sewage piled along the banks of the River Thames.

Rats lived off rubbish and burrowed into wooden houses and thatched roofs.

Many people got water from the River Thames. Other people dumped sewage and rubbish into the river.

THINK ABOUT IT

Look at the picture above.

1. Share ideas with a neighbour on why people living in this town faced death from disease?

2. Then, on your own, write down: (a) What is so unhealthy about the place? (b) Which diseases might be caused by different aspects of life in this town? (c) Why might the newly arrived Black Death spread in a town like this one? (d) What changes would be needed in order to make this town healthier?

3. Next, in small groups, share your answers and decide why people in the Middle Ages would have found it hard to make this town healthier.

STOP AND REFLECT:
Write a sentence explaining why the state of towns in the Middle Ages made life unhealthy, and which diseases you might find in one.

What can bones tell us?

The bones of dead people can tell us a lot. They can tell us about:

- Diseases which made them ill.

- Diseases which killed them.

- Living conditions and **diet**.

- Treatments of injuries and diseases.

- *But remember*: some illnesses leave no marks on bones!

We need to remember that not all illnesses, injuries or treatments leave clues in the bones of skeletons found by archaeologists. But a lot do. We are going to look at bones from some of the people who lived in the Middle Ages. Each of these bones is a clue to life in the past.

SOURCE Ⓐ

Teeth.

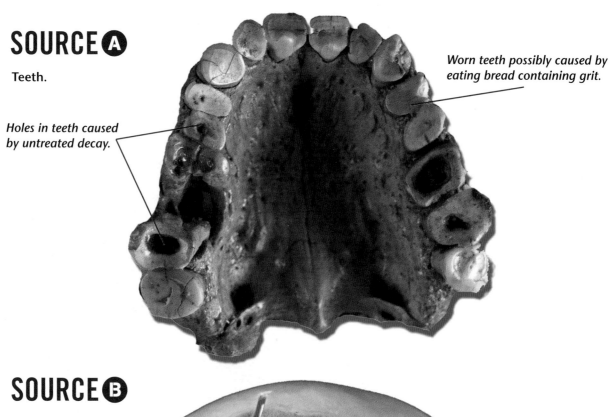

Worn teeth possibly caused by eating bread containing grit.

Holes in teeth caused by untreated decay.

SOURCE Ⓑ

Skull.

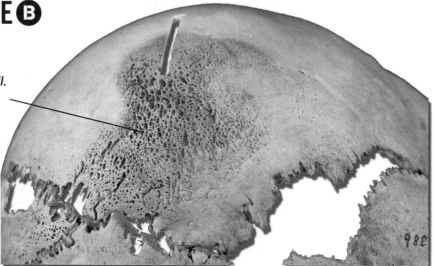

New bone growth on skull. Possibly caused by scurvy (lack of vitamin C).

SOURCE C

Eye sockets.

Holes in eye socket bones. Possibly caused by infection, or lack of iron in diet?

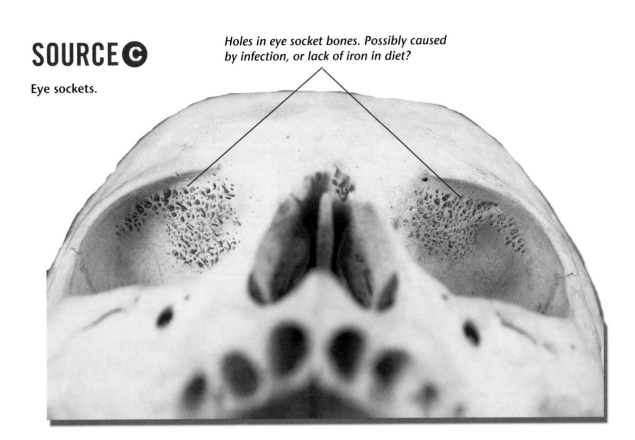

SOURCE D

Bone growth on skull.

Healed wound. Possibly caused the pain which was treated by the drilling?

Hole drilled in skull to treat a disease (pain in the head?). Healing is evident, which suggests the patient survived the operation.

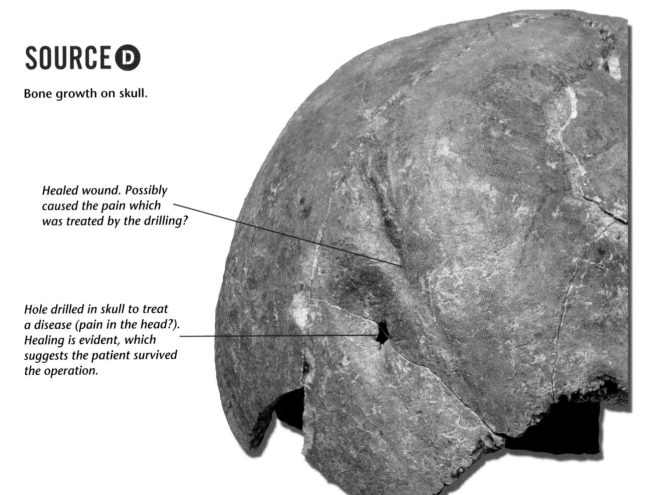

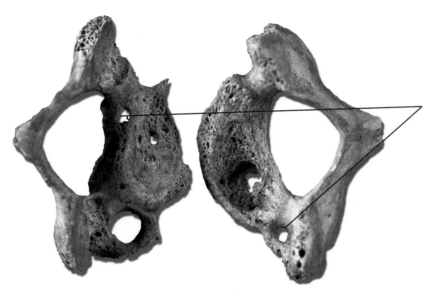

SOURCE **E**

Neck vertebrae.

Destruction of bone. Probably caused by tuberculosis.

SOURCE **F**

Foot.

Loss of toe bones, especially fourth and little toe.

Destruction of bone in arch of foot. Both caused by leprosy.

THINK ABOUT IT

1. Write an 'Instruction Guide' to tell another person how to use these bones as evidence.

   a) How useful are bones as evidence about health?

   b) Explain what different signs of different illnesses can be detected on bones.

   c) Explain what to look for to discover about living conditions or diet.

   d) Explain what to look for to find out about surgery.

2. Now get a neighbour to read your instructions. You do the same, reading theirs. Afterwards, discuss with each other how each set of instructions, of what to look for, could be improved.

STOP AND REFLECT:
Write down three sentences. One saying what you have learnt about diseases affecting Medieval people. One saying what you have learned about unhealthy living conditions or poor diet. One saying what you have learned about Medieval surgery.

Would a medieval hospital cure your illness?

'CASUALTY ...', 'HOLBY CITY ...', 'ER ...'

Have you been into hospital? There are lots of reasons why you might have. Perhaps you were sick, or injured, or visiting someone. If you've never been in one you will probably have watched TV programmes set in hospitals. Hospitals are an important part of our National Health Service. Many thousands of people would die each year if it were not for the treatment they receive in a modern hospital. Hospitals are life savers!

Hospitals in the Middle Ages

The first hospitals started in the Middle Ages. St John's Hospital in Canterbury, Kent, has been continuously in use since it was built in 1184. It was built to provide care for 30 poor men and 30 poor women. It is one of the oldest hospitals in the country. Like most Medieval hospitals it was set up by the Church to show Christian love to people in practical ways. The building itself was split into two. In one half men were cared for. In the other half were women. Behind the accommodation was the **reredorter** – a Medieval toilet. This toilet is still used over 800 years later!

SOURCE A

Cut away diagram of St John's hospital, Canterbury.

Accommodation, men and women kept separate.

Gateway

Reredorter. Toilet over running water.

Church

Hospitals and health

If there were hospitals, why did so many people die of disease? It is a good question. The most obvious reason is that hospitals in the Middle Ages were different to modern ones. They did not have modern knowledge about germs causing disease, or anaesthetics to stop people dying from shock in an operation, or powerful antiseptics and antibiotics to kill germs.

There were similarities though. They knew about herbs and some medicines which helped healing. People were given simple – but good – food and rest. As in monasteries, there was running water to remove toilet waste. Monks and nuns cared for the sick. But none of these were as effective in battling disease as modern medical ideas and technology.

SOURCE **B**

'There were about 1,200 hospitals run by the Church in England and Wales, all of which were founded after 1100. There were almost as many hospitals as there were monasteries. The name hospital comes from the Latin *hospes*, which means guest, stranger or foreigner. Hospitals in the middle ages were not places where people went to be cured. They provided shelter for travellers, the elderly and the sick. Usually they were run by monks or nuns and would offer some general nursing skills. There were no doctors in medieval hospitals until after the Black Death.

There were no cures available. The eating of rotten meat and fish is believed to have encouraged the development of disease, so giving people fresh food was sensible, effective and probably the result of the observation that a good diet halted disease.'

Kent Education website.

THINK ABOUT IT

In 1999 Time Team dug up the Medieval hospital of St Leonard in York. The picture shows a modern idea of what it looked like – with modern Time Team members drawn in! Imagine you could talk to these Time Team members. Explain to them ways in which a hospital in the Middle Ages was (a) similar and (b) different to a modern one.

STOP AND REFLECT: Write a paragraph to explain why Medieval hospitals could not cure disease as well as modern hospitals do.

Moving forward, or in the wrong direction?

New ideas and lost knowledge

During the Middle Ages there was more contact between Christian Western Europe and the Islamic countries in the Middle East. This took place because, in places like Spain and southern Italy, Christians and Muslims lived close together and because, during the **Crusades**, many Europeans travelled to the Middle East.

Books about medicine, written by ancient Greek and Roman writers, had often been lost in Europe after the fall of the Roman Empire. But these had survived in the Middle East. These ideas now spread back to Europe. By about AD 1360 the French writer Guy de Chauliac quoted ancient Greek and Roman writers 1,010 times in his books on medicine. He could only do this because the old ideas had been rediscovered.

Moving forward?

One famous rediscovered ancient writer was Galen (born AD 129 in Greece). His books encouraged doctors to record what they saw in an illness and to explore how the human body worked. These were good ideas. Islamic writers like Ibn Sinna (died AD 1037) and Rhazes (died AD 925) wrote detailed descriptions to help doctors identify different diseases. New ideas spread about setting up hospitals to treat the sick and to study diseases. In AD 1100 London had one hospital, but Baghdad (in modern Iraq) had 60! Medical schools were set up in Islamic countries and these were copied in Europe.

In the wrong direction?

But there were problems. Many people just read Galen instead of studying things for themselves. Some Islamic writers encouraged this because they had so much respect for ancient books. This was a problem because Galen had done a lot of his work on animals and some of his ideas about the human body were wrong! As well as this, an ancient Greek idea became popular that sick people should have blood let out of their bodies. This was thought to get rid of things called **humours** which were thought to build up in the body. This was wrong!

The missing piece in the puzzle

So, the spread of new ideas and the rediscovery of old knowledge helped in some ways and got in the way of improving medicine in other ways. But, most important of all, none of these writers knew anything about **germs**. As long as this was the case doctors would find it hard to fight disease and no one would know how to stop disease happening in the first place. This problem would continue until the nineteenth century. As a result, health for most people at the end of the Middle Ages would not be much better than at the beginning. On top of this, where there were advances in treatment – only the rich could afford it.

SOURCE A

Thirteenth-century medical textbook from Salerno in Southern Italy, where ideas from Islamic countries were studied.

THINK ABOUT IT

1. Look at the six pictures from the Salerno medical textbook. Some appear to show:

   - bandaging a head wound

   - putting ointment on a sore, or wound

   - a brain operation

   - letting out blood

   Write down the letters A–F. Write these four descriptions next to the 'picture-letter' you think it best applies to.

2. Which one of these treatments might have been influenced by Greek ideas from Islamic countries? Explain why.

3. Write two short paragraphs: one describing how medicine improved due to ideas from Islamic countries; one describing problems caused by these 'new' ideas.

STOP AND REFLECT:
What was the single biggest reason why health and medicine did not improve greatly during the Middle Ages?

Pulling it Together

Why was life so unhealthy in the Middle Ages?

Over the last chapter we have been trying to answer this big question. To help us answer it we have asked a number of little questions:

- **How did increasing trade links between Europe and Asia help make the Middle Ages less healthy?**
- **How did the state of towns in the Middle Ages make life unhealthy?**
- **What can archaeology tell us about disease and medicine?**
- **In what ways did 'new' ideas change medicine and health? Did things get better because of these 'new' ideas?**

We call these little questions a Route of Enquiry. They help us work through the evidence so we can start to answer our big question. Now you are ready to start doing this.

Planning a group presentation

Stage 1

In your group, brainstorm: *What things make people ill today?*
Don't just list different types of disease but, instead, think about different reasons *why* people become ill. Are some of these different reasons connected in any way? What does this tell you about how complicated it can be trying to discover why diseases happen?

Stage 2

Bring together all your answers to the little questions. Look at your notes, look again at the evidence in this chapter. Write a short paragraph which answers each of the little questions.

Stage 3

Now decide your answer to the big question. Remember to:

- Describe how we know the Middle Ages were so unhealthy.

- Explain why it can be hard deciding what causes disease.

- Explain different reasons for disease in the Middle Ages and why these made people sick.

- Identify any changes which led to illness and say why these changes caused problems.

- Explain how different areas of life in the Middle Ages worked together to make life unhealthy.

- Show how some changes bring progress in some areas of life but make things worse in other areas of life.

- Decide what you think was the biggest cause of disease in the Middle Ages. And then explain why you think this is more important that other reasons.

Stage 4

Make your presentation to the rest of the class. Decide who will talk about each area you are presenting. You should support your opinions with evidence (writing and pictures from the time) which show why you think as you do.

CHAPTER 5

Money, Money, Money ...
What was it like to live in towns in the Middle Ages?

SOURCE Ⓐ

In this chapter you will:

- **Explore different aspects of town life for different people.**
- **Explore different reasons why Bristol changed and grew.**
- **Imagine what it was like to live in a Medieval town.**

A modern artist's impression of the attack on Jewish people sheltering in Clifford's Tower, York.

'Ethnic Cleansing': York, March 16,1190

For years there had been a Jewish community in York. Like many towns, York had a royal castle in which Jews could find protection if attacked by racists. The growing town and monasteries of the city, and its local area, needed loans of money which could be borrowed from the Jews. For years there had been a Jewish community in York but then that changed.

In March, 1190, in the city of York, a mob broke into the house of Benedict, a wealthy Jewish man who had recently died, and murdered his **widow** and his children. They then stole his treasure and set his house on fire. The homes of other Jews in York were also attacked.

The English king – Richard 'the lionheart' – was away on crusade to capture Jerusalem from the Muslims and make it a Christian city. Back in England some people were keen to attack the only non-Christians they could get their hands on. These were the Jews.

The terrified Jewish community escaped to the protection of the royal castle. Here they were safe in what is now called 'Clifford's Tower', on top of its great **motte** of earth. The angry mob surrounded the tower.

The Jewish people inside were afraid that the warden of the castle (who ran the castle for the king) might let the mob in. To protect themselves, they locked the doors and would not let him in. The warden called in a local landowner, Richard Malebys, to help him. Malebys had borrowed money from the Jews of York and was keen to destroy them. Then he would not have to repay his debts. There were many like him in the mob which attacked the castle.

When the mob finally broke into the burning tower they found that most of those inside had killed themselves. Those still alive were immediately murdered. Then the mob went to York Minster cathedral. There were kept records of who owed money to the Jews. The mob took these records and burned them.

Living in towns and cities today

What is it like to live in modern towns and cities?

'... pollution, racial tension, street crime.'

'... jobs, entertainment, choice of housing.'

THINK ABOUT IT

1. Where would you prefer to live today? In a town/city or in a small village? Explain your reasons.

2. With a neighbour make a list of four positive things about living in a Medieval town, or city. Then decide which of these would be true of living in a town or city today. Use the information on these two pages to help you.

Town and city life today is a mix of positive and negative things!

Living in towns in the Middle Ages

Towns in the Middle Ages, like today, were a mix of positive and negative things. On the positive side, they were places to escape the power of the lords who controlled the villages. In a town, people had a better choice of jobs. It was easier to make money and 'get on in the world'. Towns were exciting and had more entertainment.

Like today, people from **ethnic minority** groups tended to live in the towns. Most Medieval British people were Christians, but there was a minority of Jewish people who lived in towns. Why did they choose town life? Because the only job they were allowed to do was lend money and charge **interest** to those who borrowed it. Christians were not allowed to do this Towns were useful places to live in because they were where most **trade** took place. There was always someone wanting to borrow money. On top of this, the king was keen to keep an eye on the Jews because they were forced to pay heavy taxes and to loan him money. Other minority groups gathered in towns for similar reasons. In the fourteenth century, Flemings (from what is now France and Belgium) settled in London and other towns to set up cloth making and to trade. German traders lived in London and other East Coast ports. Towns were places of opportunity.

On the other hand ...

There were negative things about towns in the Middle Ages. They were dirty and unhealthy. There was street crime. There were crowded houses. Many poorer people hated groups they thought of as 'foreign'. Many powerful townspeople encouraged attacks on Jews and Flemings, if it helped them escape from debts they owed them, or got rid of rivals. In London, during the Peasants' Revolt in 1381, Flemish merchants were hunted through the streets and killed. Thirty-five hid in the church of St Martin in the Vintry but were dragged outside and beheaded, one after the other, on a single block of wood. Altogether more than 150 were murdered.

In the towns, groups called 'guilds' made rules about how craftspeople should work and make things. Being in a guild gave workers and traders protection and encouraged good quality in things made and sold. But people outside the guild faced **discrimination**. Traders from outside a town were only allowed to sell things on special market days. And then they had to pay for the right to do so. Towns could be intolerant places.

SOURCE B

'Shops, markets, taverns, docks and churches, the great fortress of the Tower, the baths and brothels of Southwark. Large merchant houses, often with shops or business premises attached, rubbed shoulders with the hovels of the poor. An Italian observer was amazed by the 52 goldsmiths' shops which lay along Cheapside, while the country hero of a popular song described food-sellers offering 'ripe strawberries, ribs of beef and many a pie, hot sheep's feet and mackerel'. There were drapers selling cloth and taverners selling wine. The numerous guilds were run by their own leaders, but above them were the Mayor and the Aldermen who controlled the large majority of the city's inhabitants who could not vote: from the wealthy groups of German and Italian merchants to the apprentices [learning a trade], labourers and criminals. It was from among these groups that disorder was always liable to break out.'

A description of fifteenth-century London by the historian, Dr Roger Virgoe, 1989.

THINK ABOUT IT

1. With a neighbour make a list of four negative things about living in a Medieval town. Then decide which of these would be true of living in a town or city today.

2. Reading and notetaking: skim through Source B to get a general idea of its meaning. Then scan it for positive and negative things about town life. Record these on a spidergram. Colour-code it: one colour for positive, another for negative. Make a note of any words you do not understand. Look these up in a dictionary.

3. 'For the Jews of York and the Flemings of London, town life brought opportunities and terrible dangers.' Explain how this was true.

STOP AND REFLECT: Write down two sentences: one recording what you think was the best thing about living in a Medieval town; one recording what you think was the worst thing. You decide.

How and why did Bristol change in the Middle Ages?

Bristol was one of the largest towns in Britain in the Middle Ages. In 1377, 10,000 people lived there. Only London and York had bigger populations. London's population in 1377 was 23,000 and it was the biggest town in Britain.

Change over time

By looking at Bristol we can see how one town changed over the Middle Ages. This helps us:

- Understand the different ways in which it changed.

- Explore reasons for these changes.

- Write an imaginary account of life in the city.

Baseline: Bristol in 1150

Bristol first appears as a town before the Norman Conquest. Although it was some distance from the sea, it was the lowest place on the River Avon where a bridge crossed the river. Its Anglo-Saxon name, '*Bricg-stow*' means 'the bridge place'. It was a port where ships sailing up the Avon from France, Wales, Ireland and the West of England could load and unload cargoes. It was important enough for a Norman castle to be built there. There was so much trade between Bristol and Ireland that records from Dublin in 1202 record 14 Dubliners with the surname 'de Bristol' (from Bristol). We know there was a Jewish community there, because Abraham of Bristol was imprisoned in Bristol castle, in 1210, to force him to pay £6,600 to King John. Seven of his teeth were pulled out before he would pay. Bristol, like most towns, was a mixture of opportunities and intolerance.

In 1141 the writer of a chronicle, called the *Gesta Stephani*, wrote that Bristol was 'fit and safe for a thousand ships. Bristol's walls surround the city so closely that the whole city seems to swim on the water and be set on the river banks.' But Bristol had a problem which it would have to overcome if it were to keep growing.

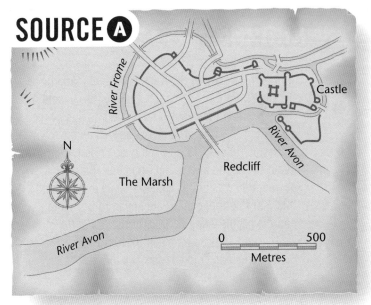

SOURCE A

Bristol in 1150.

Solving the problem

SOURCE B

'The ships of old time came up by the Avon to a place called '*the Back*' where there was and is enough depth of water but the bottom is very stony and rough. So they decided to dig a trench a little to the north-west of the old quay on the Avon, in the year 1247, and so brought the course of the River Frome that way and made a soft and comfortable harbour for great ships.'

John Leland visited Bristol and wrote this in about 1542.

An amazing solution

Historians writing between 1480 and 1623 record that the people of Bristol thought of an amazing solution to their problem. It resulted in one of the biggest engineering projects in Britain in the Middle Ages. But what was the solution? Look back at Leland and you may get an idea. Here is how this project was remembered a long time after the event:

SOURCE C

'1247: This year was the trench dug and made for the river from *Gibtailer* to the quay by the consent of the mayor and the people and as well as this by the consent of the area of *Redcliffe* as well as the town of Bristol. Before this time the river, or port, did run about the castle and so the Church of Our Lady's Assumption was and is called St Mary le Port. And this year the bridge of Bristol began to be rebuilt and the people living in the areas of *Redcliffe*, *Temple* and *Thomas* were combined with the town of Bristol. Whereas before it was two towns with two separate markets.'

Adam's Chronicle of Bristol, *written in 1623.*

SOURCE D

'The parish church of St Leonard is sited on top of St Leonard's Gate, with the tower for bell ringing on top of the gate but it is a small church. It stands there between Baldwin Street – along which street the River Frome flowed in ancient times on the south side – and the road going to the Quay and the street called Marsh Street and St Stephen's Church.'

William of Worcester who visited Bristol and wrote this in 1480.

A clue from the time

SOURCE E

'Henry, by the grace of God, King of England, Lord of Ireland, Duke of Normandy and Aquitaine and Count of Anjou, to all worthy men living in *Redcliffe*, greetings. Our beloved **burgesses** of Bristol, for the common good of the whole town of Bristol as of your **suburb**, have begun a trench in the Marsh of St Augustine that ships coming to our port of Bristol may be able to enter, or leave, more freely. We command you that, for the betterment of the whole port, not only to the burgesses but also to you, since you enjoy the freedoms that they do, you shall give as much assistance as they do, otherwise the work may be delayed if you do not assist.'

Letter written by King Henry III, April 27 1240.

THINK ABOUT IT

1. **So, what was the problem and how was it solved? Historians need to check evidence critically and carefully in order to decide just what it is telling them. Do this now, to answer this question.**

- **Look at Source A and read Source B. What *problem* did Bristol have?**

- **Now write down *anything* you find in Source B about what was done to *solve* the problem. What *extra information* can you find in Sources C and D?**

- **Why is Source E valuable for trying to decide what happened in the Middle Ages?**

- **Which of Sources B, C and D might have used Source E to help them write their history of Bristol? How can you tell?**

SOURCE **F**

Bristol in 1250.

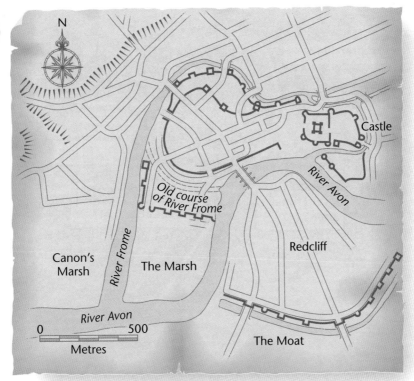

So – what happened?

THINK ABOUT IT

Look at Source F and the account written by Peter Aughton in Source G.

2. **What was it about towns and cities which made it possible for them to attempt such a huge project as this? Think about:**

- **amount of workers needed**
- **skills and organisation**
- **paying for it**
- **what was gained from all the effort.**

SOURCE **G**

'In the 1240s it is unlikely that there was another town anywhere in the world which contained so much civil engineering activity. First a new channel was cut for the River Avon. Then the whole river was dammed and diverted to flow through the new channel. A second dam was built just downstream from the bridge so that the townsfolk gazed down on a dry riverbed where their wooden bridge had stood. The foundations for the new town bridge, to be built of stone, were under construction.

In the south and west of the town the new walls took shape, complete with rounded towers and new gateways for the roads leading out of the town to the south. But it was in the north, where the great new trench was being excavated to accommodate the seagoing ships, that the most impressive works were underway. Primitive cranes were used for lifting the heavy stones to build the stone quay on the Bristol bank, but the excavation of the trench must have been entirely by hand. In the deep channel, well below ground level, hundreds of labourers scrapped at the earth, shifting the mud and muck by the barrow-load up timber-lined ramps. Other workers hauled with ropes, rollers and levers to bring the cut stone from the local quarries to build the quay wall. The cost was £5,000, an enormous sum of money and comparable to that of the great castles and cathedrals.'

Written by a modern historian, Peter Aughton, in Bristol: A People's History, *2000.*

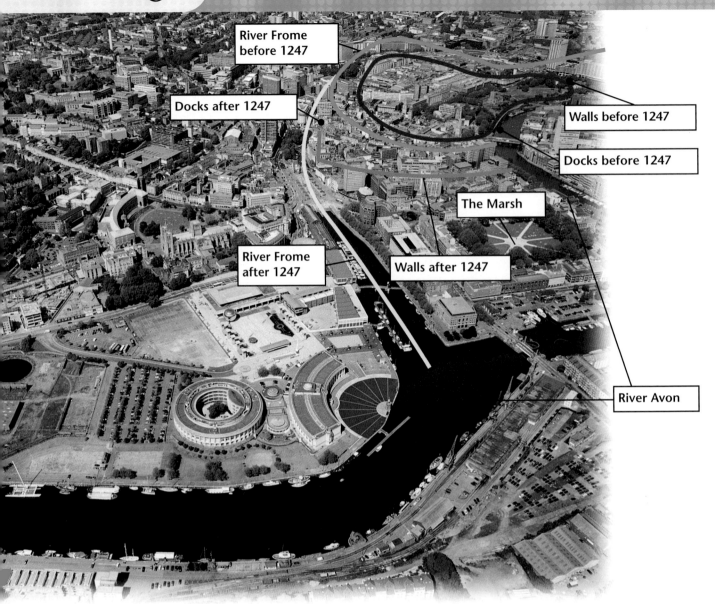

River Frome before 1247

Docks after 1247

Walls before 1247

Docks before 1247

The Marsh

River Frome after 1247

Walls after 1247

River Avon

SOURCE H *Bristol today, showing the layout of the Medieval city.*

THINK ABOUT IT

1. Look carefully at Source H. What can this tell you about the size of towns and cities in the Middle Ages compared with today? Remember that, in 1377, Bristol was the third biggest town in Britain.

2. How much did the project to change the route of the River Frome change Bristol? Write three short paragraphs describing changes (a) in size, and (b) in working as a trading place. In each paragraph you will need to first say what it was like before 1247, then how it changed, and then how important the change was in your opinion, using the evidence.

STOP AND REFLECT:
Write a paragraph to remind you what it was about towns which made it possible for them to carry out such big projects as was done in Bristol in the thirteenth century.

How was Bristol governed in the Middle Ages?

SOURCE A

All of us have roots going back into the past. Today, Bristol is a busy and bustling city. There are shops and offices, factories and lots of people! But modern Bristolians still remember their past. Every year until 1972 at 10 a.m. on the last day of September, a little ceremony marked the opening of the 'Court of Piepowder', or '*Pied Poudre*'. In the Middle Ages this was the special court which kept law and order during the great fair at Bristol. People came great distances to buy and sell at this fair. Its name means, in French, the court of 'dusty feet'. Today, of course, there is buying and selling all the year round. But this survival into the late-twentieth century is a reminder that the wealth and power of the modern city started in the Middle Ages.

During the Middle Ages the way Bristol was organised and **governed** changed as the town became more powerful. But how did it change? And why? To understand this we will build up a picture of the way Bristol was gradually given more rights and freedoms which helped it become more powerful and encouraged it to grow.

Until 1972, the medieval Court of Piepowder was opened on September 30 in this Public House!

SOURCE B

'I have granted to my burgesses [townspeople] of Bristol that they shall be free from **tolls** and **passage** [paying to use ferries] throughout my whole land of England, Normandy and Wales, wherever they shall come, they and their goods. I will and strictly command that they shall have all their freedoms and free customs fully and honourably as my free and faithful men and that I forbid anyone to disturb them on this account contrary to this my charter, or be fined ten pounds.'

A charter given by King Henry II in 1155.

SOURCE C

'For every ship coming to Bristol carrying goods other than wine: 6 pennies.
Barrel of wine: 1 penny.
Every hundred sheepskins: 1 penny.
Every ten sheep, goats or pigs: 1 penny.
Barrel of honey: 2 pennies.
Every cart from Gloucestershire: half a penny.
Every other cart: 1 penny.
Every horseload (except firewood): quarter penny.'

Some of the taxes charged on goods brought to sell in Bristol. The right to do this was given to the town in 1170.

SOURCE D

'No foreign merchant shall buy hides, corn, or wool in the town from anyone but the townspeople. No foreigner shall have a tavern except in a ship. No foreigner shall sell cloth except at the fair. No foreigner can stay in the town to sell his goods longer than forty days. No townsperson shall be arrested anywhere in my lands for any one else's debt unless it is they who owe the money or have promised it will be paid. Townspeople will be free to marry themselves and their sons and daughters and widows without needing a licence from their lords.'

Rights of the people of Bristol, given in a charter in 1188.

SOURCE E

'Know that I have granted and by this charter confirm, to our beloved son Edward, that he and his heirs forever shall hold one fair every year at Bristol for fifteen days, on the day before and on the feast day of St Lawrence and for thirteen days after. Therefore we will and firmly command that Edward and his heirs for ever shall hold this fair, every year at Bristol for the space of fifteen days with all rights and freedoms that are required for the fair.

Witnessed by Richard de Clare, Earl of Gloucester and Hertford. Given by my hand at Westminster, the 19th day of February, 1255.'

Charter given by King Henry III to Bristol, 1255. It was this charter which set up the Court of Piepowder.

SOURCE F

Picture taken from a legal document from Bristol, 1347. It shows the power of the Court of Piepowder to arrest a baker charged with some offence. Perhaps his bread was mouldy, or his loaves were not the right weight. These were the kinds of things checked by the court.

SOURCE G

Fifteenth-century painting of the mayor of Bristol and the council who governed Bristol. The mayor swears on a copy of the Bible. The people in red are councillors. Below them are merchants of Bristol. Lowest are the ordinary people. A charter in 1344 had allowed the election of 48 merchants to help a mayor govern Bristol. Another, in 1373, had made Bristol a separate county.

THINK ABOUT IT

1. Look at Sources A–G. Make a timeline from 1155 to 1373. On it mark ways in which the rights of the people of Bristol increased during this time.

2. Which of these rights do you think was the most important? Explain why.

3. Which of the sources do you think is most useful for a historian trying to explain that the increased importance of towns can be shown in the way they were given power to govern themselves?

4. 'In the Middle Ages not everyone had the same rights, or was regarded as being of equal value.' Explain how you could use both Sources D and G as evidence to prove this.

STOP AND REFLECT:
Write down three ways in which towns had power to run their own affairs.

Why did John Cabot sail to the 'New World'?

A shrinking world?

How many things are there in your home which come from abroad? These could include textiles used to make clothes, food, oil used in making plastic, medicine and so on.

All of these things remind us that we are part of a world-wide community. During the Middle Ages this world-wide community became more closely connected. It was trade with the Far East which brought the Black Death to Britain. It was trade with the Middle East which brought Arabic ideas about medicine to Britain (many of which had survived from Roman times). It was trade with Ireland and France which made Bristol into such an important port.

In May 1497 the Italian merchant, John Cabot, sailed from Bristol. He had lived in Bristol for some years and had heard of

Columbus' voyages to a New World, across the Atlantic Ocean, in 1492. Columbus had only reached the islands of the Caribbean. Cabot landed on the coast of North America. He thought he had reached Asia and hoped to bring expensive spices back from Asia to Europe. In fact he had reached Newfoundland, off the coast of Canada.

This 'New World' would soon be brutally exploited. In fact, one of the buildings in use as a warehouse by Bristol merchants in 1500 had once been the Jewish synagogue. The persecuted Jews had been driven out of England in 1290. But by 1500 the energy and skills of Bristol were beginning to discover and exploit new opportunities. This would show the same mixture of energy, co-operation and brutality that had made towns grow since 1066.

SOURCE Ⓐ

'Henry by the grace of God, King of England, France and lord of Ireland, greetings. Be it known that we have given and granted to our well-beloved John Cabot, citizen of Venice, full and free authority, rights and power to sail to all parts, countries and seas of the east, of the west and of the north to seek out, discover and find and set up our banners and ensigns in all such newly discovered lands and to subdue, occupy and possess all such places in the King's name.'

Rights given to the Italian, John Cabot, living in Bristol, by King Henry VII in 1496.

THINK ABOUT IT

1. First skim Source A to get an idea of its meaning. Then scan it and write down the *key words* which show: (a) the rights Cabot was given, and (b) the key words which show what King Henry got out of the deal.

2. Why would Cabot and King Henry have thought a voyage was a good idea?

STOP AND REFLECT:
How might Cabot's voyages increase the importance of Bristol?
Explain the possible impact of his discoveries.

Pulling it Together

What was it like to live in towns in the Middle Ages?

- Writing an Historical Fiction account of life in Bristol in 1497.

Historical **fiction** is a great way to play with history and to make serious points at the same time. It means:

- imagining that you are in the past, but

- using the evidence to try to make sure your story is as realistic as possible.

And because it is imaginative you can try to fill in the gaps in the evidence and try to explore what people might have thought and felt.

How to prepare

- Read through your **Stop and Reflect** notes.

- Decide on the ways in which Bristol changed in the Middle Ages. Think about why it changed and what these changes led to.

- Think about what it was like to live there.

- Identify ways in which different parts of life in the city had an impact on other areas of life (e.g. how trade brought more people to Bristol *and* then how this larger group of people had more skills and money to change the city *and* how this linked back and improved the trade).

Imagine if ...

- Look at the historical fiction writing on page 14 and page 43. These show you how you can use your imagination to try to picture life in the past.

- Imagine you are the mayor of Bristol watching John Cabot sail into the unknown. Write five paragraphs, written in the first person and present tense.

- In the first paragraph describe the sights, sounds and smells of the dock. Use adjectives, metaphors, similes to describe it.

- Next say who you are and how you govern Bristol. Make this a factual statement.

- Then explain how proud you are of your city. Use words which praise and excite.

- Describe how it has changed over the years. Make this a factual statement

- Say why you are so excited about Cabot's journey and why it is important for Bristol. Use words which describe the excitement of a journey into the unknown. Use vivid words to describe the valuable goods he might bring back to Bristol.

CHAPTER 6

Village Life

Did life get any better for ordinary people over 450 years?

SOURCE A

Pictures from a document drawn in about 1140. They show King Henry I having a nightmare in 1130. In the top right scene, peasants protest that they are having to pay too many taxes.

In this chapter you will:

- **Use evidence to decide why country life improved for some people, but got worse for others.**
- **Make a judgement on how far life really got better for most people.**

Better, worse, or just about the same?

According to legend, King Henry I had a nightmare in 1130. In this dream different people in his kingdom complained to him that taxes were making life too hard. According to the legend when Henry awoke he decided not to collect a tax he had planned for seven years! The legend reminds us that:

- Ordinary people often faced tough times.

- Some of these tough times were caused by the actions of other people.

- Sometimes ordinary people did things which resulted in improvements in their lives.

Between 1066 and 1500 many things happened which affected the lives of ordinary people. There were wars, taxes, plagues, disasters, good harvests and bad ones. When we think of the Middle Ages we often think of things staying pretty much the same for these 450 years. But things did *not* stay the same. In all kinds of areas of life there were changes: some religious beliefs changed, the power of the king changed, knowledge about medicine changed, towns changed. But what about the lives of ordinary people? Did they get better, worse, or stay just about the same? To find out we need to look at ordinary people. But where will we find them?

Well, in the Middle Ages most people lived in the countryside. In fact, until as late as 1851 the majority of British people lived in the countryside. They were small farmers, or **'peasants'**. So, we will need to look in the countryside. We will need to look at the people living in farms and villages and working on the land. To focus in more closely we will look at country people in one area of England – in the eastern Midlands. We will look at them in Domesday Book and then at how their lives changed after this.

What was life like in Codicote, 1086–1386?

Codicote is in Hertfordshire. Over the next three pages we will explore:

● What the village was like in Domesday Book.

● How the lives of ordinary people changed between 1086 and 1386.

● Why life got better for some people, and worse for others.

Codicote was one of the manors belonging to St Alban's Abbey. This was a powerful abbey which owned a lot of land in eastern England. The first evidence we have about the lives of peasants in Codicote was when it was recorded in Domesday Book. This great survey was carried out on the orders of William the Conqueror. Its aims were to find out who owned what land in England and what the land was worth. It also tells us about the different kinds of people living in the towns and villages of England.

CODE BREAKERS

Understanding Domesday Book code

Cottager *poorest villager, farmed 4 acres of land or less, had to do unpaid work for the lord of the village, could not leave the village without permission, had to pay the lord to marry and use the lord's mill.*

Frenchman *a Norman, probably ran the village.*

Hide *enough land for a family.*

In lordship *farmed by the lord of the village, using villagers forced to work on this land.*

Slave *a person owned by another, had no rights or land.*

Villein *(or 'serf') better-off peasants, farmed between 30–100 acres of land, but had to do unpaid work for the lord of the village, could not leave the village without permission, had to pay the lord to marry and use the lord's mill.*

SOURCE A

'Codicote is owned by the Abbey of St Alban's. At Codicote there are 8 *hides* of land to be taxed. Of these, 3 hides are *in lordship*. Living there are 16 *villeins*, 1 *Frenchman*, 3 *cottagers* and 4 *slaves*. There are 2 mills, along with meadow, pasture and woodland to feed 200 pigs.'

Many of the words used in Domesday Book are written in a kind of 'Norman Code'. If you break the code you can find out what life was like in the village in 1086.

THINK ABOUT IT

1. Each person mentioned was head of a family. If there were five people in a family, what was the Domesday Book population of Codicote?

2. Draw a triangle. At the top write the type of person who was best off in Codicote and how many there were of this kind of person. Then work down the triangle, (a) ranking the people in order and (b) noting how many there were of each type. On your triangle will appear: *Cottagers, Frenchman, Slaves, Villeins.*

3. Explain how the village was organised in order to make money for the lord of the village.

Did life change over time?

SOURCE A

The life of Hugh Cok, 1277–1306.

Look at the following sources of evidence about the lives of people living in the village of Codicote. Then decide how much life changed over time.

1277, poorest villager in Codicote.

Rented place to sell fish in the market.

Saved money and bought 6 pieces of land.

Rented one strip for 10 years and one for 4 years.

Bought a house and piece of land.

Bought a piece of land and a hedge.

Rented 3 more pieces of land.

Fined for selling bad beer!

1306, left his property to his daughter, Christina.

SOURCE B

'Up' and 'Down' in the village, 1315–32

Michael Gorman. During **famine**, sold house and 4 small pieces of land to raise money. Died 1321. Remaining piece of land taken by lord of the village.

Roger le Heldere. Bought 22 small pieces of land from poorer neighbours needing money during famine. In 1332 owned land, 2 houses, 3 shops in the market.

SOURCE C

'John Salecok has a house and garden. Owes a quarter of his income to the lord of the village. Has to plough the lord's land every winter or pay a fine. Has to do one day harrowing on the lord's land and provide his own horse. Has to bring his own horse to plough the lord's land, no meals provided. At Christmas owes his lord 1 cock, 1 hen, 1 loaf of bread. At Easter owes his lord 30 eggs. Has to work for his lord for 42 days between September and August, or pay a fine for each day missed. Owes one day carrying hay, food provided by lord. Must mow the lord's meadow. Must pay for two men to help harvest the lord's crops. Owes one day carrying corn. Owes half a day cleaning the lord's water mill.'

The kind of work a villein at Codicote owed the lord of the village in 1332. All of this work was unpaid. There were no more slaves in England because lords relied on villeins to work for them.

SOURCE D

The changing village after 1300:

- Crime went up during bad harvests in fourteenth century.

- Between 1350 and 1450, 90% of old families left the village (despite control by lord of the village) and new families moved in.

- Villeins tried to buy, or rent, more pieces of land.

- Villeins married later in life, had smaller families, few grandparents lived with their children. Parents left more land to their children.

- Villeins tried to get free from the control of the lord of the village.

Based on the historian Michael Wood's research on Codicote.

THINK ABOUT IT

1. So, did life get better for the people living in Codicote in the three hundred years after 1086? Write three headings: (a) *Life gets better*, (b) *Life gets worse*, (c) *Life stays about the same*. Under each heading write down any evidence you can find from Codicote. Ignore any information which is not relevant.

2. Explain how the following areas of life could stop things getting better for a villein family:
   - Famine
   - Duties owed to the lord of the village.

   Use the evidence from Codicote to support your answer.

3. If you were a villein, what area of your life would you most want to change?

STOP AND REFLECT:
What was the biggest barrier stopping life from getting better for country people?
Why did it stand in the way of improving the lives of ordinary people?

What do 'seals' tell us about changes in peasants' lives?

SOURCE Ⓐ

An agreement between the Earl of Chester and the men in two of his villages. The villagers could not write but fixed their 'seals' on the document to show they agreed with it.

SOURCE Ⓑ

Wax seal of Simon de Montfort, Earl of Leicester, 1258. All great landowners had their own expensive seals which were unlike anyone else's seal.

SOURCE Ⓒ

Wax seal of Diota de Luceby, from Durham, 1322. A squirrel throws nuts at a lion. The words say 'I nuts crack on a lion's back'.

Making a mark!

Most villagers in the Middle Ages could not write. But, as many of them worked hard and became better off, they found they had to agree to legal documents like an agreement over a sale of land, or an agreement about a right, or a responsibility, they had. When rich people did this they stamped their badge onto hot wax and stuck it to a document. This was called a 'seal'. The seal often showed a coat of arms – the special badge which was personal to a rich knight and landowner.

Better-off villagers soon copied these seals. They were not rich enough to have coats of arms. Instead, they chose seals with pictures on them which appealed to them in some way. Some seals made a little joke about their name. Ralph Hairun, in Durham, in 1200, had a seal with a 'heron' on it. 'Heron' sounds a bit like Hairun. Most villagers, though, could not afford their own special badge and, instead, bought one already made up. Most of these **mass-produced** seals had plants, flowers or animals on them. They looked a bit like a coat of arms but in fact lots of the same ones were made and sold. Some had a joke on them, like a picture of a monkey throwing nuts at a lion and the words: 'I nuts crack on a lion's back'! Or a sleeping lion with the words: 'Wake me no man'! But the villager who used a seal must have been proud of it. It made them stand out from the crowd.

THINK ABOUT IT

1. Can you think of ways in which some modern people copy fashions and lifestyles of richer people? Write down three of these ways. Then write a short paragraph explaining why people do this today.

2. Look at Simon de Montfort's seal (Source B), then at the villagers' seals (Sources A and C). Why were ordinary villagers keen to have their own seals? Think about:

   - Literacy (being able to read and write)

   - Fashion (things which make you seem trendy, up-to-date and important)

3. Explain how a historian might use the evidence of seals to show how life was improving for some people in the countryside.

STOP AND REFLECT:

Remember, as villagers became better off they grew to resent things like feudalism (which forced them to do unpaid work for their lords) more than ever. Write down a sentence to record this.

If life was getting better, why did the peasants revolt in 1381?

Most village people in the Middle Ages were villeins. They were forced to do some unpaid work for their lords. At Codicote, in Hertfordshire, in 1086, 79% of the people living in the village were villeins owing this '**labour service**' to their lord. In time some villeins became better off. They bought up bits of land. They sold things to their neighbours. They built better houses. But as long as any land they farmed was called 'villein land' they were not free. The lord could force them to work for him and could control their lives in many ways. And they hated this!

In 1381 things exploded into violence. Taxes to pay for wars in France, called '**Poll Taxes**', made rich and poor pay the same amounts. This unfairness added to villeins' anger. The revolt which followed has been remembered as the Peasants Revolt. But what did the peasants want? And why did it fail?

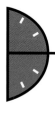

Timeline

2 June:	Royal Poll Tax collectors killed in Essex.
3 June:	Merchant arrested in Kent because he was a runaway villein.
6 June:	Riot in Kent frees him. Rochester Castle captured.
12 June:	Rebels send messages across England telling people to revolt.
13 June:	Rebels led by John Ball and Wat Tyler enter London.
14 June:	King agrees to free villeins.
14 June:	Rebels murder Archbishop of Canterbury.
15 June:	Small fight as King Richard II met rebels. Wat Tyler killed. Rebellion collapsed.

After the Revolt the king says villeins must stay as villeins!

The rich, including Church leaders, live in luxury while we work hard.

The King's just a boy and his uncle, John of Gaunt, is taking our money for himself.

It's wrong for rich and poor to pay the same Poll Tax. We hate lawyers who help rich men cheat us.

We villeins are forced to work for the lords for nothing.

The war is going badly in France. We have to pay for it.

Peasant complaints

Things are going to change around here!

SOURCE Ⓐ

'John Ball had the habit on Sundays of gathering the people and preaching like this:

"My good friends, life cannot go well in England until all things are shared by all the people. This will be when the lords stop being our masters. See how badly they treat us. But aren't we all descended from the same parents, Adam and Eve? So, why should the lords be more "masters" than us? They wear velvet and rich stuff, while we wear poor clothing. They have wine, spices and fine bread, while we have cheap bread and, when we drink, it's got to be water. They have rich houses, while we go out in the wind and rain to work in the fields. And it is our work that gives them the money to live so well.

We are like slaves and, if we do not perform the service they demand, we are beaten. We have no ruler to whom we can complain, or who would be willing to listen to us. So, let us go to the king and argue with him. He is young and we might get a positive answer from him. And if not – we must sort things out ourselves!"

The Archbishop of Canterbury had John Ball arrested and put in prison for two or three months. It would have been better if he had put him in prison for life or had him killed. When John Ball was let out of prison, he went on causing trouble like before.'

The words of the preacher, John Ball, according to the French writer, Jean Froissart, written shortly after 1381.

SOURCE Ⓑ

'He tried to prove that, "From the beginning of the world all men were created equal by their nature. And that the idea of some men serving others had been started by the cruelty of wicked men. It was not what God wanted. If God had wanted to create villeins, then surely, when God made the world, he would have said who was to be a villein and who was to be a lord. So they [the rebels] should kill the great lords. Next they should kill lawyers and judges. Lastly they should destroy all those who in the future might try to harm the common people! Then all would be peaceful and safe. For, with the 'great ones' gone, all would be equal." When he finished saying this, and other mad things, the people there thought he was such a great man that he should be the future archbishop and chancellor of the kingdom!'

The words of John Ball, according to the writer of the St Alban's Chronicle, Thomas Walsingham. He wrote shortly after the revolt.

EVIDENCE FACT FILE

- **Jean Froissart**. French priest. Wrote in French. Joined the royal court in 1361. Mostly interested in the lives of the rich. Not in Britain in 1381. Visited shortly afterwards. Got his information from rich and powerful people.
- **Thomas Walsingham**. Monk at St Alban's Abbey. Hated the rebels in St Alban's who attacked the rich abbey in 1381 and forced it to give more freedom to the townspeople. Usually correct in his facts. Wanted to keep villeins doing work on abbey land. Codicote belonged to St Alban's Abbey.

THINK ABOUT IT

1. Imagine you were a peasant in 1381. Write a short speech explaining why you are unhappy. (Effective speeches repeat key words, address the audience in the first person, use emotive language.) In your speech:

   - Explain ways in which life has improved over the years. *Look back in this chapter.*

   - Explain problems you face, which stop life getting better.

   - Explain how you want life to change.

2. Historians often have to put together information from different sources, decide how useful it is, decide how reliable, or trustworthy, it is. Look at Sources A, B and C.

   - List the demands of John Ball in Source A, and then in Source B. Underline any found in both sources.

   - What evidence is there that the writers did not like Ball's ideas? Look at words they used to describe: (a) him, (b) his ideas. Why did they not like his ideas? Look at the Evidence Fact File on page 75.

   - How useful are Sources A, B, C for finding out what the rebels were like and what they wanted? Remember, even if you do not agree with a source, its information can still be useful.

SOURCE ⓒ

John Ball preaching to the rebels. A picture painted in the fifteenth century, for a copy of Froissart's Chronicle. *Drawn by someone who usually painted knights, it makes the rebels look as well equipped as knights, with armour.*

STOP AND REFLECT:
By 1450 landowners stopped forcing villeins to work for them. They found they could get more money by renting land to them as free people. So, how important was the 1381 revolt?

Pulling it Together

Did life get any better for ordinary people over 450 years?

Stage 1 **Persuasion**

With a partner you are going to write two points of view.

(a) One of you says life got *worse*.

(b) One of you says life got *better*.

This type of writing is called 'persuasive writing'. You want a person reading it to think that what you say is correct.

How each of you will need to do this

- *Firstly, collect your ideas.* Skim through your notes from this chapter. Then scan it for evidence which shows life being good, or bad, for country people.

- *Now organise your ideas.* Create a flow chart, from 1066 to 1500, and put on it evidence for life being good, or bad, in the order in which these things happened. Colour code it: one colour for good, another colour for bad. You might create two spidergrams. One showing good things (with dates). One showing bad things (with dates).

- *Make some decisions.* Decide which pieces of evidence are 'useful' and explain why. If you think there are any parts of any evidence that are not 'reliable', explain why you think this.

- *Persuade.* Now put together all the evidence to try to persuade someone that life got worse, or better. Persuade them by selecting the evidence which shows this, repeat ideas, use rhetorical questions like: 'Isn't this clear proof that people were happy/unhappy?' Say why you reject evidence which argues the opposite way.

- Finally, read your speeches to each other. Then decide what worked best in each other's speech and what could be improved.

Stage 2 **You are the historian!**

Now you have to be an historian and decide between these two points of view. Historians have to:

- Explain what question they are exploring.

- Look at both sides of the argument.

- Decide what evidence is: (a) reliable (can be trusted), (b) useful (remember even evidence you don't agree with can still be useful as it can tell you about the ideas of people in the past).

- Reach a conclusion. This means deciding what they think the answer is. And why this is a better answer than other possible answers.

So, you do this now. Follow this approach to say whether you think life got any better for ordinary people over 500 years (1066–1500).

CHAPTER 7 ALLEYN'S SCHOOL LIBRARY

Relations with Other Countries
Was England the neighbourhood bully?

In this chapter you will:

- Decide what modern images we have of the way the English behaved in the Middle Ages towards other countries.
- Examine the changing relationship between England and its neighbours.
- Decide whether England treated its neighbours badly.

SOURCE Ⓐ

Photograph of Wallace (actor Mel Gibson) from the film, **Braveheart.**

SOURCE Ⓑ

Photograph of King Edward (actor Patrick McGoohan) from the film, **Braveheart.**

Braveheart

In 1995 a film produced by Paramount Studios became a world-wide success. The film was *Braveheart*. It told the story of the attempt by the Scottish hero, William Wallace to defeat King Edward I of England who was invading Scotland and attempting to conquer it. In the film Mel Gibson played Wallace, and Sophie Marceau, the beautiful wife of King Edward's son.

The film showed the English as the neighbourhood bullies trying to control, or destroy, a less powerful neighbour. Wallace's wife is murdered by the English. The Scots fight back against all the odds and defeat them. Wallace has an affair with the wife of the English king's son. The English finally treacherously capture Wallace and kill him horribly, in 1305. The film ends as a new Scottish hero, King Robert the Bruce, finally leads the Scots in defeating the huge English army at the Battle of Bannockburn in 1314.

Freedom!

As William Wallace dies in the film he cries out, 'Freedom!' It is the most dramatic part of the film. It has made an impact on many different people. The film is so popular that, in October 1999, the BBC carried a report that it was the most popular video amongst 'freedom fighters' in Chechnya fighting against the Russian army. William Wallace had become their hero. For them the bullying bigger country was Russia rather than England.

SOURCE C

Picture of the English army from the film Braveheart.

THINK ABOUT IT

1. Have you seen the film *Braveheart*? What was the part you most remembered and why? If you have not seen it, try to find someone who has. Ask them this question and record their answer.

2. Look at the pictures from *Braveheart* on these pages. The film-makers wanted audiences to sympathise with the Scots as they tried to resist the English. Explain ways in which these pictures from the film might do that. Think about:

   • images of a hero

   • weapons of both sides

   • appearance of both sides

SOURCE D

Picture of Wallace's Scottish army from the film Braveheart.

The past is still with us

Do you think the past is all over and done with? Think again. The past is with us all the time. It affects how we think and understand things right now. The relationship between England and its neighbours today is still affected by events which took place in the past. In 1999 elections took place for a new Parliament in Scotland – the first since 1707. Scotland had managed to remain independent in the Middle Ages but, in 1603, its king (James VI) became ruler of England too (as King James I). After that more and more power moved from Scotland to London. In 1999 a Welsh Assembly was elected too. Wales had not had its own parliament since a Welsh revolt against England in 1400–9. Before this, in 1284, the last Welsh ruler had been defeated and from that time forward Wales was ruled by England. In 1999 English control, dating from the Middle Ages, was being partly reversed. However, there is still lots of feeling in Britain that England needs reminding that it is not the only country in the United Kingdom. Feelings like that still show themselves in many ways.

SOURCE Ⓔ

Modern Scots football fans, known as the 'Tartan Army'. Even in Sport, England is still the 'Auld (Old) Enemy'.

SOURCE Ⓕ

Modern English football fans. There is still great rivalry with Scotland, Wales, France and Germany. All these countries, except Germany, were Medieval rivals. Modern feelings have ancient roots.

SOURCE G

Support the auld enemy, says SNP man

Scotland's Tartan Army is no stranger to betrayal. Usually it comes from the national team, crashing out at the first hurdle in glorious defeat. Yesterday, however, the Judas was Andrew Wilson of the Scottish National Party, who has dared to suggest that, in the absence of the Scottish team, Scotland's fans should support England in the World Cup this summer. Mr Wilson, who admits his idea is unlikely to make him 'the most popular man in town', says it is time Scots laid aside years of enmity to root for Beckham and the boys in Japan and Korea. 'We share a border, we share a culture, why on earth are we not supporting them?' he asked. 'Our real enemy is not England, it is those among us without ambition. I cannot wait for the day when we are so confident in ourselves as a nation that we can bring ourselves to support the so-called auld enemy.'

By mid-morning, Mr Wilson, shadow minister for the economy in the Scottish parliament, admitted that his mobile phone was choked with text messages, most of them unrepeatable. At the headquarters of the Tartan Army, meanwhile, an official, Hamish Husband, was adopting a more measured view. 'If you think about it, it is the mature thing to do,' he said. 'But it would take half the fun out of it. It's not anti-Englishness. It's just a football thing. It's a tradition.' And anyway, says Mr Husband, the issue is nothing new. Just last month, a member of the Scottish tourism authority posed a similar question. Shouldn't Scotland be supporting England? The Tartan Army put it to their 86-strong executive committee in a free vote. 'We had three recounts,' Mr Husband said. 'But it still came out the same. 86–0. Against.'

The Guardian *newspaper, Monday, February 25, 2002.*

Using the past?

William Wallace would probably never have believed that his exploits would be told in the Chechen language. To be fair, he would not have recognised many other parts of the film either. The film is an interpretation of the past and History was changed to fit Hollywood! Not surprisingly, William Wallace never had an affair with a princess! And King Edward I did not die at the same time as Wallace. Most of the film is based on a late-fifteenth-century romantic account of Wallace's life by a poet named 'Blind Harry'. This was written almost three hundred years after Wallace died. It is mostly made up of legends about Wallace – not history!

However, the story of Wallace in *Braveheart* still contains truth. Scotland *was* invaded by huge English armies. A little country *was* attacked by a much larger one. And it was not the first to feel the force of England. Ireland had been invaded in the twelfth century. Wales was conquered in the thirteenth century. English armies invaded France in the fourteenth and fifteenth centuries. So was England the neighbourhood bully? You decide.

THINK ABOUT IT

1. Read Source G. What was it that Mr Andrew Wilson was suggesting? What evidence is there that many Scottish people did not like his suggestion? Why do you think they felt this way?

2. What changes are happening in the way Britain is governed to try to reduce English power over other parts of the United Kingdom? Why is it important to do this?

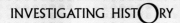

What was England's relationship with its neighbours like before the Middle Ages?

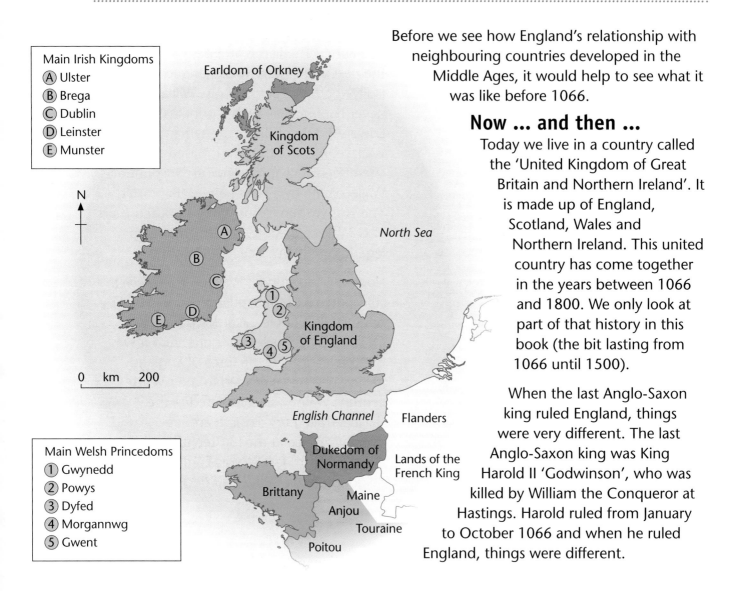

Main Irish Kingdoms
- (A) Ulster
- (B) Brega
- (C) Dublin
- (D) Leinster
- (E) Munster

Main Welsh Princedoms
- (1) Gwynedd
- (2) Powys
- (3) Dyfed
- (4) Morgannwg
- (5) Gwent

Before we see how England's relationship with neighbouring countries developed in the Middle Ages, it would help to see what it was like before 1066.

Now ... and then ...

Today we live in a country called the 'United Kingdom of Great Britain and Northern Ireland'. It is made up of England, Scotland, Wales and Northern Ireland. This united country has come together in the years between 1066 and 1800. We only look at part of that history in this book (the bit lasting from 1066 until 1500).

When the last Anglo-Saxon king ruled England, things were very different. The last Anglo-Saxon king was King Harold II 'Godwinson', who was killed by William the Conqueror at Hastings. Harold ruled from January to October 1066 and when he ruled England, things were different.

THINK ABOUT IT

1. Look at the map. In what ways was Britain in 1066 different to Britain today?

2. Imagine you are: (a) Scottish, (b) Welsh, (c) Irish, in 1066. Explain what your country is like and what your relationship with the English is like.

3. What evidence is there to show that England could not always get its own way with its neighbours?

STOP AND REFLECT:
Why was England able, at times, to dominate its neighbours in Britain?

ENGLAND

Anglo-Saxon England was the most powerful part of Britain. Between AD 450 and 1066 Anglo-Saxon kings had conquered the land we now call England. At first there had been many Anglo-Saxon kingdoms. But by the tenth century there was only one king in England. By 1066 England was a wealthy, powerful and very well organised country. It had lots of natural resources and was not divided by great mountains, or other natural features. Its farmland was rich. It was united and strong. The English kings ruled no land across the English channel, though there was a lot of trade with Normandy, France and Flanders. Also, the king before Harold II (Edward the Confessor) was half Norman (on his mother's side).

SCOTLAND

At the same time Scotland had come under the control of strong kings who ruled most of the country, although its population was much less than that of England. By 1018 the Scots under King Malcolm drove the English out of southern Scotland and kings of Scotland ruled Cumbria (which was later part of England). Only parts of northern Scotland and the Western Isles were still ruled by the descendants of Viking lords.

WALES

*Wales on the other hand was split into a number of different kingdoms. By the eleventh century the most powerful kingdom was Gwynedd. Between 1055 and 1063 its ruler, Gruffudd ap Llywelyn, managed to unite all Wales under him, but this did not last. When he died, in 1063, Wales broke up once more. The Welsh rulers found it hard to resist the power of the English. This was not helped by the fact that the Welsh were divided, had a much smaller population and were easily invaded from England. English kings found it especially easy to invade the richer parts of South Wales because these parts were not protected by mountains. At different times powerful English kings raided into Wales and forced the rulers there to accept the English king as their overlord. This meant they were forced to give **tribute** to the English king and recognise his power and authority.*

IRELAND

Ireland too had many different kings and a much smaller population than England. One of these – the kingdom of Dublin – had been set up by Vikings. But in 1014 the Irish High King, Brian Boru defeated a Viking army at the battle of Clontarf. However, Ireland remained divided amongst a number of rulers. Viking traders from Waterford and Dublin traded with Bristol. There were strong connections between Anglo-Saxon England and Ireland but Ireland, like Scotland, remained free from English control.

Why was England involved in wars in France?

Wars across the Channel

Many of the wars fought by England in the Middle Ages were in France. Between 1337 and 1360 the English king, Edward III, claimed he was also king of France. Between 1337 and 1453 English armies invaded France many times. Famous victories were won against French armies such as the Battles of Crécy (1346), Poitiers (1356) and Agincourt (1415). These battles were part of

Henry Plantagenet (Henry II of England)

I was born at Le Mans, I died at Chinon and was buried at Fontevrault. They're all in the part of France called Anjou. From my father I became Count of Anjou. I married Eleanor of Aquitaine and became its ruler also. My mother was daughter of King Henry I and through her I became ruler of England and Normandy, though we had to fight a Civil War, against her cousin Stephen, to get it. I finally became king of England in 1154 and the most powerful man in Europe. The French king is supposed to be my overlord for all the land I rule in France but I'm more powerful than him!

what historians have called the 'Hundred Years War'. In 1415 King Henry V renewed the claim that English kings should rule France. When he died in 1422, his baby son, King Henry VI, was technically king of both countries. But the English hopes collapsed and the wars ended in 1453, when England was finally defeated. By that time the only land England controlled in France was around the port of Calais.

Violence and war crimes

During the Hundred Years War English armies caused terrible harm to France. Great groups of knights and footsoldiers swept through the French countryside. They destroyed villages, **looted** towns, murdered and assaulted civilians. What we would now call 'war crimes' were committed across much of the French countryside. Many soldiers increased their pay with what they could steal. Knights **ransomed** back French knights they captured and made money from the war too. Often groups of soldiers would set themselves up as private armies, robbing and murdering.

Changes brought by 1066

Today it seems strange that any king of England would claim to be king of France as well. It looks as if England was trying to control any country it could get its hands on. But things were more complicated than this. Ever since 1066, kings of England had also owned land in France. They had a right to be there. They spoke French and continued to do so in the royal court until the fifteenth century. When a king like Henry II (king, 1154–89) fought in France, he was not an English person invading France. He was a French-speaking lord, fighting to protect his homeland from the French king, or other rivals. History can be complicated.

Things change ...

Between 1066 and 1500 English connections with land in France changed.
Here are some of the big changes, with some of the reasons for the changes.

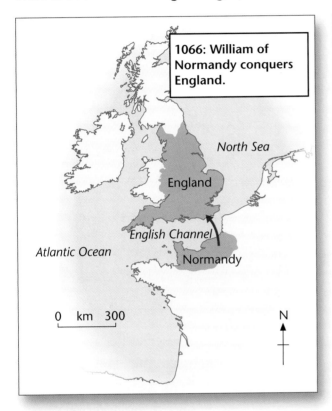

> **1066: William of Normandy conquers England.**

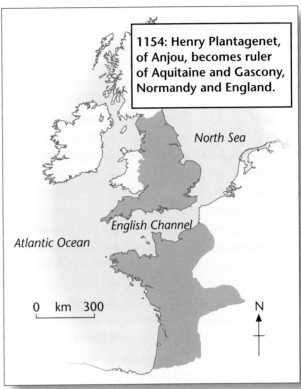

> **1154: Henry Plantagenet, of Anjou, becomes ruler of Aquitaine and Gascony, Normandy and England.**

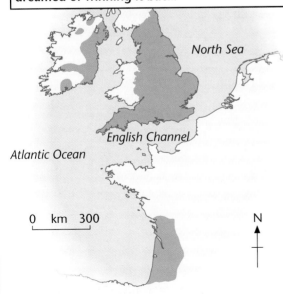

> **1214: Attacks by the king of France and revolts by barons caused King John to lose much of his lands in France. English kings dreamed of winning it back.**

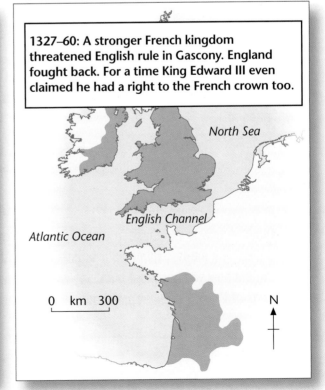

> **1327–60: A stronger French kingdom threatened English rule in Gascony. England fought back. For a time King Edward III even claimed he had a right to the French crown too.**

The purple shaded area shows the lands held by the English king.

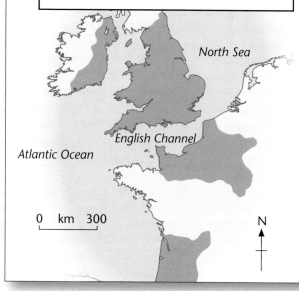

1415–22: King Henry V took advantage of problems in France to try to win back Normandy and even rule France.
Successful war made him more popular in England and promised wealth and power.

North Sea

Atlantic Ocean

English Channel

0 km 300

N

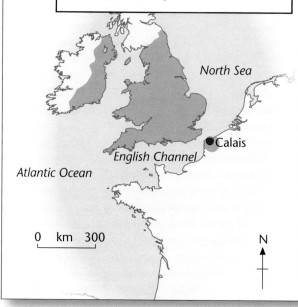

1453: France fought back. England was defeated. Gascony was lost by 1453. It had been ruled by the king of England for 300 years! Only Calais was left.

North Sea

Calais

Atlantic Ocean

English Channel

0 km 300

N

THINK ABOUT IT

Imagine you are an English king in 1400. A French person tells you that you have no right to be in France. You are just the 'neighbourhood bully' pushing your weight around in somebody else's country. Look carefully at the maps and put together an argument which justifies your right to be there. To do this you will need to:

● *Anticipate the argument against you.*
List the reasons which might be given for you having no right to be in France.

● *Prepare your defence.*
Think of answers to these arguments against you.
Look at the maps. Explain your connections with France. Explain how you have lost land. Say why you think certain parts of France should come back under your control.

STOP AND REFLECT:
On a spidergram, record reasons why English kings in the Middle Ages might be thought to have a right to rule in France.

The invasion of Ireland: a case of bullying?

In 1171 King Henry II invaded Ireland. Earlier he had been asked for help by an Irish leader named Diarmait, king of Leinster, who had been thrown out of Ireland by his enemies and wanted help getting his kingdom back. Henry was too busy himself but was happy for others to help Diarmait. The Pope had also encouraged Henry to invade, because he thought Ireland was uncivilised.

For the next eight hundred years England and Ireland would be linked together in a way which caused terrible bloodshed and sorrow. So was this just another example of the English bullying their neighbours?

It's a matter of opinion

On these pages you are going to read the opinion of a famous historian to try to find out what he thinks about this invasion. You are going to:

- Read carefully to try to spot his main ideas.

- Explore how events in history can be more complex than they might seem at first glance.

- Identify and explain why some people in the past would have had different opinions about the same events.

SOURCE Ⓐ

'The Pope had asked Henry to invade Ireland to clean up what was reported to be a corrupt and lax form of Christianity. But then, as now, Henry had more urgent things to do than get directly involved in the obscure island off to the west. On the other hand, Diarmait's appeal had presented him with a chance too good to turn down. So he gave Diarmait permission to recruit help from among his barons. This is when the trouble became *big* trouble. For Diarmait promptly went shopping for mercenaries among the nastiest and greediest possible bunch of knights. They were the **Anglo-Normans** who, around the 1160s, seemed to be on the losing end of the war against the Welsh princes of Gwynedd. They had lost castles, land and peasants. They were in an ugly mood. [Their leader was nick-named "Strongbow".] Within a year Diarmait had his throne back in Dublin. But he also now had an army of Anglo-Normans who weren't about to go away now that the job was done. In fact, from the beginning, Diarmait had known this. He not only expected but wanted the likes of Strongbow to stick around, in case his old enemies got ideas of booting him out again. At which point Henry II suddenly sat up and took notice of what was going on in the west. He had meant to use Diarmait's appeal to get a foothold in Ireland. What he had accidentally created was a monster: a **colony** of Anglo-Normans, who were led by exactly the kind of jumped-up 'superbaron' Henry was busy sitting on in every other part of his enormous **empire**. So in the winter of 1171, Henry crossed the Irish Sea himself, coming with an army big enough to give the likes of Strongbow serious second thoughts. It was then, in Dublin, that he took the **homage** of all the six Irish kings.

And though everything that happened afterwards in the sad history of England and Ireland wants to say this was the moment when Ireland lost her freedom, no one at the time saw it that way at all. The Irish kings did homage to Henry as they would to any Irish High-king. And they saw him not as conqueror at all, but as their protector *against* the Strongbows and the Anglo-Norman barons.'

Professor Simon Schama, 2002.

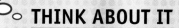

THINK ABOUT IT

1. Firstly read the passage on your own, to get a general idea of what it means.

2. Now read it to a neighbour. Get them to write down the answers to these questions as you read:

   - What was the name of the English king?
   - Which two people asked him to invade Ireland and why?
   - Why didn't Henry invade?
   - What happened next?
   - Why did this worry Henry?
   - What did Henry do next?
   - How did many Irish feel about this?

3. a) Do you think Simon Schama thought 'Strongbow' and his friends were good or bad people? What words does he use to give you clues?

   b) Do you think Simon Schama thought King Henry II was a bully to invade Ireland? What words does he use to give you his opinion?

4. People in the past would not always have agreed about events. Finish the sentences of the three people below, saying what they might have thought about the impact of knights from England on Ireland.

Knights of the English king came to Ireland because …

Diarmait, king of Leinster

I went to Ireland because …

Strongbow

I went to Ireland because …

Henry II

STOP AND REFLECT: 'Not every English king's invasion of a neighbouring country was bullying.' How does the invasion of Ireland show this?

How was the legend of King Arthur used to try to increase English power over other countries?

GLASTONBURY CHRONICLE, EASTER, APRIL 19, 1278

Huge crowds turned out here today to see King Edward I and Queen Eleanor as they visited Glastonbury Abbey. Many royal watchers were surprised when our warrior king chose this Somerset town as the meeting place for the court this Easter. And now the place is heaving with nobles and there's even a foreign royal visitor in the person of the Count of Savoy.

This afternoon the king and queen visited the abbey. It's almost one hundred years since the monks dug up a body which they claimed was that of the legendary King Arthur. Arthur as you will recall is supposed to have ruled Britain after the end of the Roman Empire. He was an ancestor of the Welsh and fought the invading Anglo-Saxons who, of course, were ancestors of us English. Legends say he conquered the whole island and even invaded France. Now we English rule land which once belonged to Arthur. Welsh legends claim Arthur did not die but will one day return to help them fight the English. Now King Edward has come to see these famous bones.

King Edward amazed everyone with the rich cloth he gave in which to wrap the bones. He ordered that the bones should be placed before the High Altar in the holiest place in the church. He put his royal seal on the tomb so no one else will disturb these bones.

The power of the past

King Edward I, of England, understood the power of the past. He knew that the Welsh believed Arthur would live again and defeat their enemies. He knew the legends which said that Arthur had once ruled all of Britain. For Edward, Arthur was a very useful 'piece of the past' and Edward knew how to use him. Edward claimed that because the English were living in land once ruled by Arthur, then English kings had the right to rule all of Britain! More than this, by being so respectful to bones believed to be Arthur's, he was saying two things. Firstly, Arthur is dead and will not return to help the Welsh. Secondly, I am the **heir** of Arthur. Everything which once belonged to him now belongs to me.

King Edward showed his links to Arthur in many ways. He visited the 'bones' at Glastonbury, he held Round Table feasts at Winchester, and when he conquered Wales in 1284 he held a Round Table feast deep in Wales, at Nefyn, where once the Welsh kings of Gwynedd had one of their courts. After the defeat of the Welsh he captured a crown, said to be 'the Crown of Arthur' and brought it back to Westminster Abbey. He used the power of the past to support his claims to rule Wales.

SOURCE Ⓐ

*King Arthur's 'Round Table', still hangs on the wall in Winchester Hall. It was really made in about 1275 for a **tournament** put on by the English king, Edward I. Edward wanted people to think of him as a new 'King Arthur'.*

The Welsh point of view

A

After the Norman's conquered England, Norman barons took land by force in South and East Wales. They succeeded because Wales is divided and weaker than England.

Edward I crushed us by force. He built castles to control us. He forced English laws on us.

E

The English King Henry II raided Wales and made the Welsh princes accept him as overlord.

B

King Edward I of England refused to accept Wales was independent of England. He invaded Wales in 1277. Then again in 1282–3.

Great Welsh leaders like Lord Rhys (died 1197), Llywelyn the Great (died 1240) and Llywelyn ap Gruffudd (died 1292) fought back. English King Henry III was forced to accept Welsh independence in 1267.

D

C

THINK ABOUT IT

1. Imagine you are King Edward I. Give two reasons why it is useful for you to be associated with the famous 'King Arthur'?

2. How could you use the evidence of *The Welsh Point of View*, to argue that Edward I used the legends of Arthur to excuse what English kings were determined to do anyway? Think about: how Wales had suffered attacks from England before 1066 (look at page 83); how Wales was treated after 1066.

STOP AND REFLECT:
Write a sentence explaining how the English used history as a way of excusing their conquest of Wales.

And now the turn of Scotland

By 1290 English kings had lost much of their land in France. With it they had lost power and wealth. They turned to other neighbours as a way of making up for this. By 1283 they had conquered Wales. Then in 1291 King Edward I was given a great opportunity to increase his power in Scotland. The Scottish king, Alexander III, had died in 1286 and Scotland faced Civil War over who should be the next king. King Edward I was asked to decide which Scottish lord had the best claim. He chose a man named John Balliol. But Edward did more than this. Edward wrote to all the great English monasteries asking if they had any old evidence in their records which described the relationship between England and Scotland. Their replies mentioned Arthur again!

Before Edward would agree to help the Scots he insisted that he was recognised as the overlord of Scotland. Reluctantly the Scots agreed. But Edward wanted to turn this into total power. He demanded that when Scots had legal problems they had to bring them to courts in London. He demanded that Scottish nobles should fight for him. This was too much. The Scots refused.

SOURCE B

'Arthur, king of the Britons, that most famous leader, made subject to his authority rebellious Scotland, and destroyed nearly all its people and then appointed as king a man named Auguselus. When later the same king Arthur had a celebrated feast at Caerleon, all the kings subject to him attended, among them the king of Scotland. And since then, all kings of Scotland have been subject to all kings of the Britons.'

Written by King Edward I, to Pope Boniface, in 1301.

Our saint is bigger than your legendary king!

The Scots denied Edward's right to control them. Firstly they said Arthur had died without any children so nothing of his power was passed on to later kings. They also used some legends of their own! They claimed Scotland had been converted to Christianity by St Andrew. Since the real St Andrew had been a close friend of Jesus, the Scots were saying 'We're an ancient people and God cares about us, so England should leave us alone!' The real St Andrew, of course, had never come anywhere near Scotland, although some of his bones may have been brought there centuries later as holy relics.

War

In 1296 Edward invaded and defeated the Scots. But the Scots refused to give in. William Wallace (as in the film *Braveheart*) united ordinary Scots against the English. The war was bloody and terrible. It went on despite the execution of Wallace. From 1306 until 1329 a new Scottish king, Robert the Bruce, fought the new English king, Edward II, and defeated him at Bannockburn in 1314. The English were forced to recognise the independence of Scotland in 1328. English kings never gave up their claims to rule Scotland but they were unable to crush them. Scotland stayed independent. 'St Andrew' had beaten 'King Arthur'.

SOURCE C

'The King of kings and Lord of lords, our Lord Jesus Christ, after His Death and Resurrection, called them [the Scots], almost the first to His most holy faith. Nor would He have them confirmed in that faith by merely anyone but by the first of His **Apostles** — the most gentle St Andrew, the Blessed St Peter's brother, and desired him to keep them under his protection forever.

So our nation lived in freedom and peace up to the time when that mighty prince, the King of the English, Edward, the father of the one who reigns today, when our kingdom had no head and our people had no malice or treachery and were then unused to wars or invasions, came in the disguise of a friend and ally to harass them as an enemy. The deeds of cruelty, massacre, violence, pillage, arson, burning down monasteries, robbing and killing monks and nuns, and yet other outrages without number which he committed against our people, sparing neither age nor sex, religion nor rank, no one could describe, nor fully imagine, unless he had seen them with his own eyes.'

The Declaration of Arbroath, *which was sent to the Pope by Scottish leaders in 1320.*

SOURCE D

'Although Scotland was not conquered by the Normans, many Normans did in fact settle there. Because the Normans came into Scotland as followers of the Scottish kings, their powerful military might, based on knights and castles, was used to support the Scottish crown, not destroy it. Edward I's attack on Scotland was something new. He was attempting to conquer another united 'Norman' kingdom, in which the ruling group did not support the English, as the Norman landowners in Wales did, but provided the backbone of the Scottish resistance.'

Written by the modern historian, Alexander Grant, in 1985.

THINK ABOUT IT

1. What reasons would Edward I of England have used to support his claim to be overlord of Scotland?

2. What reasons would many Scots have put forward to disagree with him? Read Source C carefully. Make a note of the key words in this source which explain why Scotland was (a) an independent country, (b) with good reasons to be angry with the English.

3. This source is *useful* for finding out why Scots opposed the English but not very *reliable* as history. Explain why both these statements are true.

4. Both the Scots and English used legends, not real history, to defend their actions. Despite this, which of the two do you think had the strongest argument against the other? Why?

5. Reading to find the meaning.
   Read Source D carefully. According to this historian how was the Scottish experience of the Normans different to the English one? In what ways did this make Scotland hard for the English to conquer?

STOP AND REFLECT:
Suggest a reason why the English failed to defeat the Scots when they had beaten the Welsh.

Pulling it Together

Was England the neighbourhood bully?

Design a website giving information about England's relationship with its neighbouring countries. This gives you opportunities to:

- **Recount information. Retell events, often in chronological order. Select only that which is relevant and which supports the point you are making. Use connectives related to time (e.g. 'later', 'after this') or to cause (e.g. 'because') or to contrasting ideas (e.g. 'although', 'however'). Remember you are trying to answer a question.**

- **Put arguments from different points of view, to balance arguments fairly. Keep from giving your own decision until you have looked at different views. As you write use connectives explaining ideas (e.g. 'as a result'), and phrases which introduce evidence (e.g. 'This view is supported by ...') and phrases which help build the argument (e.g. 'Although it seems that ... other evidence shows ...')**

- **Show critical use of evidence. Show how the past can be used and understood in different ways by different people. Explain why this happens.**

- **Combine information from different sources.**

- **Decide what evidence is *useful* (can tell you something) and what evidence is *reliable* (you can trust what it says). The two are not always the same!**

Home page

Your homepage should recount what you have learned about who England's main neighbours were and describe something of the background to the relationship with them.

Links

Your Home Page should have links to:

- France
- Wales
- Scotland
- Ireland.

These should take you onto other pages where there is more information about each of these neighbours.

Link pages

These pages should say:

- Where these countries are.

- What they were like in the Middle Ages.

- How their relationship with England developed.

- Your assessment of how England treated them. Were the English wrong in their efforts to win power over them? (e.g. Was England the 'neighbourhood bully'?) Or did the English have points in their favour? If there are arguments on both sides, then show both before you reach your conclusion.

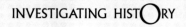

GLOSSARY

Anglo-Normans population mixed between English and Normans after 1066

Apostles the leading followers of Christ in the Bible

Archbishop Church leader, over a number of bishops

banish forcing someone to leave a country

barons powerful men given land directly by the king

biography a life story of someone else

bishops Church leaders

burgesses townspeople

castrated cutting off a man's private parts

Chancellor official in charge of parts of the government

charter list of rights, responsibilities and freedoms

Chronicle an account of events in the order in which they happened (sometimes written later)

clergy someone educated by, or employed by, the Church (e.g. a priest)

clerk an educated person

colony land controlled by another country

Commons the elected people who decide the country's laws (MPs)

confessions telling someone about the wrong things you have done and how you want God to forgive you

corrupt rotten and dishonest

Crusades going to the Middle East to try to recapture Jerusalem from Islam. There were a number of Crusades in the Middle Ages.

desmesne land run directly by the lord of the manor

diet kinds of food eaten

discrimination treating some people differently to others (often in a worse way)

empire when one country conquers and controls other countries

ethnic minority group of people whose race, language, or way of life is different from most people in a country

excommunicated cut off from the Christian Church and from God

famine shortage of food

fast going without food

Feudal System system where monarchs give land to their followers in return for them fighting for the monarch

fiction story which is not true

germs microscopic organisms which cause disease

governed ruling a place

heir person who inherits property after another person's death

holy living a good life, approved by God

holy order a priest or other full time worker in the Church

homage showing respect and accepting the authority of another person

humours the idea that the body contains four different substances and that illness is caused by too much of one substance

interest repaying borrowed money, plus extra money

interpretations a point of view

labour service having to do unpaid work on the lord of the manor's land

laity ordinary members of the Christian Church

looted stolen

Lords the great landowners in the country; today people with a title like duke or earl who are part of the House of Lords, the unelected group who help decide the country's laws

martyr a person who dies for their beliefs

mass sharing bread and wine in memory of the Last Supper before Christ's crucifixion

mass-produced made in large quantities (like in a modern factory)

monasteries place where monks live, worshipping God

motte and bailey an early castle; 'motte' was an earth mound with a wooden tower on top and the 'bailey' was a courtyard surrounded by a wooden wall

oppress treat badly

Parliament the group of people who decide on the country's laws

passage travelling somewhere

peasant owner of a small amount of land

peat bog wet, marshy land; sometimes preserves human bodies

persuasion to get someone to agree, or do, something by the power of your argument

pimp someone who finds clients for a prostitute (an insulting term)

Poll Taxes everyone paying the same amount of tax regardless of their wealth

ransomed paying money to free someone

reredorter toilet

saint a holy person

seal stamp made in wax to show who has agreed to a document

sermon a talk given in Church, explaining Christian beliefs

shire area of England (e.g. Somerset)

state the way government is organised to run a country

suburb area on the edge of a town

taking the Cross becoming a Crusader

technology skills and ways of working and making things

thanes Anglo-Saxon nobles

tithe giving one tenth of your income to the Christian Church for the work of God

tolls paying money to visit a place

tournament knights fighting to entertain others

trade buying and selling

tribute forced to pay something to a conqueror

tried brought before a court

vigils praying through the night

widow woman whose husband has died

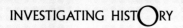

INDEX